Hungary

Second Edition

RAYMOND HILL

Facts On File, Inc.

Nations in Transition: Hungary, Second Edition

Facts On File, Inc.
132 West 31st Street
New York NY 10001

Library of Congress Cataloging-in-Publication Data

Hill, Raymond.
  Hungary / Raymond Hill.—2nd ed.
    p. cm. — (Nations in transition)
  Includes bibliographical references and index.
  ISBN 0-8160-5081-3
  1. Hungary. 2. Hungary—History—Chronology. I. Title. II. Series.
  DB906.H45 2003
  943.9—dc21   2003049011

Facts On File books are available at special discounts when purchased in bulk quantities for businesses, associations, institutions, or sales promotions. Please call our Special Sales Department in New York at (212) 967-8800 or (800) 322-8755.

You can find Facts On File on the World Wide Web at
http://www.factsonfile.com

Text design by Erika K. Arroyo
Cover design by Nora Wertz
Map by Patricia Meschino © Facts On File

Printed in the United States of America

MP JT 10 9 8 7 6 5 4 3 2 1

This book is printed on acid-free paper.

CONTENTS

ACKNOWLEDGMENTS   v

INTRODUCTION   vii

PART I: HISTORY   1
1. Ninth Century to World War I   3
2. World War I through World War II (1918–1945)   23
3. Hungary under Communism   53

PART II: HUNGARY TODAY   91
4. Politics and Government   93
5. Economy and Trade   109
6. Foreign Policy and Defense   137
7. Arts and Media   155
8. Snapshots: People and Places   177
Conclusion: Into the Future   189

CHRONOLOGY   193

FURTHER READING   201

INDEX   204

4022

ACKNOWLEDGMENTS

The author wishes to thank Ms. Agnes Bodnar of the Hungarian Commercial Counselor's Office and Ms. Aniko Polgar of the Hungarian Tourist Board for their kind assistance in the gathering of information and photographs for this book. He also wishes to thank Mr. Joseph Magyar for agreeing to be interviewed by a complete stranger.

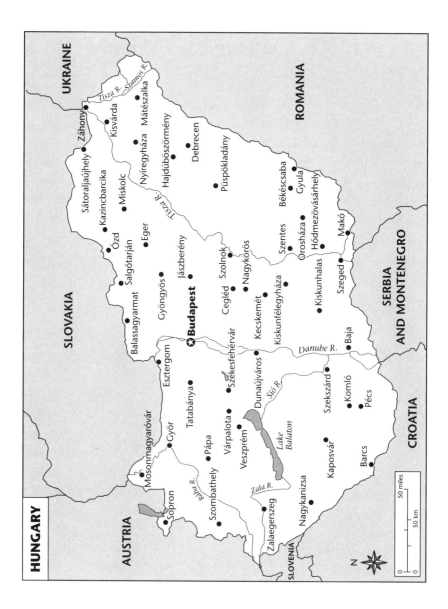

HUNGARY

UKRAINE

ROMANIA

SLOVAKIA

SERBIA
AND MONTENEGRO

CROATIA

AUSTRIA

SLOVENIA

Záhony
Sátoraljaújhely
Kisvárda
Mátészalka
Kazincbarcika
Miskolc
Nyíregyháza
Hajdúböszörmény
Debrecen
Ózd
Eger
Püspökladány
Salgótarján
Jászberény
Szentes
Békéscsaba
Gyula
Balassagyarmat
Gyöngyös
Szolnok
Orosháza
Hódmezővásárhely
Budapest
Cegléd
Nagykörös
Makó
Kecskemét
Szeged
Esztergom
Székesfehérvár
Kiskunfélegyháza
Kiskunhalas
Mosonmagyaróvár
Tatabánya
Dunaújváros
Baja
Győr
Várpalota
Szekszárd
Komló
Pápa
Veszprém
Pécs
Szombathely
Kaposvár
Sopron
Zalaegerszeg
Nagykanizsa
Barcs

Lake
Balaton

Tisza R.
Szamos R.
Tisza R.
Danube R.
Sió R.
Zala R.
Rába R.

N

0   50 miles
0   50 km

INTRODUCTION

The date was September 11, 2002. At nightfall on Gellert Hill, overlooking the beautiful city of Budapest, Hungary, two powerful spotlights were switched on and turned skyward. The twin beams of light represented New York City's World Trade Center towers, which had been destroyed by terrorists one year earlier.

The spotlights, erected by the Budapest city council, were part of a series of solemn events in Hungary marking the first anniversary of the September 11 attacks. Earlier in the day, Hungary's president, Ferenc Mádl, and premier, Péter Medgyessy, visited an official ceremony hosted by the U.S. embassy in Budapest.

Premier Medgyessy told the attendees, "We in Hungary followed the events of September 11 [2001] on TV, radio, newspapers and the Internet with shock, fear and enormous sadness. . . . As far as we know, no Hungarian citizens were killed in the attacks, but we remember all those with Hungarian surnames who died, particularly the policemen and firefighters who lost their lives." Medgyessy noted that the governor of New York State, George Pataki, and New York City's deputy police commissioner, Tibor Kerekes, are both of Hungarian descent.

The events in Hungary were not unusual; many of the world's nations marked the September 11 anniversary in 2002. But consider this: A scant 14 years earlier, the United States had regarded Hungary as an enemy of everything for which America stood.

More than 700,000 Americans are of Hungarian descent. But the number of Hungarians who immigrated to the United States is tiny compared with, say, numbers of German, Irish, Italian, Polish, or Chinese immigrants to America. This in part explains why Americans in general know so little about Hungary.

A few facts are in order. Hungary is a small, landlocked county in central Europe. Some people like to say that Hungary is an eastern European country, reflecting the nation's former membership in the "Eastern bloc." (The now-defunct Eastern bloc was a group of European communist nations, led by the Soviet Union, that was located geographically to the east of the capitalist democracies of Western Europe.) During the cold war, the 45-year period of East-West tensions that followed World War II, the Hungarian people were forced to endure more than 40 years of Communist dictatorship and Soviet domination.

Hungary is a miniature country compared to the United States. Its total area, 35,919 square miles, is smaller than that of the state of Indiana. Its population, approximately 10.2 million people, is less than that of the state of Illinois.

Seven nations share Hungary's 1,407 miles of external borders: Austria on the west and northwest, Slovakia on the north, Ukraine on the northeast, Romania on the east and southeast, Serbia and Montenegro (the new designation for Yugoslavia) on the south, Croatia on the south and southwest, and Slovenia on the west.

Hungary has three major waterways. The mighty Danube River—Hungarians call it the Duna—forms part of the Slovakia border and flow south through Budapest and central Hungary to Serbia and Montenegro, a journey of 375 miles. East of the Danube, the Tisza River runs from the northeast to Serbia and Montenegro. West of the Danube is Lake Balaton, the largest lake in central Europe. Balaton is 50 miles long, nine miles wide, and it occupies an area of 102 square miles.

Hungary has a temperate climate with, on average, about 25 inches of rain a year. The country's mean temperature is 50 degrees Fahrenheit (10 degrees Celsius). Winters tend to be damp, chilly, and cloudy, with only moderate snowfalls. Summers tend to be warm and humid but rarely oppressively hot.

The nation's terrain is mainly grasslands, rolling hills, and low mountains. Forests and woodlands make up less than 18 percent of Hungary. Hungary's rich black soil yields wheat, barley, corn, sugar beets, potatoes, and sunflowers in great abundance. About 52 percent of the country's land is used for growing crops.

The nation's natural resources include large deposits of bauxite (the mineral that is processed into aluminum) and coal. Its mines also yield iron ore, copper, and small amounts of gold and uranium.

The Buda side offers a view of Parliament and the Danube River in Budapest.
(Courtesy of David and Margaret Roberts)

Magyars, descendants of warrior horsemen from central Asia, are the predominant ethnic group in Hungary. Since Magyars have their own language and culture, Hungary's majority population is very different from the Slavs and ethnic Germans who populate neighboring nations. The Magyars' origin means that they are not so much Europeans as Europeanized Asians.

For those who may be wondering, the word *Hungary* has no connection whatsoever to the word *hunger*. According to the Hungarian News Agency (MTI Corporation),

> Between the 3rd and 5th centuries A.D., the nomadic Hungarian tribes came into contact along the southern Russian steppes with Turkish and other tribes. . . . The name that came to refer to the Hungarians . . . originated from the ethnic name Onogur, translatable as "ten tribes" in the Bulgarian-Turkish language. The Hungarians, however, call themselves Magyar, taking this name from the magyer/megyer tribal name of Ugric origin.

Hungary's official language is Magyar (Hungarian), although many older Hungarians speak at least some German. Young Hungarians increasingly are learning English as a second language. Linguists classify the Magyar tongue, which shares some common traits with the Finnish and Estonian languages, as an Ugro-Finnish language. There are 44 characters in the Hungarian alphabet. Names are reversed when written or spoken in Magyar. Thus, István Dobo Square in the city of Budapest is Dobo István ter in Hungarian.

Hungary is a multiethnic country, but Magyars make up at least 90 percent of the population. The remainder of the population includes Rom, or Romany (Gypsies), ethnic Germans, ethnic Slavs (Slovaks, Croats, Serbs, and Ukrainians), and ethnic Romanians. Sixty-seven percent of Hungarians are Roman Catholics; about 20 percent of Hungarians are Calvinists (the largest Protestant denomination).

About 65 percent of Hungary's population lives in the cities and large towns. The nation's capital, Budapest, is one of the world's most beautiful cities. (Some people call it the "Paris of Central Europe.") It is not only the political capital but Hungary's cultural and financial center as well. The city was once three separate towns: Buda, Obuda, and Pest. The

Danube divides the hilly Buda section from the flat Pest. (Looking south, in the direction of the river's flow, Buda occupies the right bank and Pest the left bank. Nine bridges over the Danube link the two sections.) Obuda is a present-day suburb of Buda.

Authentic Hungarian goulash (Courtesy of Hungarian National Tourist Board)

Budapest, with 1.8 million residents, is by far the largest city in Hungary. Hungary's other largest cities—as of 2001—are Debrecen (211,038), Miskolc (184,129), Szeged (168,276), Pécs (162,502), and Győr (129,415).

When some Americans think of Hungary, two things may come to mind: goulash and the 1956 uprising. Actually, the two are connected in an odd way. The thousands of Hungarians who fled their country following the uprising introduced goulash (*gulyas leves*)—a hearty stew—to Western Europe, Canada, and the United States in the late 1950s.

The 1956 uprising—discussed in chapter 3—was a bloody, failed attempt by Hungarians to throw off the chains of Soviet domination. Picture David and Goliath, with the giant winning. The Hungarian people had the last laugh, however. Hungary adopted a softer brand of communism (so-called goulash communism) in the late 1960s. And with Hungary peacefully leading the way, the entire Eastern bloc began to crumble in the late 1980s. Shortly thereafter, the Soviet Union itself ceased to exist.

The transition to a free-market democracy has not been easy. Hungary endured a drastic economic downturn in the 1990s, wrestling with the demons of high unemployment, rising prices, mounting government debt, increased crime, and the lure of nationalism (an obsessive national self-interest.) But look at Hungary today and you see a small nation that is taking its place on the world's stage. It has embraced the global economy. It has become a member of the North Atlantic Treaty Organization and is now poised to join the European Union. This book will attempt to explain where Hungary has been, where it is now, and where it is going.

NOTES

p. vii "'We in Hungary . . .'" Fraser Allan "Hungary Marks September 11." Budapest Sun Online, September 19, 2002. Available on-line. URL: www.budapestsun.com. Downloaded October 2002.

p. x "'Between the 3rd and 5th centuries A.D. . . .'" *Hungary: Essential Facts, Figures and Pictures* (Budapest: MTI Corporation, 1997), p. 27.

PART I
History

1
NINTH CENTURY TO WORLD WAR I

The Magyars Arrive

Late in the ninth century A.D., thousands of fierce horsemen swept westward through passes in the Carpathian Mountains of central Europe and spread over the Carpathian Basin—the broad lowlands situated between the Carpathians and the Alps of south-central Europe. The invaders were short and stocky, with black wavy hair that framed sun-weathered faces with dark eyes, high cheekbones, and prominent noses. They rode strong, agile ponies—their most prized possessions—that were bred for both speed and endurance. The horsemen's favorite weapon was the bow, and they could shoot arrows with terrifying accuracy, even when riding their ponies at a thundering pace. They were the world's best mounted bowmen.

These were the Magyars, the ancestors of most modern-day Hungarians. They were a proud, independent people whose ancestry remains something of a mystery. Most historians believe the tribe originated somewhere in central Asia and settled for a time in the foothills of the Ural Mountains of Russia. As early as the fourth century B.C., some Magyars were thought to have migrated to the Baltic coast of northern Europe and settled in areas that became the present-day nations of Finland and Estonia. That might explain why the Magyar language is loosely related to Finnish and Estonian.

The bulk of the Magyars left the Ural Mountains and wandered south and west to the Caspian Sea some time in the early seventh century A.D. More than a hundred years later, they left the Caspian region and pushed onto a steppe, or plain, north of the Black Sea. From the Black Sea region, the tribe moved northwards along the eastern flank of the Carpathian Mountains and then into central Europe.

Throughout their wanderings, the Magyars encountered and mixed with other peoples. Hungarian historians are convinced that the Magyars were blood relatives of the Huns, a fierce central Asian tribe that had terrorized Europe, and then returned to Asia, in the fifth century A.D. Also, it is likely that the Magyars interbred with the Khazars and other Turkic-speaking peoples of the Caspian Sea region.

Although little is known about the Magyars' social structure, historians believe the tribe was made up of seven clans, or subtribes, united by blood ties and customs. One observer, a ninth-century Arab trader, offered his impressions of the Magyars (whom he mistook for "Turks") in the Caspian Sea area. It was one of the first recorded sightings of the tribe:

> The Magyars are a race of Turks and their leader rides out with 20,000 horsemen. They have a plain which is all dry herbage and a wide territory . . . They have completely subjugated the Slavs, and they always order them to provide food for them and consider them as slaves . . . These Magyars are a handsome people and of good appearance, and their clothes are of silk brocade, and their weapons of silver encrusted with gold. They constantly plunder the Slavs.

The Slavs in question were the ancestors of today's Russians. Throughout the eighth and ninth centuries there had also been a steady eastward migration of Slavic peoples to Russia from central Europe. The Slavs were generally a peaceful folk who preferred farming, cattle-raising, and trading over fighting. The Magyars—nomadic horse-breeders and warriors—no doubt felt crowded by the numerous Slav farms and villages that sprang up in the steppes of the Caspian region. It was their need for wide-open spaces, more than any other factor, that most likely forced the Magyars to leave the area.

Under a powerful leader named Árpád, the seven clans migrated south and west. Their destination, a plain north of the Black Sea, turned out to be only a temporary stop. There the Magyars encountered the Pechengs, a warlike Turkic tribe that was already established in the area. Unlike the passive Caspian Slavs, the Pechengs offered fierce resistance to the intruding Magyars. The Magyars chose to move on. They crossed the Carpathian Mountains and descended into the Carpathian Basin in the winter of 895–96.

The Terrors of Europe

The Carpathian Basin was far from uninhabited when the Magyars arrived. A thousand years earlier, it had been sparsely settled by Asiatic tribesmen known as Scythians. Then there had been successive waves of other settlers: Celts from northwest Europe, Avars (a nomadic Asian tribe), Romans, and Slavs. The Romans—who had one of the great empires of the ancient world—established a large colony in west-central Europe in the first century A.D. The Roman colony called Pannonia encompassed what is today western Hungary, lower Austria, and Croatia. The Slavs cohabited the region with the Romans from the third century A.D. until the fifth century, when the invading Huns pushed out the Romans. After the Huns returned to Asia, Germanic tribes dominated the northern part of the basin, but the rest of the area was Slavic.

After descending the Carpathian Mountains, the Magyars moved south and set up a settlement on the site of the current northeastern Hungarian town of Eger. From there, they rode through the Great Plain, the vast *puszta* (grasslands) of eastern Hungary, which in those days contained some forests. The plain—which resembled the Russian steppes—was much to the liking of the horsemen, who spread throughout the region, establishing settlements along the way.

Late in 896, Magyar clan chieftains gathered on the site of what is today the town of Szeged, in south-central Hungary, and pledged loyalty to their king, Árpád. According to legend, the chieftains sealed their pledge by drinking from goblets filled with human blood. Europeans were more than willing to believe the grisly legend, given the Magyars' bloodthirsty ways.

The Slavs were the first residents of the basin to find out the Magyars were bad neighbors. The Slavs were a collection of separate tribes that shared a common language and culture. The Carpathian Basin was the hub of the Slavic world. It was there that the lands of the Western Slavs (Moravians, Bohemians [Czechs], Slovaks, and Poles) converged with the lands of the Southern Slavs (Serbs, Croats, and Slovenes). When the Magyars arrived, they cut off the Western Slavs from their southern kinsmen. That division would have repercussions into the 20th century.

One of the earliest Slav states, the kingdom of Greater Moravia, had been created by the Western Slavs in the seventh century and reached its height early in the ninth century. Greater Moravia included the regions that now form modern Austria and Croatia. But the heart of the kingdom was the lands of Bohemia, Moravia, and Slovakia. (Today, Bohemia and Moravia form the Czech Republic. Slovakia, on Hungary's northern border, is now the Republic of Slovakia.)

Unfortunately for the Slavs, the kingdom was in decline when the Magyars arrived. The Magyar horde invaded Greater Moravia in 896, and soon afterward defeated the kingdom's forces in a battle fought near Bratislava (the capital of modern Slovakia). The horsemen overran most of the kingdom with the notable exceptions of the territories of Moravia and Bohemia, these states having been brought under the protection of some German states.

As in the Caspian region, the warrior Magyars regarded the relatively civilized Slavs as weak and inferior. The Slavs in the occupied remnants of Greater Moravia became the slaves of the Magyars. Those Slavs not taken directly into bondage were made to pay tribute—in the form of gold, food crops, cattle, and young women—to their new masters.

The Slavs were not the only Europeans to suffer at the hands of the Magyars. Beginning in 896 and for the next 60 years, the Magyars were the terror of the continent. From their camps in the Carpathian Basin, they launched massive hit-and-run raids that carried thousands of horsemen as far west as France and as far south as Italy. The mounted bowmen struck towns, villages, and Christian monasteries, looting, raping, and killing with barbaric glee. Their deadly rain of arrows easily defeated the small armed forces that opposed them. Larger forces declined to pursue the Magyars because the horsemen, while retreating at full speed, would turn around in their saddles and fire arrows at any riders who dared to chase them.

The sound of thundering hooves and the alarm, "The Magyars are coming!" was enough to make trembling villagers throughout Europe cram into their churches and pray for mercy. According to British historian Rowlinson Carter:

> To Europe, the Magyars were savages, barely human in character and interested only in rape and plunder. . . . Their arrival was interpreted as a sign that the Day of Judgment was at hand.

To the Magyars, Europe was one great treasure chest of booty. The marauders returned from their raids with stolen gold, silver, horses, cattle, weapons, rich cloth, wealthy hostages for ransoming, and young women. Captured women were forced to bear children by Magyar men and thus increase the tribe's population.

During their raiding period, which lasted until the middle of the 10th century, people began referring to the Magyars as "Hungarians." However, many Hungarians believe that the name, which can be translated literally as "those from the land of the Huns," comes from the fact that the Huns had launched their ferocious attack on Europe in the fifth century from the same area later occupied by the Magyars. (To this day, the townspeople of Szeged, Hungary, boast that the Huns' fearsome and famous leader Attila once had his headquarters on the site of the town.) Historians differ on the matter, with some holding that the word *Hungarian* is probably derived from the Turkic word *Onogur*, meaning "ten tribes." At any rate, the Magyars were widely known as "Hungarians" by the end of the 10th century. Today, the Hungarian word *Magyar* translates into English as "Hungarian."

Defeat and Christianization

At its height, the empire established by Charlemagne (742–814), a German, in A.D. 800 in alliance with the powerful Roman Catholic Church, included most of western and northern Europe and parts of southern Europe. But internal bickering and political intrigues had weakened and divided the empire to the point that it was a mere shadow of its former self when the Magyars appeared.

By the 10th century, north-central Europe was dominated by a collection of feuding German principalities that included Saxony, Prussia, Bavaria, and Austria. These German states made up the eastern portion of the crumbling Carolingian Empire, or Empire of the West, the Christian successor to the former Roman Empire.

One mission of Charlemagne's successors was to hold back the encroachment of the Eastern Orthodox religion, which rivaled the Roman Catholic Church. The Slavs made up the bulk of Eastern Orthodox worshipers in Europe. The German states helped to contain the spread of the Slavs and their religion from the Carpathian Basin. When the Magyars invaded the basin, the Slavs lost all hope of pushing any farther into Europe than they already had.

From Germania's perspective, the Magyars themselves were the problem. The Germans regarded the newcomers as dangerous, godless savages who had to be subdued at all costs. One German prince in particular, Otto I, managed to rally the German states to fight the horsemen from the East.

The Magyars were experts in raiding but never before had confronted large, organized armies on open battlefields. They were unfamiliar with the systematic rules of warfare that had evolved in Europe. Consequently, forces under Otto I routed the Magyars at the Battle of Augsburg (also known as the Battle of Lechfeld), in Germany, in 955. Otto was crowned emperor of a newly established Holy Roman Empire in 962.

The Battle of Augsburg all but ended the Magyar raids. The tribesmen settled down to consolidate the territories they still held, which were still considerable. Magyar territories included all of Slovakia, a sliver of northeastern Croatia, part of northern Serbia, part of what is today Ukraine, and Transylvania, now part of Romania. The wealthiest Magyars in these regions had large landholdings. Slavs formed the core of slave labor on these holdings.

The Magyars were wary of the Holy Roman Empire, but they were also fascinated by the Germans' social structure, culture, and religion. The Germans, like the rest of the more refined parts of Europe, were evolving a feudal social structure. In such a structure, the king was on top, nobles in the middle, and the poorest classes—peasants and slaves—on the bottom.

Little is known about the Magyar religion. They were most certainly some sort of pagans, in that they probably did not worship a single deity. Perhaps, like other nomadic horsemen, they worshiped natural elements, like the wind. German Catholic missionaries found willing converts among the Magyar nobles. More and more, missionaries began to appear at the side of Magyar leaders.

The Crown of St. Stephen

Géza, the great-grandson of Árpád, the leader who had led the tribe to its new home, converted to Christianity in the year 972. Géza's son Stephen (István) (977–1038) ordered all Magyars to adopt the religion and even invited the Vatican (the center of the Roman Catholic religion located in Rome, Italy) to send priests to help convert all his people. Stephen took his religion seriously. Any Magyar who disobeyed his order to convert was buried alive, along with his family and beloved horses. Still, there were some who resisted the idea of giving up the old ways in favor of a "love-thy-neighbor" religion.

Bishop Gerard, an Italian, came to Hungary to observe the progress of the mass conversion. He preached to a crowd at the top of a 770-foot hill in the town of Buda, overlooking the Danube River. It is not known what he said to the Magyars, but he apparently angered a number of people. The bishop met a terrible fate after his speech. As recounted by travel writer Phyllis Meras: "Some of those who did not wish to be Christianized captured him, tied him to a barrel studded with nails, and rolled him off [the] hill into the Danube."

The unfortunate bishop was canonized as St. Gerard. Hungarians know him as St. Gellert (the Magyar version of Gerard). A statue of him converting pagans stands atop that fatal Budapest hill, now known as Gellert Hill.

Murdered bishop aside, the Vatican was encouraged by the conversion efforts in Hungary. Pope Sylvester II was so grateful that he appointed Stephen an apostle of the church and crowned him a Christian king on Christmas Day in the year 1000. King Stephen established a strong Roman Catholic tradition in Hungary, and the church declared him a saint after his death. Stephen's crown, formally called the Holy Apostolic

Crown, is the centerpiece of Hungary's royal jewels. Since his death, Hungarian monarchs were said to wear the "Crown of St. Stephen."

King Stephen's contributions were not only in the realm of religion. He married a German noblewoman to solidify ties between Hungary and Germania. From his seat of government in Gran (today's town of Esztergom), he handed down Hungary's first written laws and had the Magyars adopt the trappings of European civilization. He brought scholars from all over the continent to teach and study in Hungary. He invited artists and craftspeople to settle in Hungary and pass along their creative skills to the Magyars.

Stephen also established a social order that placed all Magyars, no matter how poor, over non-Magyars. Non-Magyars fell into two categories: those who had been in the Carpathian Basin when the Magyars arrived, and those who came to Hungary as "guests and immigrants." Of those guests and immigrants, according to British historian Carter:

> Many were Germans (lumped together misleadingly as "Saxons"), a mixture of knights, miners, artisans and town-dwellers. There also were Jewish merchants ("Ishmaelites"), Moslem Bulgars (in charge of the royal mint) and Slavs who were often invited to settle in waste land or forest and bring on cultivation. Foreign nobles who entered Hungary were invariably given the equivalent of Hungarian rank and status.

Stephen's descendants were neither as wise nor as strong as he was. The Magyar nobles nearly revolted against King András II after he plundered the royal treasury and sold off royal lands to support an extravagant lifestyle. The pope had to step in and act as a mediator. The result was the papal bull (document) of 1222. It effectively ended the monarchy's absolute power over the Magyar nobility.

The Mongols, who were Asiatic horsemen much like the old Magyars, invaded Hungary in 1241 and wiped out nearly half the population. King Béla IV led an army against them at the Battle of Mohi, and he barely escaped when the Mongols annihilated the Magyar forces. The invaders reached the royal capital, the town of Pest, across the Danube from Buda, and burned it to the ground. King Béla learned a crucial lesson: never build your capital on low ground. He moved the royal court across the

An altar containing the right hand of St. Stephen. (Courtesy Free Library of Philadelphia)

river to the more defensible high ground of the Buda Hills. The Mongols did not stay in Hungary for long. Internal political conflicts in their Asian homeland compelled them to leave Europe.

Power-hungry nobles murdered King András III in 1301, ending a long line of monarchs descended from King Árpád. The nobles put a Frenchman, Louis of Anjou, on the Hungarian throne. After Louis, the Crown of St. Stephen passed to several other foreigners. One was Mátyás Hunyadi, a Romanian, who defeated an invading Turkish army at Belgrade (the current capital of Serbia, part of Serbia and Montenegro, the country formerly known as Yugoslavia) in 1377. Another was Mátyás's son, who was known as Matthias Corvinus (Latin for "crow," from a heraldic symbol on his family's coat of arms), who died in 1490.

Corvinus ruled from 1458 to 1490. During his reign, Hungary was the strongest, richest, and most admired country in central Europe, and Buda was a center for scholars and artists. He established Hungary's first library, the Corvina. During his reign, advantageous marriages between Hungarian royals and the members of other royal families gave Hungary part of lower Austria, all of Moravia, and Silesia (now part of Poland).

There is suspicion that Corvinus was poisoned, perhaps by jealous nobles. After his death, the country was beset by disputes over succession and by serious internal disorders. There was a bloody peasant uprising in 1514 and the Turks once again moved against the country's borders. Hungary got no help from the Holy Roman Empire. The Germans were too busily engaged in a feud with the papacy to offer any assistance.

Hapsburg Domination Begins

A Turkish army of Sultan Suleiman II, the Magnificent, crushed the Hungarian army under King Louis II at the historic Battle of Mohács on August 29, 1526. Louis had led an army of about 20,000 against a Turkish force numbering 200,000 and was drowned while trying to retreat across a river.

Louis (Lajos)II had been married to noblewomen of the Hapsburg family, the powerful dynasty centered in Austria. With Louis's defeat, the Crown of St. Stephen eventually passed into the hands of his Hapsburg in-laws. Hungary would remain under Austrian domination for the next 462 years.

Nearly all of Hungary was occupied by the sultan's forces but for two notable exceptions. One was the Principality of Transylvania, whose Magyar nobility avoided absorption by paying tribute to the Turks. The other was called "Royal Hungary," a small area in what is now Slovakia.

The Turks held Hungary in an oppressive grip for 150 years, imposed crushing taxes on the populace, built mosques (Muslim places of worship) in Hungarian towns, and converted many Christian churches into mosques. They cut down the forests of the Great Plain to prevent Magyar rebels from having a place to hide, but the people were determined to keep their language and customs alive. Most Magyars staunchly resisted pressure to convert to Islam. (That was not true in other parts of Turkish-occupied Europe. In Bosnia-Herzegovina, south of Hungary, many Slavs converted, which is why today the majority of Bosnians are Muslims.)

Most of Hungary's aristocracy fled to Royal Hungary and Transylvania during the Turkish occupation. The peasants remained, but they were probably no worse off under the Turks than they had been under the Magyars.

Hungary's aristocracy had to rely on the armies of Austria to gradually push the Turks out. That was accomplished by 1697. The Turks left two enduring legacies. One was paprika, a pepper that Hungarians use to season many of their dishes. The other legacy was Turkish baths. Today, attending baths and spas is a regular social ritual in Hungary.

In return for the Austrians' help, Hungary was compelled to accept the rule of the Hapsburgs. For one thing, only the powerful Austrians could return order to Hungary. Land ownership was in dispute. The rural middle class (owners of small landholdings) and peasants resented a return of the Magyar aristocracy.

The Magyars chafed under the thumb of the Hapsburg Empire until 1740, when the Hapsburg crown passed to Empress Maria Theresa. Austria was threatened with an invasion of joint Bavarian and French forces, and much of the Austrian army refused to fight because it had not been

Turkish baths, like this one in Budapest, are very popular. The Turks occupied Hungary for 150 years. (Courtesy of David and Margaret Roberts)

paid for some time. History tells us that Maria Theresa, mounted on a white horse and clutching her newborn son, made a dramatic appeal to Hungarians for help. The six regiments (about 6,000 troops) of loyal Hungarians that rallied to her banner played a key role in halting the invaders. Maria Theresa was forever grateful to Hungary. Hungary, in turn, recognized the empress as its legitimate ruler. She was the only woman ever to wear the Crown of St. Stephen.

Joseph II, the son of Maria Theresa, had little regard for Hungary. He refused to wear the royal crown. He taxed Hungary's aristocrats (something no monarch had done since 1222), and he attempted to put an end to Hungarian feudalism. The Hapsburgs wanted to shape Hungary in Austria's image: a highly centralized and bureaucratic government structure coupled with a fledgling industrial economy. The foundation of Hungary's political and economic power lay in its great rural estates.

About 200 aristocratic families, and 3,000 wealthy but untitled families, owned nearly half of the arable land in Hungary. The Roman Catholic Church also held vast tracts of land. Although some members of the peasant class earned viable livings as farmers (the so-called smallholders—owners of up to 130 acres each), most peasants lived in or on the edge of poverty.

The majority of Hungarian peasants were landless. They lived in villages on the great estates and endured lives of hardship only a step above slavery. (The Austrians ended slavery in Hungary in the 18th century.) Under ancient tradition and law, they were bound for life to work for the landowning elite. The landowners had the right to punish any peasant who attempted to leave the land. Other peasants worked as itinerant farm laborers. They moved from estate to estate, cultivating the soil and picking crops for subsistence wages.

Hungary's Magyar population in the mid-1800s was 5.5 million. Due to the acquisition of outlying territories, the Magyars were far outnumbered by other ethnic groups that were part of the kingdom of St. Stephen. These included more than 2 million Romanians, and more than a million each of Slovaks, Germans, Serbs, and Croats. There were also ethnic Ukrainians, ethnic Slovenes, and others.

The ethnic minorities (who together constituted a majority) were content to maintain their own languages and customs, just as the Magyars resisted Austrian influence. But in 1843, Magyar was declared the official language of Hungary and all Hungarian territories. It was the first act of "Magyarization," or the policy of forcing other ethnic groups to adhere to Magyar culture. The policy would inspire separatist movements in the lands under Hungarian rule that would be active for more than 70 years.

Revolution and Absolutism

Nationalist and political unrest brewed in Hungary and throughout Europe in the mid-1800s, inspired in part by concepts first introduced in the French Revolution of 1789. One concept held that no nationality or ethnic group had a right to rule another. Another held that, within a given country, citizens were entitled to a truly representative government, not one controlled by monarchs or aristocrats. Both of these concepts played a role in the Hungarian Revolution of 1848–49. First, most Hungarians wished to be rid of Austrian rule. Second, many of the key figures in the revolution supported moves toward democracy.

Count István Széchenyi and Lajos Kossuth were two figures who sought broad social changes in Hungary. Széchenyi, although an aristocrat, called for sweeping reforms, including universal suffrage and education for Hungary's illiterate masses. Kossuth, a left-wing lawyer, swayed intellectuals and radical politicians with demands for independence from Austria and for an end to feudalism.

Austria's emperor Ferdinand I sought to defuse the situation by making concessions. In 1847, he granted Hungary limited autonomy, created a Hungarian diet (parliament), and allowed limited voting rights. In order to be eligible to vote, Hungarians had to own property and have some education. Count Lajos Batthányi became Hungary's first elected premier, and he appointed Széchenyi and Kossuth to cabinet posts.

Armed friction between Magyars and independence-minded ethnic Romanians, Croats, and Serbs (among others), however, brought requests in Austria for a tougher stance toward the unruly Hungary. Ferdinand abdicated the Hapsburg throne in 1848 and was succeeded by his young nephew Francis Joseph (1830–1916).

The new emperor rejected Ferdinand's more tolerant approach toward the Hungarian people. He ordered nothing less than Hungary's absolute obedience to the Hapsburg monarchy. The order precipitated a nationalist revolt in Hungary in 1848 led by Kossuth. In April 1849, the Hungarian diet declared an independent Hungarian republic with Kossuth as its "governor."

Hungary's hastily recruited "revolutionary army" defeated Austrian imperial troops in several skirmishes, but the success was to be short-lived. A humiliated Francis Joseph appealed to czarist Russia for help and in May 1849, Russian troops entered the fray. Together, Austria and Russia put nearly 300,000 soldiers in the field. The small, badly equipped Hungarian revolutionary army was overwhelmed. The ragtag insurgents, under General Artur Görgey, surrendered to the Russians on August 13, 1849, at the village of Világos, Hungary. Kossuth and several other members of the revolutionary government fled to Turkey. Premier Batthányi was captured and executed.

There followed 18 years of Austrian absolute rule in Hungary, which had the status of a "royal land." In effect, Hungary was the emperor's personal property. Francis Joseph divided the non-Magyar lands into four separate administrative regions of Austria: Transylvania, Croatia, Slovenia, and Vojvodina (northern Serbia). Austria took Moravia from Hungary.

A POEM BY SÁNDOR PETŐFI (1823–1849)

Sándor Petőfi was the poet of the 1848–49 Hungarian Revolution against Hapsburg Austrian rule. He was a Magyar patriot and a democrat. Petőfi not only despised the emperor of Austria; he hated all monarchs. Here is one of his poems:

A knife in the heart of Lamberg,*
a rope around the neck of Latour,*
And after them others may follow;
You begin to be mighty, O people!
This is all right, this is perfectly fine,
But this has achieved little.
Hang the kings.

*High-ranking Austrian government officials in 1848, at the start of the revolution

---

During this period of absolutism, Hungary had no parliament. It was ruled by a governor-general, Prince Felix Schwarzenberg, who filled the government bureaucracy with Germans and Czechs. Hungary's police forces were run by another Austrian, Interior Minister Alexander Bach. The so-called Bach era was characterized by the brutal treatment of any Hungarians suspected of harboring nationalist tendencies.

The Hapsburgs made German the official language of Hungary. Hungarians were barred from using their native language in government offices, courts, and schools. In addition, Hungarians were stripped of all civil rights. Austrian officials confiscated Hungarian property without hearings, and thousands of Hungarians suspected of revolutionary activities were jailed without trial.

Amid the simmering discontent, a Magyar tailor's apprentice, János Libenyi, attempted to kill Francis Joseph with a knife on a Vienna street in 1853. He failed—the emperor was wounded but recovered—and Libenyi was executed.

The Dual Monarchy

While holding Hungary in an iron grip, the Austrian Empire fared badly in wars against Italy, France, and Prussia. Relations with Russia deteriorated. The setbacks helped convince Emperor Francis Joseph of the wisdom of consolidating the empire. He accepted a petition from a group of Hungarian moderate nationalists, led by Ferenc Deák, to restore Hungary's autonomy under a unique framework—the Dual Monarchy.

The Compromise of 1867 made Francis Joseph the king of Hungary as well as the emperor of a combined Austro-Hungarian Empire. Austria and Hungary each had its own elected parliament and separate government. The important areas of defense, finance, and foreign relations were handled by the consensus agreement of representatives from both part of the empire. Issues such as trade and commerce between Austria and Hungary were governed by renewable 10-year agreements. Hungary regained its non-Magyar territories with the exception of the Czech land, which were held by Austria.

Austria did not allow heavy concentrations of Hungarian troops in Hungary. Those forces were dispersed throughout the empire. Austria

An equestrian statue of Austro-Hungarian emperor Francis Joseph in the Austrian capital, Vienna. (Library of Congress)

based Croat troops in Hungary. Although Slavs, Croat men regarded service in the Austrian military to be an honor. On the other hand, the Croats had an intense dislike for Magyars, partly because of the arrogant rule of the Magyars in Slavonia (northeastern Croatia). The basing of Croat soldiers in Hungary was not accidental.

Francis Joseph was one of the craftiest political thinkers of the day. He held the empire together by continually playing one ethnic element against another. The groups were too busy quarreling with each other to notice who was pulling the strings. In a conversation with the French ambassador in Vienna, the emperor disclosed

> My people are all estranged from one another and this is all for the good. . . . I send the Magyars to Italy and the Italians to Hungary. Each of them watches his neighbor; they do not understand each other and they hate each other. Out of their mistrust order is born and from their mutual hatred a lasting peace arises.

The Dual Monarchy was fully supported by Hungary's two most powerful classes, the landowning aristocrats and the middle-class farmers. There remained an undercurrent of anti-Austria feeling in Hungary, but the only organized opposition came from the 48 Party (later renamed the Independence Party), a leftist organization that drew its inspiration from Lajos Kossuth, the revolutionary hero.

Hungary's dominant political organization during the Dual Monarchy was the Liberal Party. Its platform, a mixture of moderate left-center nationalism and a desire to maintain the social status quo, was popular with the upper and middle classes.

Until World War I, the empire was stable and relatively prosperous. Hungary accounted for almost half of the empire's agricultural production. There was steady industrialization in Hungary during the last half of the 19th century. More and more people moved to the cities. By the early 1900s, the percentage of agricultural workers in the total workforce had declined from 75 percent to 60 percent.

Conditions in Hungary's factories were harsh. Workers labored for long hours at low pay. Women and children made up about three-fifths of all factory workers. However, for unskilled laborers, life in the cities and large towns was better than the dawn-to-dusk drudgery of laboring on the large estates.

A new urban middle class appeared in Hungary, made up mostly of Jews who had immigrated to Hungary from Russia, Poland, and other

Slavic countries. Due to a tolerant atmosphere in Hungary's cities, Jews thrived as business owners, bankers, financiers, lawyers, doctors, teachers, and government bureaucrats. Jews formed about 4.5 percent of the population in 1910 (932,000). Most of Hungary's larger cities had at least a 12 percent Jewish population. Prior to World War I, Budapest was 23 percent Jewish.

Educational opportunities also expanded under the Dual Monarchy. Improvements in basic education reduced the illiteracy rate from 55 percent in 1867 to about 41 percent in 1914. Although the poorest Hungarians rarely received higher education, there was a sharp increase in university attendance among the wealthy and middle classes. In the mid-1800s, there were only about 800 university students in Hungary. By 1914, the number increased to more than 16,000.

Cultural nationalism, a romantic attachment to all things Magyar, also flourished during the Dual Monarchy. The writings of Zsigmond Móricz and Endre Ady, the plays of Ferenc Molnár and the musical works of composers such as Franz Liszt, Béla Bartók, and Zoltán Kodály were lionized.

The Hungarian Royal Guard, dressed in uniforms that reflect a bygone era, used to be present at official government functions. (Courtesy Free Library of Philadelphia)

While Austria-Hungary was a model of stability, the political situation in the rest of the Balkan region was not. (The region, encompassing southeast Europe, has long been a volatile area. Hungary occupies the northernmost part of the Balkan region.) At the turn of the century, the empire was increasingly at odds with the Kingdom of Serbia. The Serbs wished to unite with Hungary's Serbs, Croats, and Slovenes to form a southern Slav kingdom. Russia was Serbia's ally and protector.

Two Balkan wars were fought in 1912–13. In the first, Serbia, Bulgaria, Greece, and Montenegro pushed the remnants of the Turkish Ottoman Empire out of Europe. In the second, Bulgaria attacked Serbia but was defeated when Romania, Greece, and Turkey came to Serbia's aid. Austria-Hungary was not involved in the Balkan wars, but the proximity of the conflicts made Francis Joseph nervous. In casting about for allies against Serbia and Russia, he moved diplomatically closer to Germany.

A big war was looming in Europe. It was triggered on June 28, 1914, when a radical Serb student, Gavrilo Princip, assassinated the heir apparent to the Austrian throne, Archduke Francis Ferdinand, in the Bosnian capital of Sarajevo.

Hungary had nothing to do with the assassination, but at first some Austrians suspected that Magyars were behind the plot. That is because Archduke Francis Ferdinand hated Magyars, whom he viewed as treacherous. The archduke, who was very unpopular in Hungary, made no secret of his bias. While the Austrian press was barred from openly criticizing the Hapsburg royal family, the Hungarian press frequently mocked the archduke as a fool and a bigot. Here Francis Ferdinand rails in a letter to the German leader, Kaiser Wilhelm:

> The so-called gentlemanly Magyar is a most infamous, antidynastic, lying, unreliable fellow. . . . All the difficulties which we have in the Monarchy arise exclusively from the Magyars.

Following the assassination, the Central Powers—Austria-Hungary and its ally, Germany—declared war on Serbia. The Allies—Russia, Britain, and France—came to Serbia's aid. World War I had begun.

Hungary's Liberal premier, Count István Tisza, doubted the Central Powers could win. At first he sought to avoid Hungarian involvement in the conflict, but then reluctantly relented. Hungary could not sit out the war while Austria—its partner in the Dual Monarchy—took part. Tisza publicly disavowed the notion that Hungary had territorial designs on Serbia or any other neighbor. As it turned out, Hungary would be the one to lose most of its territory to its neighbors when the war ended.

NOTES

p. 4 "'The Magyars are a race of Turks . . .'" Rowlinson Carter, *Insight Guides: Eastern Europe* (Singapore: APA Publications, 1993), p. 238.

p. 7 "'To Europe, . . .'" Carter, p. 238.

p. 9 "Some of those . . ." Phyllis Meras, *Eastern Europe: A Traveler's Guide* (Boston: Houghton Mifflin, 1991), p. 209.

p. 10 "'Many were Germans . . .'" Carter, p. 239.

p. 19 "'My people . . .'" Vladimir Dedijer, *The Road to Sarajevo* (New York: Simon & Schuster, 1966), p. 118.

p. 21 "'The so-called . . .'" Dedjer, p. 136.

2

WORLD WAR I
THROUGH
WORLD WAR II
(1918–1945)

The Great War

World War I was fought between 1914 and 1918 and resulted in more than 8 million deaths, to both soldiers and civilians. It was mainly a conflict between two major European power blocs: the Allies (Great Britain, France, Italy, and Russia) and the Central Powers (Germany and Austria-Hungary). The United States entered the war in 1917 and helped speed the Allied victory. At stake in the conflict was domination of global economic markets, although U.S. president Woodrow Wilson viewed the outcome as a triumph of the forces of democracy over the forces of tyranny.

World War I was the catalyst of Hungary's independence from Austria. But Hungary was on the losing side of the war and as such received drastic punishment from the Allies.

Hungarians generally were enthusiastic about World War I when it began. Magyars viewed the conflict as a means of punishing Russia for its

Austro-Hungarian troops march into Serbia in 1916 during World War I.
(Library of Congress)

role in smashing the Hungarian revolt of 1848–49. The kingdom's loyal Slavs regarded themselves as Hungarians first and foremost, and therefore were willing to fight their ethnic cousins in Serbia and Russia. Nationalist Slavs knew enough to be patient, believing that they would eventually win their freedom regardless of the war's outcome.

The leaders of the Austro-Hungarian Empire had visions of regaining its past glory, but it was too weak militarily to have more than a secondary role in the Central Power alliance. Germany planned the overall war strategy, and German troops did the bulk of the fighting against French and British forces on the all-important western front (the fighting in France and Belgium). Hungarians mainly fought on the eastern front, where the kingdom's principal military role was to defend the many passes in the Carpathian Mountains against advances by Serbian and Russian troops.

Premier Tisza turned the entire Hungarian economy toward support of the war. Farmers, miners, and industrial workers labored around the clock to produce raw materials, weapons, and food for the Central Powers. Calls for political, social, and economic reforms were set aside in the name of national unity.

Hungarian forces suffered heavy losses in the early years of the conflict, but the fact that Hungary itself was under a real threat of invasion from the east helped to fuel patriotic spirit. Hungarian troops played a pivotal part in the Central Powers' capture and occupation of Serbia, in 1915, and Montenegro, south of Serbia, in 1916. However, the conflict dragged into 1916 with no end in sight, and Hungary's population grew increasingly weary of the war. The kingdom's economy had been drained by supporting the war effort. Civilians were worn down by the exhaustive work schedules, food shortages and soaring prices for goods.

Germany unwittingly contributed to a growing discontent in Hungary. Hungarians resented Germany's arrogant leadership of the Central Powers. German propaganda, which characterized the war as a "Germanic" crusade against "Slavdom," not only ignored Magyar sacrifices in the war but trampled on sensitivities of the loyal Slavs in Hungary. On the other hand, the Allies actively encouraged Slavic nationalism in Hungary's territories, prompting some Hungarian military units to stage mass desertions to the Allied side.

The political unity of 1914–15 fell apart. A new Hungarian Independence Party (actually a splinter faction of the old Independence Party) was formed in the summer of 1916 by the reform-minded leader Count Mihály Károlyi. The party defied Tisza's ruling Liberal government by calling for Hungary to end its participation in the war and focus attention on internal reforms. The Independence Party began to gather widespread support as the war continued and defeat loomed for the empire.

Emperor Francis Joseph, the Hapsburg monarch since 1848, died in November 1916 at the age of 86. King Charles IV of Hungary succeeded Francis Joseph on the dual throne, taking the title Emperor Charles I of Austria-Hungary. Charles realized that Germany was leading the Central Powers to defeat. He quietly—and unsuccessfully—sought a separate peace with the Allies, hoping to salvage the empire.

Peace protests and work stoppages hit the empire in 1917, compelling Emperor Charles to place the most important sectors of the Austro-Hungarian economy under the control of the military. Charles dismissed Hungarian premier Tisza in May 1917 following a massive antiwar demonstration in Budapest. (Tisza would be murdered by disgruntled Hungarian soldiers in 1918.) The new premier, Sándor Werkele (who had held the post twice before), could do little to halt the unrest. Left-wing movements sprang up throughout Hungary, denouncing the war and demanding democratic reforms. The government cracked down on reformers, jailing as many of the leaders as they could find. But the reform movements had already gained wide support among urban workers throughout the empire.

A strike by munitions workers, first in Austria and then spreading to Hungary, paralyzed the empire's production lines in January 1918 and finally ended through army intervention. Army units mutinied in May 1918 in the Hungarian city of Pécs. The mutiny was put down bloodily by loyal army units.

In June 1918, Hungarian workers staged a nine-day nationwide general strike. The government responded by declaring martial law. Only mediation by the Social Democratic Party convinced the strikers to return to their jobs. Slavic nationalists took advantage of the chaos by asking the Allies to recognize formally their right to independence from the empire. In the summer of 1918, the Allies recognized the Czech National Council as the true representative of the Czech people. The South Slav and Romanian National Councils also gained Allied recognition.

In October 1918, a month before the end of World War I, Hungary experienced a massive political upheaval. Charles I issued a manifesto on October 16 that declared Austria-Hungary's willingness to end its participation in the war. The same day, Hungarian premier Wekerle proposed an end of the Dual Monarchy, with Austria and Hungary to function as separate nations. Neither the manifesto nor the proposal addressed the issues of Slav independence or far-reaching reforms in Hungary.

Wekerle resigned as premier on October 23, 1918. On October 25, the Independence Party, Social Democratic Party, and leading left-wing movements announced the formation of an opposition front called the Hungarian National Council. The council issued a 12-point program calling for an immediate separate peace with the Allies, as well as for democracy, universal suffrage, and meaningful land reform in Hungary. The program also acknowledged the "right of self-determination" of the non-Magyar peoples of Hungary. Within a four-day period, October

27–30, the Romanians of Bukovina, the Ukrainians of Galicia, the Czechs, and the Slovaks all announced secession from the empire.

On October 28, police in Budapest fired at demonstrators on the Chain Bridge. The protesters were demanding the appointment of the reformer Count Károlyi as the new Hungarian premier. Rather than bow to reform, the defiant emperor picked Count János Hadik—a favorite of the landed elite—to lead the government. But the Hadik government had no effective control of the streets of the capital, where the residents were on the verge of revolution.

Units of the Territorial Army, which had pledged their support of the Hungarian National Council, seized Budapest railroad stations, the central telephone exchange, and key government buildings on the night of October 30. Hadik resigned the following day, and the alarmed emperor named Count Károlyi premier. Károlyi quickly created a center-left government that promised policies based on the Hungarian National Council's 12-point plan. Among other things, the plan called for universal suffrage, land reform, and much-improved conditions for workers in the cities.

World War I ended for Austria-Hungary on November 3, 1918, when the empire signed an armistice with the Allies in Padua, Italy. The old Hapsburg regime had attempted to regain past glory by going to war. As it turn out, the war destroyed their empire.

Postwar Struggles

Emperor Charles I announced on November 11, 1918, that he would no longer take "any part in the affairs of government." He then moved to Switzerland as a private citizen. The Austrian parliament regarded the statement as an abdication of the throne, and the lawmakers proclaimed Austria a republic on November 12. The Dual Monarchy officially ended on November 16, 1918, when the Károlyi government proclaimed Hungary a republic. The proclamation marked the beginning of Hungary as a modern, independent country.

Károlyi quickly learned that proclaiming a republic, and maintaining a strong, viable government were two very different things. Although he was a capable politician and administrator, the new premier was by nature a centrist who relied on the consensus of diverse political elements in his decisions. Getting a consensus to deal with the overwhelming problems of the postwar period was nearly impossible.

First of all, Hungary's economy was in a shambles. The dissolution of the Dual Monarchy destroyed the integrated financial system that Austria and Hungary had shared for more than 50 years. Second, the Allies had imposed economic sanctions on Hungary that were to remain until the matter of war reparations was settled.

French troops occupied much of eastern Hungary and parts of the Slavic lands that had been under Hungarian and Austrian rule. The French did not object when, in the period between October 1918 and January 1919, the formerly subjugated nationalities seized Hungarian property in those lands. Romania in January 1919 annexed all of Transylvania, with no opposition from the French occupation forces in that region.

Even though the Károlyi government professed support for "self-determination," it was stunned by the land seizures and embittered by the Allies' indifference. The Allies were of a mind to punish Austria-Hungary for siding with Germany in the war, so Károlyi's appeals to preserve Hungarian territorial integrity received little sympathy. Inside Hungary, political elements of the far left and far right tugged, pushed, and prodded the government toward extreme actions.

The far left—Communists and radical Socialists—had been influenced by Russia's Bolshevik Revolution of 1917. Some had been prisoners of war in Russia during the revolution and returned to Hungary inspired by Marxist-Leninist ideals. Others were Hungarians who actually had fought on the side of the Bolsheviks in Russia, and who were determined to lead a similar revolution in Hungary. One such man was Bélá Kun, who considered himself a protégé of V. I. Lenin, the father of Soviet communism. Kun founded the Hungarian Communist Party in Budapest in November 1918.

Communism, as defined by German social theorists Karl Marx and Friedrich Engels, would create an ideal society in which all means of production (as well as political power) would be in the hands of the workers. Marx and Engels regarded capitalism as a necessary interim phase between feudalism and communism. Lenin took their theory a step further. He believed only through revolution, not evolution, could capitalism be overcome and communism implemented.

While the far left openly organized industrial workers, miners, and peasant farmers, the far right—mainly current and former army officers—established secret paramilitary groups. The most prominent figure of the extreme right was Gyula Gömbös de Jafka, an aide on the Hungarian general staff who attempted to unite the paramilitary groups under his own organization, the National Militia Association.

The Hungarian parliament and the Károlyi government swiftly instituted major reforms in 1918. Laws were passed guaranteeing freedom of the press, freedom of speech, and freedom of assembly. Any person over 21 who had been a Hungarian citizen for at least six years was granted the right to vote, and elections were to be held by secret ballot. The new laws were popular with everyone except the elite landowners, who feared their power would be eroded by popular democracy.

Early in 1919, while parliament wrestled with land reform, Hungary was swept with a series of crippling industrial strikes that were instigated by the Communists. Károlyi stepped down as premier and was replaced by a former justice minister, Denes Berinkey, and the leftist Social Democrats took a more visible role in the ruling coalition. (The Social Democrats asserted that they, not the Communists, were the true representatives of the working class.) Károlyi became the republic's first president in January 1919.

Parliament passed a law giving the police power to jail anyone suspected of being an enemy of the state. But rather than being used against the Communists, the law was used to jail right-wingers in the army, whom the government believed might pose the threat of an eventual military takeover. The authorities banned Gömbös's National Militia Association.

On February 6, 1919, parliament finally passed a land-reform law. (Land reform had been discussed in political circles, but not implemented, over the course of more than 70 years.) Under the statute, all estates of at least 741 acres were subject to expropriation by the government, with the land being distributed in parcels to small- and dwarf-holding peasant farmers. (Dwarfholders were farmers who owned less than seven acres of land.) The owners of the expropriated lands, however, were to be compensated in part by taxes on those who received the parcels. If the taxes were not paid, the land was returned to its original owner.

The law satisfied no one. The big landowners opposed the legislation. Smallholders and dwarfholders complained that they could not possibly meet the tax burden. Landless peasants, who made up 96 percent of the

This 1919 propaganda poster reflects the spirit of the far-left Revolutionary Ruling Council, which controlled Hungary for a brief period. (Library of Congress)

peasant class, were to receive nothing at all. Poor farmers, with the urging of the Communists, began seizing estates outright soon after the law
was passed. Communist-controlled "peasants' committees" took over several rural county governments.

In response to this, the government jailed approximately 50 Communist leaders—Kun was not among them—on February 21. That did not
halt their activities; not only did the leaders continue to give orders from
their prison cells, but they also used the opportunity to radicalize fellow
prisoners. Communist agitators on the outside gathered strength for a
mass protest to free their leaders by force.

It appeared that widespread political violence was on the horizon.
President Károlyi took a gamble that he hoped would bring some peace
and stability: he attempted to quiet the far left, while at the same time
undercutting the Communists, by having the Social Democrats lead a
new government. But the Social Democrats realized that they would have
no credibility with the masses unless the Communists also had a major
political role. The two parties combined to form one ruling body, the
Revolutionary Governing Council, on March 21. The chairman of the
council—a rank equivalent to premier—was a moderate Social Democrat named Sándor Garbai. But the person really in charge was Communist Party boss Béla Kun, who modestly took the post of foreign minister.

The first official act of the Revolutionary Ruling Council came on
March 22, 1919. It abolished parliament, announced its intent to form a
"dictatorship of the proletariat" (working class), and proclaimed the
Hungarian Soviet Republic. Hungary thus became the first nation in history outside Soviet Russia with a communist government.

Red Terror/White Terror

Between March 25 and March 30, 1919, the Revolutionary Ruling Council issued a series of decrees aimed at a radical transformation of Hungarian society. The council nationalized all banks, insurance companies,
mines, and transportation systems. It handed over factories to "workers'
councils." It placed all private and church schools under state control.
(The Roman Catholic Church owned more than 60 percent of Hungary's
elementary and middle schools.) It abolished the regular court system and

replaced it with "workers' tribunals." The council also reorganized the army as a pro-Communist Hungarian Red Army, and created the Hungarian Red Guard, a Communist-controlled militia charged with maintaining internal order.

On April 3, the council took its biggest step: it abolished all private property and decreed a massive land-reform program. All middle-sized and large estates were expropriated by the state with no compensation for the owners. However, the program contained an important catch: the peasants would not receive any private plots. Instead, the estates were transformed into collective farms.

There was no strong opposition to these decrees. Centrist and right-wing politicians either fled the capital (or the country), or were cowed into silence by the Red Guard. The church and big landowners complained, but were politically powerless to stop their property from being seized. Landless peasants resented the fact that they still were not going to receive any land of their own, but soldiers and militia kept them quiet. On the other hand, tens of thousands of industrial workers applauded the changes.

Outside Hungary, the Allied countries were alarmed. At the time the council took power, the United States, Britain, France, and other countries were attempting to militarily overthrow the Communists in Russia. Now, suddenly, there was a Marxist-Leninist state in central Europe. They feared that Hungary might attempt to spread communism to Austria, or even Germany. Soviet Russia was the only country to give Hungary's new government diplomatic recognition.

Romania, apparently with the quiet approval of France, invaded southeast Hungary in mid-April in order to secure its hold on Transylvania. When Hungarian troops failed to halt the onslaught, Romanian forces pushed all the way to the Tisza River, in eastern Hungary. In May, a frightened Revolutionary Ruling Council directed units of the Red Army into Slovakia and Ruthenia so as to open a corridor between Hungary and Russia. The council hoped that Russia would send troops to help Hungary battle against Romania, but the Lenin regime was too preoccupied with the Allied military intervention in Russia to offer any such aid. The Hungarian Red Army was fought to a standstill in Slovakia by troops of the newly formed Czech army. On June 3, 1919, Hungarian opposition figures formed a coalition rival government in the southeastern Hungarian city of Szeged, which the Communists had abandoned before the Romanian invasion. Count Károlyi, who had once been Hungary's president, assumed leadership of the rival government. Count Pál Teleki, a political moderate, was the foreign minister. Admiral Miklós Horthy de Nagybánya—a former military aide to Emperor Francis Joseph—led the so-called National Army, a force recruited by right-wing activist Gyula Gömbös de Jafka.

As June progressed, both domestic and foreign situations deteriorated rapidly for the Revolutionary Ruling Council. The inability to defeat the Czechs in Slovakia and the Romanians in eastern Hungary discredited the Red Army. Shortages of fuel and food made the population restless. Communism lost favor in the countryside because landless peasants refused to accept collectivization. As public disorders mounted, the council used the police and Red Guard to crack down on the public. The crackdown, which included arbitrary jailings and torture, became known as the "Red Terror."

By the end of July, Romanian troops had crossed the Tisza and were approaching Budapest. The Allies proposed to intercede with the Romanians—to prevent a takeover of most of Hungary by Romania—but only if the Revolutionary Ruling Council stepped down. The council initially resisted the proposal, but gave in when the Social Democrats (who resented the Communist domination of the council) withdrew from the ruling coalition. The council formally resigned on August 1, 1919, and its leaders quickly left the country. The Hungarian Soviet Republic was no more. Romanian troops entered Budapest on August 3, 1919, with no resistance and remained in Hungary until October of that year.

Hungary endured nearly a year of political instability and social chaos following the end of the Communist reign. The period became known as the era of "White Terror." The term *white* signified "anticommunist." As many as 5,000 people were killed during the White Terror, and tens of thousands were imprisoned without trial. Known or suspected Communists and radical Socialists, as well as Jews—who were identified with communism in the public mind—were hunted down and jailed by the authorities or murdered by right-wing vigilante groups.

Taken together, the two periods of terror—the Red Terror and the White Terror—revealed to Hungarians a vicious social undercurrent that they had never experienced in modern times. It would surface decades

Admiral Miklós Horthy de Nagybánya, pictured here in 1921, was Hungary's head of state from 1920 to 1944. (Library of Congress)

later in the form of fascism during World War II, and after that in the guise of the Communist secret police.

The most significant political event prior to the summer of 1920 was the appointment by parliament of Admiral Miklós Horthy to the post of regent. (A regent is someone, not necessarily of royal blood, who rules in place of a monarch.) Horthy had returned to Budapest on November 16, 1919, at the head of the 25,000-strong National Army, the fighting force of the Szeged opposition government.

Horthy assumed the regency after a lengthy debate in parliament over the future of Hungary's king Charles IV (the former emperor Charles I), the last of Austria's Hapsburg rulers. Charles had been living in Switzerland since renouncing the throne of Austria-Hungary in 1918. Since he had never formally abdicated as king of Hungary, some members of parliament—backed by wealthy landowners and the Roman Catholic Church—supported his return. Others argued that Hungary should only have an elected, figurehead king, if any king at all. The Horthy regency was the result of a compromise.

From August 1919 to July 1920, Hungary was ruled by a series of interim governments. National elections were held in January 1920 and the new National Smallholders' Party, which mainly represented middle-class landowners, won 40 percent of the seats in the newly restored National Assembly (parliament). Smallholder Sándor Simonyi-Semadam became the premier in March 1920.

Together, these different governments repealed nearly all the decrees of the Revolutionary Ruling Council. Private property was again legal and land reform was rolled back. The elite landowners got back their estates, but their political power was in decline. The governments not only failed to improve Hungary's ruined economy, but they were also unable to keep Hungary's territories from being snatched away by the victorious Allied powers.

The Treaty of Trianon

The victorious Allies, known as the "Great Powers" after World War I, and the defeated Central Powers began peace talks in Paris in April 1919 over such issues as war reparations and the disposition of territories. The 'owers did not accept Hungary's argument that it had been only a reluctant partner of Germany and had not sought any territorial gains in the war. The victors, particularly France, were in a punitive mood, and the result was the Treaty of Trianon.

The treaty, signed on June 4, 1920, dismembered what had been the prewar Kingdom of Hungary. The terms outraged Magyars and inspired a popular slogan of resistance: "No, no, never!" To this day, many Hungarians resent what was imposed on them in Paris in 1920. The treaty wounded Hungary's national pride. To the average Hungarian in 1920, the neighboring Slav lands were as much a part of Hungary as the city of Budapest or the Great Plain. It was inconceivable to most Hungarians that those lands could be taken away by the stroke of a pen. The Allies and the Slavs, of course, had a much different view. They regarded the Magyars as persecutors and tyrants. The treaty was the price Hungary had to pay to end the Allied economic boycott of Hungary and to reenter the world community of nations.

In essence, the treaty forced Hungary to relinquish 89,748 square miles of territory and 13.3 million people. Prewar Hungary had comprised 125,641 square miles and a total population of 20.9 million. The treaty reduced Hungary to an area of 35,983 square miles and a population (according to a 1920 census) of 7.6 million. The treaty awarded all of Transylvania, plus two small neighboring regions, to Romania. That amounted to 31.6 percent of Hungary's prewar land and 5.3 million people. The new nation of Czechoslovakia, which incorporated Slovakia and Ruthenia, received 19.34 percent of Hungary's prewar lands and 3.3 million people. The new Kingdom of Serbs, Croats, and Slovenes (which would be renamed Yugoslavia in 1929) received 6.4 percent of prewar Hungarian territory and 1.5 million people.

A major concern of Hungary was that the treaty left 3.3 million Magyars living in areas that were now under Romanian or Slavic control. That figure included 1.7 million Magyars in Romania (mainly in Transylvania), 1 million in Czechoslovakia (mainly in Slovakia), and more than 500,000 in the soon-to-be Yugoslavia (mainly in northern Serbia). About 350,000 Magyars immigrated to Hungary from the ceded territories soon after the treaty was signed. With its economy wrecked, Hungary could barely absorb the immigrants.

In addition to the Treaty of Trianon stripping Hungary of its subject territories, the document also prohibited Hungary from having a standing army of more than 35,000 men—with no tanks or heavy artillery. So, Hungary entered the postwar period with vastly shrunken borders, a devastated economy, and no military to speak of. The stage was set for the Horthy Era.

The Horthy Era Begins

The authoritarian Horthy Era—the period of the regency of Admiral Miklós Horthy de Nagybánya—which began in 1920 and peaked in 1930, was one of the most stable periods in Hungarian history. But it also laid the groundwork for Hungary's slide toward fascism and its disastrous alliance with Nazi Germany in World War II. It was because of that alliance that Hungary ended up a satellite of the Soviet Union from the late 1940s until the early 1990s.

In July 1920, when Count Pál Teleki took over as premier, the economy was in a shambles. One-half of the nation's workforce, including 150,000 workers in Budapest alone, were unemployed. Inflation (uncontrolled price rises) was running at about 6,000 percent, meaning the national currency, the crown, was worth 1/6,000 of its prewar value. Crop yields were a fraction of what they had been before the war.

The Teleki government was unsuccessful in easing the country's economic plight, but it did institute a modest land-reform program. Under the program, the owners of large estates voluntarily distributed 1.1 million acres of land to about 100,000 landless peasants and 300,000 smallholders. The program left more than 19 million acres in the hands of the rich, however.

Teleki resigned as premier in April 1920 and was succeeded by the government leader who was to be most closely associated with the Horthy Era, Count István Bethlen. Bethlen had a talent for gaining the respect of many political and social factions. The landed gentry respected him because he was from a wealthy landowning family. The right wing respected him because, in 1919, he had organized a group of Hungarian exiles in Vienna to oppose the Hungarian Communist regime. The center-left, most particularly the reformed Social Democrats, respected him because of his vigorous efforts to free jailed leftists and halt the remnants of the White Terror.

Hungarian peasant farmers walking to market in 1924. (Library of Congress)

The new premier was faced with a crisis in October 1920, when King Charles IV came back to Hungary from Switzerland with the support of some army units that wanted him to return to the throne. Premier Bethlen and Admiral Horthy rallied a force of army troops and right-wing militiamen (led by Gyula Gömbös) to defeat the king's forces in a battle west of Budapest on October 23. Horthy captured King Charles and later exiled him to an island off the coast of Portugal. Charles, the last monarch to wear the Crown of St. Stephen, died in exile in 1922.

Bethlen's power base was the Christian Social Party (renamed the Unity Party in 1922), which he forged into a broad-based alliance of wealthy landowners, impoverished gentry (those who had owned land in the Slavic territories taken away from Hungary), the urban Christian middle class, government bureaucrats, and, for a time, extreme-right civilian and military figures. The far-right faction, led by Gömbös, broke away from the party in 1923 and formed its own political organization, the Party of Racial Defense. Gombos later returned to the Unity Party and became one of its most powerful figures.

Even with a degree of political stability, the country's economic recovery was slow. The government attempted to counter rampant inflation—16,300 percent in 1924—with wage and price controls. The government banned businesses from raising their prices or increasing their workers' pay. The controls inevitably led to shortages and a decline in the standard of living, particularly in the rural areas. Industrial production continued to lag: it was only 60 percent of prewar levels in 1924. High tariffs (taxes on imports) in the other countries of Europe made it more difficult for Hungary to export goods.

Hungary joined the League of Nations (a forerunner to the United Nations) in 1923 and the following year was able to get a loan from the league of 250 million gold crowns at an annual interest rate of 7.5 percent. The loan was conditioned on Hungary honoring the terms of the Treaty of Trianon. The loan was crucial because the Hungarian national treasury was empty and no international banks or individual countries were willing to lend Hungary money to aid its economic recovery. Bethlen used the loan to help stabilize Hungary's currency and subsidize exports. In 1927, the government replaced the crown with a new currency, the pengő, to fight inflation. One pengő was equal to 1,250 paper crowns.

Hungary became increasingly protectionist. It placed high tariffs on imported goods in the late 1920s, thus shielding domestic industries from foreign competition. With the aid of foreign capital investment and more foreign loans, unemployment dropped to about 15 percent and overall production picked up.

But the recovery was painfully slow, and Hungarian workers were angry. A series of strikes instigated by the far left failed to dampen the recovery. The Communist Party had been banned in 1921, but underground Communists and other radicals united to form the Socialist Workers' Party in 1925. The party had little support on the national level, but it began to attract some dissatisfied laborers in the major cities in Hungary.

Bethlen's only real political challenge came from the so-called Democratic Bloc, a center-left coalition of the Social Democrats and the new National Bourgeois-Democratic Party (a forerunner of the current Alliance of Free Democrats). The bloc drew support from Jews, moderate leftist intellectuals, and people who wanted Hungary to be ruled as a constitutional monarchy. The bloc demanded labor reforms, more land reform, and an end to the government's anti-Semitic policies. (Right-wingers blamed Jews for Hungary's economic problems. Official anti-Semitism was on the rise and would greatly increase in the late 1930s, when Hungary was aligning itself with Nazi Germany. Jews would be banned from government work and universities, and prohibited from owning real estate and certain businesses.)

Bethlen outflanked the opposition by issuing a decree in 1926 to re-create an upper house of parliament that would be filled by hereditary members of the aristocracy. These members would be appointed by the regent. Since the aristocracy supported the ruling Unity Party, the government could effectively block any opposition legislation. In the parliamentary elections of December 1926, the Unity Party captured 60 percent of the vote and 170 seats, solidifying the government's hold.

Hungary dutifully adhered to the Treaty of Trianon throughout the 1920s, although the document inspired simmering resentment among the proud Magyars over the lost Slavic lands. However, the country was too weak militarily to recover by force the territories that were taken away, and the flow of foreign loans, upon which Hungary's economic recovery depended, would cease if Hungary violated the treaty.

The closest Hungary came to breaking the treaty was in 1925, when it was revealed that the government had counterfeited French and Czechoslovakian bank notes in order to finance Magyar opposition activities in Slovakia. (Bethlen and former premier Pál Teleki were apparently behind the forgery operation.) France was angered, and Czechoslovakia briefly threatened to invade Hungary. But the scandal was played down by the other Great Powers on the ground that no real harm had been done.

Flirting with Fascism

The Great Depression hit Hungary in 1931, reversing the country's modest economic recovery of the 1920s. The depression was a worldwide economic downturn triggered by the collapse of the U.S. stock market in October 1929. It was characterized by massive unemployment, bank failures, business shutdowns, and falling agricultural prices. The economic upheaval drove many Hungarians into movements of the extreme right, which promised better times to come.

The depression shattered Hungary. Almost overnight, 15 percent of the country's factories shut down and 30 percent of the industrial labor force was unemployed. Those who retained their jobs in the government and private sectors were forced to accept drastic pay cuts. Agriculture industry was crippled by declining prices and mounting surpluses. More than 60,000 small and medium-sized farms were abandoned when their owners defaulted on bank loans. Nearly 500,000 farm laborers could not find work. The country's biggest bank, the Hungarian General Credit Bank, narrowly averted bankruptcy.

To make matters worse, Hungary's foreign debt stood at $1 billion (in 1930 U.S. dollars), at that time an astronomical sum for such a small country. The foreign credit that had fueled the economic recovery now was a weight around the nation's neck. Unrest spread throughout Hungary. Unemployed workers and jobless farm laborers rioted, triggering harsh responses by the police. And nearly a decade of political stability crumbled.

Two key factions of the ruling Unity Party—wealthy landowners and middle-class farmers—left to form their own political organization, the Independent Smallholders' Party. One of the founders, Zoltán Tildy, would play a major role in the post–World War II era. The Unity Party narrowly won the parliamentary elections of June 1931, but Premier Bethlen resigned two months later. Admiral Horthy named Count Gyula Károlyi to the post.

The Károlyi government was unable to ease the impact of the depression, and he personally was unable to mediate among quarreling factions in the Unity Party. As a result, Horthy fired Károlyi in September 1932 and appointed the popular war minister, Gyula Gömbös de Jafka, premier.

Gömbös was the most visible of Hungary's right-wing nationalists. He was an open admirer of such Fascist leaders as Benito Mussolini, who had come to power in Italy in 1922, and Adolf Hitler, who came to power in Germany in 1933. He favored an alliance of Hungary with the two great Fascist powers.

Under fascism, all the key elements of society—political, economic, and military—unite, usually under a dictatorial leader, to achieve a national purpose set by the leader. Nationalism, meanwhile, is a strong, sometimes obsessive, devotion by a people to their own interests. According to historian Hans Kohn, nationalism goes beyond simple pride in one's culture or traditions. Nationalism is, he says,

> The conviction of being a people chosen by God or History has, in ancient and again in modern times, sometimes even fused with a biological belief in the value of common descent and racial purity, in the embodiment of the true faith or the true civilization in people of one "seed" or "blood."

Taken to an extreme, Kohn argues, nationalism results in the belief that only your own ethnic group should rule, and that people outside of your group should be ruled. In other words, "Fascism [is] an exaggerated, self-centered form of nationalism."

Gömbös's political good fortune inspired the founding in the 1930s of a host of Hungarian fascist parties and organizations. They included the National Socialist Hungarian Workers' Party (later renamed the Scythe Cross Movement), the United National Socialist Party, the Party of National Will, and the Racial Defense Socialist Party.

Although differing slightly in agendas, all of these fascist groups were virulently anti-Semitic (while espousing "Christian values") and antiforeigner (while emphasizing Magyar "racial" and cultural superiority). They opposed Hungary's traditional aristocracy and exalted the working classes. They disparaged "bourgeois [middle-class] democracy" as practiced in the United States, Great Britain, and France. And they called for a return of Hungary's "stolen lands," using hatred of the Treaty of Trianon as a tool to recruit followers.

In spite of Gömbös's popularity, Hungary never became a true fascist state, except for a brief period in 1944–45. There were other prominent leaders of the extreme right—Ferenc Szálasi, Count Fidel Palffy, and Zoltán Boszormeny—and they were each too personally ambitious to unite under Gömbös. Also, Hungary's aristocrats and leftists in the 1930s still posed a formidable political opposition.

But the most significant factor contributing to Hungary's failure to become a fascist state in the 1930s was Gömbös's sudden death—apparently of natural causes—in October 1935, while on a visit to the Nazi German capital of Berlin. A few months before he died, the Unity Party won a narrow victory in parliamentary elections that were tainted with widespread vote-rigging.

During his three years as premier, Gömbös had succeeded in drawing Hungary closer to Italy and Germany. The Gömbös government was able to persuade Germany to open its market to Hungarian produce, and did secure some loans from the German government. However, the premier had a more important motive behind his drive to align Hungary with the Fascist powers: he wanted Hitler and Mussolini to use their influence to help Hungary recover its lost territories.

Gömbös's successor as premier was Kálmán Darányi, a cautious conservative who was wary of aligning Hungary too closely with Germany, remembering the ill-fated Hungarian-German alliance in World War I. Under Darányi, there was a modest crackdown on the extreme right, which he regarded as a threat to the status quo. One of those sent to jail in 1938 was Ferenc Szálasi, who had become Hungary's most prominent fascist since the death of Gömbös.

Szálasi was the creator of "Hungarianism," a philosophy that incorporated Magyar nationalism with German National Socialist (Nazi) principles. Szálasi founded the Party of National Will in 1937, but it was banned by the government. In 1939, while he was in prison, his followers founded the Arrow Cross Party/Hungarist Movement, a fascist organization that became one of the two most important far-right groups in Hungary in the late 1930s. The other was the National Socialist Hungarian Party.

The Darányi government quietly accepted Germany's forced takeover of Austria, in March 1938. The takeover, combined with Hitler's open designs on Czechoslovakia, scared all but the most right-wing Hungarians. Darányi redirected government spending toward rearmament and ordered a buildup of Hungary's army far beyond the 35,000-man limit set by the Treaty of Trianon. The Great Powers did not care about this treaty violation because they were too preoccupied with Germany's activities.

Admiral Horthy dismissed Darányi in May 1938 and appointed as premier Béla Imrédy, the head of the National Bank. Imrédy attempted to steer a neutral course by balancing Hungary's ties to Germany and Italy with closer Hungarian ties to Great Britain and Poland.

The Munich Agreement of September 1938 forced Czechoslovakia to cede its Sudentenland region to Germany. Hitler then made it clear to the Imrédy government that if Hungary wanted German help in recovering its lost lands, then it would have to actively support any further German moves against Czechoslovakia. Germany would absorb most of Czechoslovakia in mid-March 1939, with no objection from Hungary.

Following the Munich Agreement, Hungary held talks with Czechoslovakia over a "voluntary" return of Hungarian territories. German foreign minister Joachim von Ribbentrop and Italian foreign minister Galeazzo Ciano acted as mediators. On November 2, 1938, at a conference in Vienna, Ribbentrop and Ciano ruled that Hungary was the rightful owner of 4,615 square miles of the eastern Czechoslovak regions of Slovakia and Carpatho-Ukraine (formerly Ruthenia). The affected areas contained 1.1 million people, including 590,000 Magyars.

At first, the Hungarian public rejoiced at the return of land and the repatriation of the Magyars, but the mood soured into complaints that the ruling, known as the Vienna Award, only encompassed a relatively narrow strip along Hungary's border with Czechoslovakia. Imrédy had hoped for, and did not receive, a common border with Poland, which was north of a point where Slovakia touched Carpatho-Ukraine in an area not included in the Vienna Award. When Hungary made preparations to take the remainder of Carpatho-Ukraine by force, Hitler adamantly forbade the move.

Imrédy resigned on November 23, 1938, but again accepted the premier's post when Horthy was unable to find anyone willing to take the job. Imrédy formed a new cabinet, this one with a noticeable right-wing cast. It included as foreign minister Count István Csaky, who made no secret of his admiration for Nazi Germany.

Imrédy's second term as head of the government lasted only until February 1939. Horthy dismissed him on the pretext of discovering Jewish ancestry in Imrédy's family. Count Pál Teleki, a former premier, once again headed the government. But Foreign Minister Csaky and other right-wingers remained in the cabinet and wielded great influence.

Teleki, bending to cabinet pressure, forged closer Hungarian-German relations. Hungary received its reward in March 1939, when Germany did not interfere with Hungary's seizure of the entire Carpatho-Ukraine. A month later, Hungary occupied an adjacent chunk of Slovakia, thus attaining its coveted common border with Poland. Together, the seizures gave Hungary an additional 4,800 square miles of territory and more than 500,000 people, a majority of whom were ethnic Ukrainians.

Recovering portions of the lost lands boosted the credibility of the right wing among the Hungarian populace. Teleki's own center-right organization, the Party of Hungarian Life, won 181 of 260 contested seats in the elections of March 1939. Extreme-right parties captured 48 seats, making them the second-strongest political force in parliament.

In the Axis

Germany invaded Poland on September 1, 1939, beginning World War II, the bloodiest conflict in history. By 1945, at the end of the war, more than 50 million people were dead, and property damage was in the trillions of dollars. The issues surrounding the war were simpler and more straightforward than those in World War I. The Allied nations successfully defeated an attempt by the Axis powers to achieve worldwide military domination. The major Allies were the United States, Great Britain, the Soviet Union, China, France, and Canada. The main Axis countries were Germany, Japan, and Italy.

Hungary, Romania, and Bulgaria were among the less powerful Axis partners. Hungary did not formally join the Axis alliance until a year after the war began. It would deeply regret its involvement.

In the beginning, Hungary wanted no part of the war. Premier Teleki quickly declared Hungary a "nonbelligerent" nation following the German invasion of Poland. In addition—as if to show its independence from the Nazis—Hungary opened its new border with Poland and granted political asylum to approximately 150,000 fleeing Poles.

Teleki attempted to navigate a very difficult course: Hungary increasingly supplied the German war machine with raw materials (oil, bauxite, iron) and farm goods, while at the same time refusing to commit any troops to the Axis cause. He justified the policy with the explanation that Hungary's friendship with the Fascist powers was based solely on a desire to get back all of its lost territories. He even privately assured the British that Hungary was not completely on the side of the Germans.

Teleki's caution was not popular at home. Many Hungarians were dazzled by the Axis powers' initial military successes, and they wanted Hungary to get some of the bounty, or at least to get back all of the lost lands. With the economy on a war footing, thousands of new jobs opened up and wages rose. The ranks of Hungarian fascist groups swelled, particularly Ferenc Szálasi's militant Arrow Cross movement. When in 1940 the Soviet Union bullied Romania into handing over Bessarabia (a region on the Soviet-Romanian border), public pressure impelled Teleki to try the same tactic to force Romania to return Transylvania. Since Romania was a major supplier of oil to Germany, Hitler did not want to risk the disruption of a Hungary-Romania war. As a result, Germany and Italy again decided in favor of a Hungarian territorial claim. The Second Vienna Award, made on August 30, 1940, gave

THE JEWS OF HUNGARY

The first Jews arrived in Hungary at the invitation of King Stephen in the 12th century. By 1787, Jews numbered 83,000, or 1 percent of Hungary's population. There followed a heavy Jewish immigration, particularly from Galicia (a region in east-central Europe) and from the Czech land of Moravia. In 1880, there were 700,000 Jews in Hungary.

The Jewish people did not find it difficult to assimilate. They willingly adopted the Magyar language and some aspects of Magyar culture. Laws in 1859 and 1867 gave them full legal protection and civil rights equal to those of other Hungarians. Unlike other countries in central Europe, few Hungarian Jews lived in rural communities. Most settled in large towns and cities, especially in Budapest, and on large estates.

Jews made up Hungary's first real middle class. They became business owners, bankers, lawyers, doctors, and teachers. Jewish capital financed the growth of Hungary's major industries.

After World War I, Hungary's Jews suffered from increasing persecution. First, they were blamed unfairly for the brief Communist dictatorship of Béla Kun. Then, in the 1930s and early 1940s, a succession of profascist Hungarian governments passed laws that took away their legal protections and civil liberties. Many Jews, such as renowned playwright Ferenc Molnár, chose to leave Hungary.

In 1944, an estimated 450,000 Hungarian Jews were displaced to Nazi German concentration camps, where most perished. Today, about 80,000 Jews remain in Hungary.

Hungary 16,500 square miles of northern Transylvania. The recovered region contained 2.5 million people, mainly Magyar residents.

Teleki continued on a contradictory course. Lured by the prospect of recovering more lost territory, on November 20, 1940, Hungary formally joined the Axis by signing the Tripartite Pact (the alliance of Germany, Italy, and Japan). But less than a month later, Hungary signed a friendship pact with Yugoslavia—in spite of the fact that Germany had plans to take over Yugoslavia.

When the Germans invaded Yugoslavia in March 1941, Hitler demanded that his troops be allowed passage through Hungary. Teleki refused and was vilified, not only by the Hungarian political right, but by the regent, Admiral Horthy. On April 3, a despondent Teleki committed suicide.

The new premier was László Bárdossy, who had replaced István Csaky as foreign minister in February 1941. Bárdossy did not like the Nazis but was convinced Germany was going to win the war. He wanted Hungary to be firmly on the winning side.

Bárdossy directed Hungarian forces to follow the German army into Yugoslavia and take over the Bacska region, about 4,200 square miles that had been taken away from Hungary in 1920. With this move, Hungary regained a significant amount of territory—more than 50 percent of its pre-Trianon lands—and got back more than 5 million people, including more than 2 million Magyars. The Bárdossy government immediately launched the same kind of "Magyarization" program among its recaptured Slavic subjects that had caused so much resentment prior to World War I. Once again, Hungary forced its Slavs to adopt Magyar customs and use the Magyar language.

Hitler would not let Hungary enjoy the rewards of Axis partnership without exacting a price: Hungary's active participation in the war. When Germany invaded the Soviet Union in June 1941, Hungary sent along about 40,000 troops. The Nazi offensive stalled several months later, and the compliant Bárdossy acceded to a German demand for many more troops. The Second Hungarian Army, more than 200,000 men, was sent off to fight in the Soviet Union in January 1942.

Bárdossy's willingness to commit large numbers of troops to the Russian Front—where the Axis offensive had slowed and casualties were frighteningly high—worried Admiral Horthy. The regent removed

Livia Nador, pictured here in 1945, was a prominent stage actress before World War II. She survived the Holocaust, unlike many thousands of her fellow Hungarian Jews. (Still Picture Records LICON)

Bárdossy as premier in March 1942 and named Miklós Kállay (or Kállai), an aristocrat, to the post. Under Kállay, Hungary made no fur- ther large-scale commitments of troops to the war, but the country's resources and production continued to be bled by Germany. As Germany was slow in paying for the goods, and stopped paying Hungary altogether in 1943, inflation soared.

Hungarians at home felt the bitter impact of the war in early January 1943, when the Second Hungarian Army was annihilated in a Soviet counterattack near the Russian town of Voronezh. Anti-German sentiment in Hungary rose sharply when it was learned that the army unit had been sacrificed by the Nazis in order to cover retreating German troops. In all, 40,000 men of the Second Army died in the battle. Another 70,000 were taken prisoner by the Soviets, and many of them would die in captivity.

The bloodshed on the Russian front fueled antiwar sentiment in Hungary. In 1943, Kállay opened secret contacts with the British on the possibility of Hungary withdrawing from the conflict. The sole condition he proposed was that Hungary be allowed to keep its recovered territories when the war ended. But the British insisted that it would not be enough for Hungary to simply stop fighting; Hungary would actually have to declare war on Germany. Kállay's government rejected the idea of Hungary turning against the Axis.

By 1944, Soviet forces were steadily advancing westward toward Hungary, and Hungary was being bombed by the Allies. On March 17, 1944, Hitler ordered Horthy to fire the premier and appoint to the post Lieutenant General Dome Szótjay, a longtime Hungarian ambassador to Germany who was a well-known Nazi sympathizer. Szótjay filled his cabinet with members of the Hungarian National Socialist Alliance, a coalition of fascist groups.

On March 19, 1944, eight German divisions (about 150,000 troops) moved into Hungary, purportedly at the request of the Szótjay government. With German army and SS (elite guard) units backing him up, Szótjay was free to neutralize all domestic opposition. Thousands of leftists, including leading Social Democrats and Smallholders, and intellectuals and journalists were imprisoned or sent to German concentration camps. The police and Arrow Cross militia rounded up as many as 450,000 Hungarian Jews for deportation to Nazi death camps, a move protested by Horthy and by the Catholic Church.

Up to 20,000 Hungarian Jews escaped deportation thanks to a courageous Swedish diplomat, Raoul Wallenberg. He gave Swedish identity papers that allowed them to leave Hungary under the diplomatic protection of his country. Sweden was officially neutral in the war. Therefore, persons carrying Swedish identity papers were not regarded as combatants. Wallenberg disappeared at the end of the war. He is believed to have been arrested by the Soviets and to have died in a Soviet prison.

The government banned all political parties in August 1944. Horthy gathered the courage to dismiss Szótjay on August 24 and replaced him with a trusted aide, General Géza Lakatos. In September, when Soviet troops crossed the border into Hungary, Lakatos entered secret talks with them over an armistice. Like the British in 1943, the Soviets demanded that Hungary join the fight against Germany. Lakatos reluctantly agreed.

Horthy, with no prior consultation with the Hungarian military, made a nationwide radio broadcast on October 15, 1944. He ordered Hungarian soldiers to stop fighting the Soviets, but he did not order them to turn against the Germans. The reaction was immediate: Arrow Cross militiamen took over government buildings, and German troops seized the Buda Palace (the regent's official residence) and arrested Horthy. SS commandos kidnapped Horthy's youngest son and took him to Germany as a hostage. The Hungarian military High Command reaffirmed its loyalty to its Axis partner.

The Germans threatened to kill Horthy's son and coerced the former regent into withdrawing his announcement. They also forced Horthy to name Ferenc Szálasi—the head of the Arrow Cross—as Hungary's new head of government. Szálasi, using Hitler as role model, gave himself the title of "leader of the nation." The Nazis kept Horthy under house arrest in the palace. The Horthy Era, which began in 1920, was finished.

For the next four months, the SS and Arrow Cross murdered thousands of people in a reign of terror. As noted by Hungarian historian Joerg K. Hoensch:

> This terror was directed against the new government's political opponents and Jews who had not yet been deported. During the winter of 1944–45, over 80,000 Jews, mainly older people and children, were driven into concentration camps and perished. . . . Most of Hungary's provincial Jews fell victim to the extermination measures carried out by the Germans and the Arrow Cross.

During the reign of terror, the Hungarian army collapsed, with thousands of soldiers either surrendering to the Soviets or deserting their units. German forces could not hold back the Soviet offensive. The Germans were forced to pull back to the Buda Hills, across the Danube River, when the Soviet Red Army captured the Pest section of the capital in January 1945. One elderly Hungarian interviewed in 1987 recalled:

"The Germans defended Buda until the middle of February. They had set up a hospital in the caverns under the castle. As the Nazi troops prepared to retreat, they killed their own men who were too badly wounded to walk, killed them with flamethrowers, instead of surrendering them to the Russians."

The Soviets captured Buda Castle (freeing Horthy) on February 13, 1945, after heavy fighting that destroyed much of the city and killed many civilians. The last German troops exited Hungary in early April 1945. The remnants of Szálasi's Fascist regime fled with them.

The toll of the conflict was horrendous. No one knows how many Hungarians (including Hungarian Jews sent to Nazi death camps) perished in the conflict, but the figure definitely is in the hundreds of thousands. The capital of Budapest—already heavily damaged by Allied bombings in 1944—was largely destroyed in the street fighting in 1945. Hungary's economic structure was wrecked. And the conflict opened the door to a political takeover by the Communists and four decades of subjugation by the Soviets.

NOTES

p. 42 "'The conviction . . .'" Hans Kohn, *The Age of Nationalism* (New York: Harper & Brothers, 1962), p. 17.

p. 42 "'Fascism [is] . . .'" Kohn, p. 26.

p. 50 "'This terror . . .'" Joerg K. Hoensch, *A History of Modern Hungary: 1867–1986* (New York: Longman, 1988), p. 157.

p. 51 "'The Germans . . .'" Hans Magnus Enzensberger, *Europa, Europa: Forays into a Continent* (New York: Random House, 1989), p. 129.

3

Hungary under Communism

The Rise of Communism

At the end of World War II, Hungary faced an uncertain future. Hundreds of thousands of its people had died in the conflict. Transylvania, Carpatho-Ukraine, and the other neighboring territories restored to Hungary in 1938–40 were once again lost. The economy was in ruins. Inflation made the national currency, the pengő, worthless. All of the bridges over Hungary's two main rivers, the Danube and the Tisza, had been destroyed. The fighting had demolished one-half of all the nation's industrial plants. One-half of Hungary's farm livestock was gone. And one out of every four houses in the country had been damaged in the war.

Worse still, the country was occupied by the Soviet Red Army, which had looted and raped its way across Hungary in the last stage of the war. In the name of "reparations," the Soviets had dismantled and shipped back to the USSR much of Hungary's undamaged factory equipment. In addition, the Soviets deported more than 250,000 Hungarians to labor camps in Russia's cold, desolate Siberia region. Many of the deportees—soldiers, accused fascists, and anticommunist activists—would not survive the freezing temperatures, backbreaking work, and filthy conditions in the labor camps. Most of those who survived the ordeal returned to Hungary broken in mind, body, and spirit.

Although few Hungarians realized it, their proud little country was about to become an integral part of the Soviet sphere of influence in Eastern Europe. Hungary was destined to become a Soviet satellite, just like neighboring Romania and Czechoslovakia.

With the departure of the Fascists, Hungary was ruled initially by a provisional government of the National Independence Front under General Béla Dálnoki-Miklós. The front had been formed in the city of Szeged in December 1944 under the protection of the advancing Soviet Red Army. The organization was a coalition of Hungarian leftist opposition parties: Communists, Social Democrats, National Peasants, and Bourgeois-Democrats. The only major opposition party not represented in the front was the Independent Smallholders, led by Zoltán Tildy and Ferenc Nagy. It was the front that signed an armistice with the Allies on January 20, 1945.

The coalition enabled the Communist Party, which had been banned in Hungary since 1921, to emerge into the open. The party was careful to present itself publicly as just another member of the front, but in fact, it was secretly planning to become Hungary's dominant political force. The architect of the plan was Mátyás Rákosi, a Hungarian disciple of Soviet leader Joseph Stalin.

Rákosi (1892–1971) had commanded the Red Guard during the short-lived Hungarian Soviet Republic of 1919. He had spent most of the pre–World War II and war years in the USSR, where he had become an enthusiastic follower of the Stalinist style of communism. Stalinism emphasized rigid obedience to the party and the party leader. On the orders of the Soviet dictator, Rákosi returned to Hungary in 1945 and took over the leadership of the Hungarian Communist Party from Ernő Gerő, another Hungarian Marxist who had received his political training in the USSR.

One aspect of Rákosi's plan called for large numbers of Communists and Communist sympathizers to infiltrate the other parties in the National Independence Front without revealing their true allegiance. Once entrenched in the other parties, they could influence members of those organizations to support policies proposed by the Communist Party. As it turned out, the plan worked very well.

In 1945, the provisional government took two major actions. First, it decreed a large-scale land-reform program. Second, it signed a treaty of friendship and economic cooperation with the Soviet Union.

Under the land-reform decrees of March 1945, the properties held by "fascists" (real or accused), banks, and other financial institutions, as well as much land owned by the Catholic Church, were seized and distributed to the landless peasants, farm laborers, and smallholders. The decrees encompassed almost 8 million acres, or nearly 40 percent of Hungary's arable land. More than 600,000 people received parcels of land averaging about seven acres in size. Some 3.2 million acres of the expropriated lands became the property of the state.

The friendship/economic treaty was signed with the USSR in August 1945. The action was protested by the Western democracies, which viewed it as a move by Stalin to bring Hungary under the Soviet wing. The protest died down when the Soviet government agreed to permit free elections in Hungary.

The 1945 Elections

National elections were held in Hungary on November 7, 1945, under the watchful eye of the Allied Control Commission. The commission, which included representatives of the victorious Allied powers, monitored postwar developments in the former Axis nations.

The elections were perhaps the most free ever held in Hungary up to that time. The Independent Smallholders captured 57 percent of the vote and 245 of the 409 seats in the newly revived National Assembly. The Communist Party, which boasted of having more than 600,000 members, won only 70 seats. The Social Democrats finished third, gaining 67 seats.

The surprisingly weak showing of the Communists was attributed to several factors. The party was linked in the public's mind with the Soviets, whose military occupation was widely unpopular. Second, the wealthy and middle classes leaned toward the Smallholders, who promised liberal democracy coupled with moderate socialism. The urban working class and trade unions resurrected their prewar loyalty to the Social Democrats.

Perhaps the key factor in the Communists' poor showing was the unwillingness of the Hungarian people to replace fascism with the opposite political extreme. They remembered the widespread violence and

A Hungarian collective farm in 1959. Farmers were forced to use oxen due to a shortage of tractors. (AP/Wide World Photos)

disorder of the 1919–20 era, when the Red Terror of the far left had been countered by the White Terror of the far right (see chapter 2). Voters in 1945 endorsed social change without radicalism.

Zoltán Tildy of the Smallholders became Hungary's first postwar premier. Citing the need for national unity, he created a cabinet that had representatives of all of the major parties. The Communists had only four posts in the cabinet, but two were crucial: Mátyás Rákosi was one of the government's two deputy premiers, and Imre Nagy, a Rákosi aide, took over as interior minister.

Nagy (1896–1958) would become the key figure in the anti-Soviet uprising of 1956. He had turned to Marxism while a prisoner of war of the Russians in World War I. In 1945, Nagy was an enthusiastic Stalinist. He formed the Allamvedelmi Osztaly (AVO), or State Security Department, a police organization that would be used eventually to intimidate opponents of the Communists. Illness forced Nagy to give up the post in 1946, but his successor, László Rajk, was another Rákosi aide.

Pro-Soviet Communists regarded Imre Nagy as a traitor. He was executed in 1958, the year this photo was published. (Library of Congress)

"Salami Tactics"

Rákosi and the Communists were much more politically astute, and much more treacherous, than their partners in the postwar ruling coalition. Rákosi's intent was simple: to use any means at his disposal to slice away the opposition piece by piece until only the Communists were left in power. He would later characterize the stratagem as "salami tactics."

One of the first cuts of the "salami" came in February 1946, when he convinced Premier Tildy of the need for a Supreme Economic Council to oversee the recovery of the national economy. The council, which was not answerable to the cabinet, had sweeping powers, including the granting of government loans to industry and the distribution of raw materials. Not surprisingly, Communists dominated the council.

At the other end of the spectrum, Communists infiltrated Hungary's trade unions and workers' committees in numbers large enough to sway decision making in those bodies. They also instigated periodic work stoppages, which in turn played into the hands of the Communists in the government, who advocated state control of industries. At the insistence of the Communists, the government took over Hungary's ironworks in November 1946, and nationalized all of the country's banks and more than 200 large commercial enterprises a year later.

Meanwhile, Communist-dominated "people's courts" prosecuted more than 40,000 people for war crimes between 1945 and 1948. About 20,000 defendants were convicted and, of those, some 500 were executed. (Among those executed were former fascist leader Ferenc Szálasi and former premiers Béla Imredy, László Bárdossy, and Dome Szótjay.) Although the prosecutions were popular with some Hungarians, they contributed to an atmosphere of fear in the country. Communists in parliament used the fear to increase the government's police powers.

In February 1946, the National Assembly proclaimed a new Republic of Hungary, one that for the first time had no monarch or regent. Premier Tildy became Hungary's first president (head of state). Ferenc Nagy of the Smallholders took over as premier.

The ongoing war-crimes prosecutions inevitably spilled over into the political arena. In early 1947, the Communists claimed to have discovered a right-wing plot to overthrow the government. Several high-ranking figures in the Smallholders' Party were implicated and put on trial.

Although their guilt was debatable, it was enough to plant the seeds of discord in the party, which began to splinter with internal bickering. Moderate Smallholders either quit the party or were expelled as it increasingly came under a radical left-wing faction led by István Dobi. Dobi backed an alliance with the Communists.

Ferenc Nagy resigned as premier in May 1947 and was replaced by another Smallholder, Lajos Dinnyés, who was forced to call new elections. By then, the Smallholders were so badly divided into pro- and anticommunist factions they could barely function as a party. The nation's third leading political force, the Social Democratic Party, was filled with Communist sympathizers and therefore provided no real opposition to Communist initiatives. Several small, moderate parties had sprung up in 1946–47, but they were too weak, or too frightened, to provide any real opposition. In the national elections of August 1947, the Communists finished with 100 seats (of 411 contested seats), compared to the Social Democrats' 68 and the Smallholders' 67.

The success of Rákosi's "salami tactics" was now evident. To maintain the illusion that the Communists were not in charge, Rákosi engineered Dinnyés's return as premier. Because he owed his position to the Communists, the premier filled all but four cabinet posts with Communist ministers. That meant that the Rákosi's followers held sway in cabinet votes to determine government policies. Premier Dinnyés was so weak politically that he was compelled to bow to the initiatives of his Communist ministers.

On the foreign scene, Hungary was forced to accept a peace treaty with the Allies that formally returned the country to its 1920 Trianon borders (see chapter 2). On February 18, 1948, Hungary joined the Communist Information Bureau (Cominform), a Soviet-led treaty organization supposedly dedicated to the mutual friendship of Communist parties in Eastern Europe. In fact, Cominform was the earliest manifestation of what would be known as the "Eastern bloc," the USSR and its satellites.

Hungary's first president, Zoltán Tildy, resigned in July 1948. The Communist-dominated parliament picked the Communist-leaning Social Democratic leader Árpád Szakasits to succeed Tildy. Tildy was the last prodemocracy figure to hold high office in Hungary in the late 1940s.

In December 1948, Smallholder István Dobi—by now an open ally of Rákosi—formed a new government. Communists manned all of the significant cabinet posts. Rákosi was a deputy premier, László Rajk was the foreign minister, and an up-and-coming young Marxist named János Kádár was the interior minister. This would be Hungary's last official non-Communist government until the downfall of communism in 1989.

Stalin's Shadow

In 1948, the Communist Party and the Social Democratic Party merged into a single organization, the Hungarian Workers' Party. Hungary proclaimed itself a "people's republic." Several governments came and went, but Communists dominated the cabinets. Mátyás Rákosi, the Workers' Party boss, was in firm control of the country.

There was no longer any true political opposition in Hungary. By 1949, all of the opposition parties had either disappeared or been consolidated into something called the Independence Popular Front. The front was a Communist-controlled organization, with no real independence or political power, that pretended to be an opposition party. The Communists offered the organization as proof to the West that Hungary still was a democracy.

According to Paul E. Zinner, an American expert on Eastern Europe, Rákosi had a simple and cold-blooded concept of how Hungary should be ruled:

> He is said to have expounded his philosophy of government in terms of a "law of large numbers." This, he explained, meant "killing some [people] and corrupting the rest."

Rákosi took his cues from his idol, Soviet leader Joseph Stalin (1879–1953). In power since 1929, Stalin had gained worldwide admiration for rallying his people to turn back the German-led invasion of the USSR in World War II. (An estimated 20 million Soviets died in the war.) However, he was also a ruthless dictator who presided over a brutal police state. Stalin's policies, including the forced collectivization of agriculture (the confiscation of private farms by the government), the mass deportation of ethic minorities to remote areas of the Soviet Union, and the use of secret police and the military to crush dissent, brought suffering to millions of Soviets.

Under Stalin's direction, Soviet-trained Communists like Rákosi gained a foothold and took over the countries of Eastern Europe. Stalin regarded the "satellite" countries as a necessary geographic buffer between the Western democracies and the USSR. He was determined that if his

The brutal policies of Communist leader Mátyás Rákosi, pictured here in a wheat field, spurred Hungary's 1956 uprising. (Library of Congress)

country ever went to war with the West, the battles would be fought in Eastern Europe, not on Soviet soil. The postwar period of tensions between the Soviet Union and the Western nations, lasting roughly from 1945 to 1990, became known as the cold war.

Rákosi emulated Stalin in every way. As Stalin had done in the USSR, Rákosi saw to it that the party had its tentacles in every union hall, every classroom, every factory in Hungary. As described by Zinner, the Communists instituted regimentation and fear in the country:

> . . . Invasion of privacy in a variety of ingenious and highly irritating ways was used to brutalize human sensitivities. Work schedules, compulsory participation in supervised social activities, including [political] seminars and lectures in factories and offices, . . . reduced the amount of leisure time of individuals and the opportunity of families to be together away from the probing scrutiny of their behavior. . . . It was as if the whole working population was under continuous security investigation. Personnel files were kept meticulously to determine the class origin and occupational history of job applicants, and to record entries about their political loyalty and personal demeanor. Called cadre cards (*kader lapok*), . . . they were in fact police files whose very existence put people on guard and impeded social and occupational mobility.

Rákosi's opponents were jailed, executed, or simply disappeared. Even his allies were not safe from Stalinist "purges." A purge was a method by which Communist leaders got rid of political rivals or people whose loyalty was in question. Such people were subjected to "show trials," that is, they were prosecuted on false charges, and through torture or threats were made to publicly confess their guilt. Stalin used purges to imprison, exile, and execute what some estimate at millions of Soviets in the 1930s. As communism advanced in Eastern Europe after World War II, Rákosi and other Stalinists adopted the purge tactic to instill fear among party and government officials in their own countries. In turn, fearful officials were less likely to challenge or disobey Communist leaders.

Hungary's most infamous show trial was held in 1949. The target, László Rajk, the Communist former interior minister, was prosecuted for "nationalist deviance," a phrase that encompassed a vague notion of conspiracy against the party. Rajk was made to confess that he had been an "agent of imperialism" since the 1930s. Of course, he was found guilty and executed.

The AVO (Allamvedelmi Osztaly), the State Security Department, became a more effective tool of terror with the help of advisers from the Soviet NKVD (a forerunner of the KGB secret police). Although the AVO had an undercover arm, the organization was typified by armed thugs in blue uniforms who used threats, beatings, and torture to carry out the will of the party.

As if the AVO was not enough, the party created another brutal security organization, the Allamvedelmi Hatosag (AVH), or State Security Authority. In addition to keeping watch on ordinary citizens, the AVH kept surveillance on party and government officials to root out disloyalty in high places. As detailed by Hungarian historian Joerg K. Hoensch:

After 1950, the dynamic Peter Gabor reorganized the various police organizations with the help of Soviet experts. In the new AVH, he developed a perfect technique of fabricating appropriate conspiracies and confessions at the most opportune moment to exploit a political situation. Thanks to its purges, the secret police, which comprised sixteen departments, kept records on over a million citizens and could rely on some 300,000 informers. . . . It became a semi-autonomous institution which eventually only Moscow could control directly. At the same time, the Soviet police kept its own independent secret-police apparatus in Hungary.

Hungary was a police state from the late 1940s through the late 1950s. Hungarians had to be careful of what they said, the places they went, and whom they met. Informers were everywhere. Some informers were paid by the secret police to gather information. Others were coerced into informing on coworkers, friends, and even family members. Still others felt they had a duty to the country or the party to inform on others.

Hungarians suspected of political crimes—espionage, treason, or counterrevolutionary activities—had no legal protections, unlike criminal suspects in the Western democracies. The AVO and AVH could, and did, enter suspects' homes without warrants and kidnap suspects off the streets. The suspects could be held for questioning as long as the security organizations wanted. Some were tortured until they confessed, even if they had done nothing wrong.

High-ranking religious figures were no more immune to persecution than ordinary Hungarians. When the party placed more than 5,000 religious schools under government control, the move was strongly resisted by József Cardinal Mindszenty, the Roman Catholic primate of Hungary. He was jailed in 1948 as a "subversive," and bravely refused to confess, even when the authorities promised to release him if he would admit guilt. The Vatican (the seat of the Roman Catholic Church) and the Western nations protested Mindszenty's mistreatment, but to no avail.

Economic Failure

Rákosi launched a series of disastrous economic programs in the late 1940s. He attempted to push Hungary, an agrarian country, to rapid Soviet-style "Socialist industrialization." Simply put, Hungary spent millions on heavy industries, particularly iron and steel production. To pave the way for the program, the government nationalized all companies with 10 or more employees and banned the right to strike.

In rural areas, the government confiscated the lands of the remaining small private farmers and forced thousands of rural families into farm cooperatives and collective farms. Cooperatives were state-owned farms that were run by groups of farmers, who sold their produce to the government. As an incentive, they were allowed to own small parcels of land, from which they could keep some produce for themselves, or even sell it on the private market. Collectives, or state farms, were run by the government with the farmers as paid employees.

The only resistance to collectivization came from the *kulaks*, or middle-class landowning farmers. The government maintained control by heavily policing the *kulaks*. No one in the rural areas was safe.

> Police interfered in [country dwellers'] lives just as arbitrarily as in the lives of urban dwellers. Flying squads of secret policemen (the dreaded

blue-uniformed AVO) swooped down on villages, usually to "aid" with the organization of a collective farm or to "improve" compulsory deliveries of crops. The techniques they employed were simple and effective. Beating or placing a person on a hot stove usually sufficed to soften up resistance to joining a collective or to surrendering hoarded grain.

At one point, the Rákosi regime formulated a list of about 38,000 opponents and potential opponents in Budapest. They were all rounded up by the security forces and forced to move into the countryside to work as laborers on collective farms. The government confiscated all their property. The victims of the forced resettlement included 14,000 Jews, more than 100 former aristocrats, 85 military generals, plus numerous anticommunist politicians, factory owners, bankers, and business executives. The forced exodus had a double benefit from the party's point of

Workers in the Manfred Weiss Steel Company plant at Csepel Island in 1947. Although production increased by 39 percent under Rákosi's industrialization plan, workers were poorly paid. (AP/Wide World Photos)

view. It got rid of any potential organized opposition in the capital, and it brought much needed labor to the state farms.

Rákosi's economic plans were a complete failure. With 90 percent of all businesses in the hands of the government, economic decisions had to pass through layers of bureaucrats before anything could be accomplished.

INTERVIEW: THE ODYSSEY OF JOSEPH MAGYAR*

In some ways, the story of Joseph Magyar embodies the will and tenacity of all Hungarians. Even his last name means Hungarian.

Magyar is a cheerful, friendly man who is now retired and living in Florida. Perhaps his neighbors do not know his background. If they did, they would be impressed at what it took to get him where he is now.

He was born Jozsef Magyar in the eastern Hungarian city of Debrecen on October 28, 1921. His father was a lawyer and an active anticommunist.

During World War II, Magyar was drafted into the Hungarian army and fought on the eastern front. He wound up spending three years as a prisoner of war of the Russians. He was lucky to survive that ordeal. More than 70,000 Hungarians did not survive the Russian campaign.

When the Communists came to power in Hungary after the war, Magyar's family was in trouble. His father and mother were jailed. He and his older brother, a major in the Hungarian army, had to work hard to convince the authorities to release their parents.

Magyar and his older brother often discussed the terrible conditions in the country under communism. They had to whisper, even in the family house, because of the presence of a younger brother who was just a schoolboy. In those days, Hungarian teachers encouraged their students to inform the authorities of antigovernment or anticommunist sentiments among family members.

One day, Magyar had had enough. He fled illegally to neighboring Yugoslavia, where he was put in an overcrowded refugee camp. Conditions were so bad there, he made his way to Austria but was arrested for illegal entry by the British occupation forces in that country. He escaped from the British and crossed into West Germany, where he was again arrested. But the United States military saved him. The Americans needed his language skills: Magyar is fluent in English,

By 1950, as many as 400,000 Hungarians worked in government offices, an enormous number for so small a country. For example, if the manager of a local steel plant needed some vital new equipment, he was required to submit his request to the central government, where it would be studied by bureaucrats in dozens of departments, and perhaps even be

French, and German. He ended up working as a clerk-typist on a U.S. Air Force base.

Magyar was officially classified as a "stateless person," a man without a country. He had only a special United Nations passport. But it was enough to get him entry into the United States in 1949. "I always thought it was easier to get to heaven than to get to America," he says today. In honor of his new home, he Americanized the spelling of his first name to Joseph.

He worked for a time at a copper-smelting plant in New Jersey while living at a local YMCA. He earned enough money to allow him to travel. He lived for a while in Washington, D.C., and then in Seattle. It was the mid-1950s and the Hungarian uprising erupted. His older brother battled alongside the freedom fighters against the Soviets, and was later kicked out of the army for disloyalty.

Magyar was among the first generation in America to learn about computers. He worked as a key-punch operator in a Seattle bank in the late 1950s and took courses in the new field of data-processing. He became a United States citizen on January 19, 1961.

Armed with a degree in computer science, he joined the United States Export-Import Bank (a federal agency that loans money to foreign interests that want to buy American products) in 1964. Magyar worked at the Eximbank and rose to the major position of director of management systems and data-processing. He retired in 1987.

Magyar has returned to Hungary several times, and he likes the changes he sees there. When asked about the potential for political turmoil in the country, he laughs and notes that Hungarians always disagree with one another. "If two Hungarians are together, you will have three different opinions," he says.

And is there a lesson to be learned from his life? Yes, he answers: "Defeat is not the absolute end. It is a new beginning."

*Based on an interview with the author, April 11, 1995

reviewed by party officials. It could take months for the request to be approved or disapproved. Even if it was approved, there was no guarantee the equipment was available.

Also, the industrial production targets had been set much too high, forcing employees into exhausting work schedules. The plants were inefficient, and their equipment was in need of modernization. Workers had no incentive to work harder, since their salaries were low and fixed.

Similarly, the only decent farm production was on the few remaining private plots. The families that worked on the cooperative farms rejected the low prices offered by the government. They thought it made better sense to slaughter their livestock and use the money to purchase scarce consumer goods. Farm production actually dropped. Because of this, the government was forced to ration beef and pork.

Hungary's economic woes embarrassed its Soviet masters and lowered Rákosi's stature. When Stalin died in March 1953, his temporary successor, Georgi Malenkov, did not hesitate to humiliate Rákosi by reducing his power. Malenkov handed the Hungarian government to Imre Nagy, a former interior minister who had all but retired from public life. Nagy, once a devoted follower of Rákosi, had been disgusted by the party leader's disregard for civil liberties. Rákosi stayed on as the chairman of the Hungarian Workers' Party, but his role and stature were diminished.

The Gathering Storm

Premier Nagy did not remain in office for long. Rákosi forced him out in April 1955, shortly after the Soviet Communist Party removed Malenkov (Nagy's sponsor in Moscow) from power. But during his two-year tenure, Nagy managed to correct some of the harm caused by the party boss. He placed the independent State Security Authority (AVH) under the charge of the interior ministry, giving him at least a minimum of control over the organization. He freed some political prisoners from jail. He redirected government spending away from the heavy industries. He allowed more than 1,500 agricultural cooperatives to break up, and their land to return to private ownership. All in all, Nagy gained the respect of a populace wearied by Rákosi's terror tactics and grandiose, impossible economic schemes.

Nagy's cautiously liberal course emboldened some intellectuals and dissatisfied workers to form a loose-knit coalition known as the Petőfi Club, named after Hungary's 19th-century revolutionary poet, Sándor Petőfi. The club advocated a flexible, reformed communism without a police state. The Petőfites supported a continuation of Nagy's moderate policies, and Nagy's replacement as premier, András Hegedüs, permitted the club to function.

Rákosi, however, could not leave well enough alone. In June 1956, he publicly accused Nagy and the Petőfi Club of an anticommunist "conspiracy" against him. The speech was so paranoid, so reminiscent of Stalin, that the Soviet Union removed Rákosi and replaced him with Ernő Gerő. Typically, the Hungarian Workers' Party announced that Rákosi had stepped down for "health reasons." Gerő himself had been a Stalinist. However, he was smart enough to sense the way the wind was blowing in the Kremlin, the seat of the Soviet Communist Party. The heavy-handed approach was out. "De-Stalinization" was in.

Led by Nikita Khrushchev, the new Soviet boss, the Soviet Communist Party was rejecting the police terror of the Stalin era in favor of "Socialist legality." That meant the Soviet security agencies were supposed to respect the civil liberties guaranteed to the people under the Soviet constitution. In fact, they did not, but they were less openly brutal than they had been under Stalin. De-Stalinization also meant a pretense that Hungary, Poland, and the other Soviet "satellites" in Eastern Europe were free to develop their own kinds of communism. In reality, the Kremlin had not stopped pulling the strings. It was just more subtle about it.

Some Eastern Europeans were fooled into believing that a de-Stalinized USSR would not intervene if liberal forces challenged their countries' Communist hard-liners. Early in October 1956, there was unrest among workers in Poland that was squashed by that country's security forces. Hungarian university students mobilized in support of the Polish workers and confronted the Hungarian government with a list of demands. The demands included a free press, the withdrawal of Soviet occupation troops, a multiparty political system, guarantees of personal freedom, and a return of Imre Nagy as premier.

On the afternoon of October 23, 1956, as many as 100,000 joined a student-led march through Budapest. The security forces confronted the

Soviet tanks in the streets of Budapest during the 1956 uprising. (Library of Congress)

marchers and attempted to break up the demonstration. Mayhem erupted as the demonstrators fought back. A mob of protesters used ropes to pull down a 60-foot-tall bronze statute of Stalin in Dozsa György Street. It was the beginning of the Hungarian uprising.

The 1956 Uprising

Experts disagree on whether the majority of Hungarians who took part in the 1956 revolt were seeking Western-style democracy or simply a freer, more responsive type of communism. One thing is certain: they all wanted to be rid of the Soviet chains that bound their country.

Regardless of their aim, people in the West would later call them "freedom fighters." The name stuck to the degree that, throughout the rest of the 1950s, the words *Hungarian* and *freedom fighter* seemed to go together.

On October 24, with no signs of order being restored, the Central Committee of the Workers' Party ousted András Hegedüs as premier and replaced him with Imre Nagy. The government radio station, Radio Kossuth, appealed for calm, but the appeals were ignored. Workers were now joining students in the street. They were increasingly armed with rifles and homemade gasoline bombs that came to be known as "Molotov cocktails" (sarcastically named after the Soviet foreign minister, Vyacheslav Molotov). Soviet armored units left their bases throughout Hungary and rushed to Budapest. British journalist Reg Gadney described the fighting this way:

> Soviet tanks thundered through the streets, blocking off bridges and main road intersections. The freedom fighters, moving in small groups, armed with petrol bombs and guns, ran circles around them. If the tank crews made to clamber out, they were met with sniper fire from the windows and rooftops. This game of cat and mouse served as a major delaying tactic until such times as an effective opposing force could be mustered.

The Hungarian army had not yet made an appearance, but its loyalty was determined almost as soon as the Soviets appeared. According to Gadney,

> Many officers and men were in sympathy with the rebels; they showed their support by handing over arms and ammunition. So far, they had not joined the battle. But the appearance of the Soviets, foreigners fighting compatriots, friends and relatives, left them no doubt with whom to side. It had been the Soviets, no less, who had diligently trained the Hungarians to fight invaders on their streets.

High-ranking Soviet Communist officials Anastas Mikoyan and Mikhail Suslov were on the scene in Hungary to make sure order was restored. Under their direction, the Workers' Party dropped Ernő Gerő as party leader and named János Kádár to the post October 25. Rákosi had purged Kádár from the party in 1951, and Kádár had been tortured and imprisoned for three years. Now, he was back and would have a much greater role in the course of Hungarian history than anyone might have imagined at that moment.

Kádár (1912–89) was a pragmatist, or someone who generally took the most expedient means to an end. He seemed to be less motivated by ideology than by sheer practicality. In public life, he was a humorless, gray man who sought decision by consensus. He was also capable of taking bold action, for good or bad, as Hungarians would soon discover.

Nagy and Kádár pleaded for an end to the violence in radio addresses on October 25. Both made vague promises about a negotiated withdrawal of Soviet forces from Hungary and a reorganization of the ruling Workers' Party. (It was renamed the Socialist Workers' Party.) But things were out of control. AVO units fired on demonstrators in Parliament Square in Budapest, killing scores of people.

The revolt was not limited to Budapest. By October 26, rebels had taken over the city halls and radio stations of the industrial centers of Győr and Miskolc. AVO men shot into a peaceful crowd, killing dozens of people in the town of Magyaróvár, about 50 miles from the capital. A mob hunted down the AVO gunmen and literally tore them to pieces:

Shop workers and patrons watch rebel Hungarian soldiers fire on secret-police units during the 1956 uprising. (AP/Wide World Photos)

Within the hour news of what had happened in Magyarovar reached Budapest and the rebels unleashed their hatred of the AVO with extreme savagery. Innumerable secret policemen were hunted out, lynched or hanged from the branches of trees in the streets and squares. The crowds stood in silence peering at the bloody corpses. Many spat at them. Some AVO men tried to disguise themselves hurriedly in plain clothes. One who had done so failed to change his boots. The boots were spotted. He was chased, caught and lynched.

A mob swarmed into AVO headquarters in the capital and ransacked the place. Another crowd found six unarmed blue-uniformed men hiding in the headquarters of the Greater Budapest Communist Party. Even though they had their hands raised and were begging for mercy, the AVO men were gunned down on the spot. Soon afterward, a pale, frightened woman in civilian dress emerged from the building. Some members of the crowd—believing she was a collaborator or police informant—wanted to kill her. Others argued that she should be spared. They let her live, but only after one angry man knocked her to the ground with the butt of his rifle.

There were many examples of bravery as well as savagery. One Hungarian known as "Uncle Szabo" led a squad of youths that ambushed Soviet tanks with Molotov cocktails. According to one account, the band destroyed as many as 30 tanks, one at a time. Soviet tanks soon learned not to go alone through the streets of Budapest. They began traveling in convoys.

Young people played a prominent role in the uprising. Foreign reporters on the scene saw boys and girls who appeared to be no older than 11 or 12 firing rifles at the Soviets and AVO units.

The uprising wrecked the capital. Tanks fired their cannons into buildings to wipe out snipers. The freedom fighters tore up tram tracks and paving stones to build barricades to halt the Soviet advances. There were dead bodies and burned-out tanks and trucks everywhere.

On October 30, freedom fighters took over Felsopeteny Castle, the AVO prison outside of Budapest. They released the most prominent inmate, József Cardinal Mindszenty, the Roman Catholic primate of Hungary, who had been jailed under the Rákosi regime. Mindszenty had been in prison for nearly eight years.

Most of the Hungarian army went over to the freedom fighters on October 30, led by a young colonel, Pál Maleter. Premier Nagy promoted Maleter to general and named him deputy defense minister for his courageous action. At the same time, Nagy—with Kádár's apparent support—decided that the only way to save his country from a wholesale Soviet intervention was to appeal to world opinion. In a radio broadcast November 1, he announced Hungary's neutrality and withdrawal from the Warsaw Pact, the Soviet-bloc military alliance. By portraying Hungary as an independent nation, one no longer tied to the USSR, Nagy hoped that the Western countries might be encouraged to halt the Soviet intervention somehow. He was too late. Massive Soviet military forces, an estimated 250,000 men, swept into Hungary from Czechoslovakia and Ukraine. They were approaching Budapest November 3, when Kádár mysteriously disappeared.

Kádár turned up in the Soviet Union November 4 and declared his support for the Soviet invasion of Hungary. He also announced that he, not Nagy, was Hungary's true leader. It turned out that Kádár had cut a secret deal with the Kremlin: he would become Hungary's leader in return for public backing of the Soviet intervention.

Soviet troops and tanks entered Budapest November 4 and crushed the rebellion by sheer force of numbers. Thousands died in the fighting. And many more thousands fled the city and the country. Droves of Hungarians crossed illegally into neighboring Austria. Nagy, Maleter, and several of Nagy's aides were arrested by the Soviets. Cardinal Mindszenty, so recently freed from prison, gained sanctuary in the United States embassy in Budapest.

The Soviets characterized the uprising as a "Fascist counterrevolution" instigated by the West. The Western nations did little more than lamely protest the USSR's actions. The United States might have wanted to help Hungary, but at the same time it did not want to provoke a confrontation with the Soviets and trigger World War III. Britain and France could not come to Hungary's aid because they were preoccupied by potential war with Egypt over the Suez Canal. The United Nations General Assembly condemned the Soviet intervention, but that did not change the situation in any material way. To no one's surprise, the Soviets installed János Kádár as general secretary of the Hungarian Socialist Workers' Party.

According to the official figures of Hungary's Communist government, the uprising left 3,000 dead and 13,000 injured, with 4,000 buildings destroyed. (The true figures were probably much higher.) In addition, as many as 200,000 Hungarians fled the country.

An estimated 2,000 Hungarians were executed in the wake of the uprising. Nagy, Maleter, and other prominent rebels were convicted of treason in secret trials. They were put to death in 1958.

The uprising, with all of its tragic consequences, nevertheless reaffirmed the proud, rebellious spirit of the Magyars. As in the revolt against Austrian rule in 1848–49, the Hungarians had risked their lives and their livelihoods to stand up to oppression. Paul Zinner viewed the uprising as an ironic confirmation of a theory of V. I. Lenin, the father of Soviet communism:

> According to Lenin, revolutions will occur when the rulers cannot, and the people will not, continue in the old way. In Hungary, both conditions were met.

The New Economic Mechanism

Hungary was a sad, demoralized place for the next decade. The economy was lackluster—no sharp downturns, but no real economic growth, either. The people, still reeling from the 1956 uprising, were low-spirited. János Kádár stepped down as premier in 1965, turning the government to Gyula Kállai. However, he remained party leader, and as such he held the most important reins of power.

Worst of all, from the ordinary Hungarian's perspective, the Soviets had about 70,000 soldiers based in Hungary, and there was no sign they would ever leave. Hungary was a member of the Warsaw Pact, the Soviet-led military alliance created in the mid-1950s. The Soviet leadership regarded the coalition as essential to the forward defense of the USSR itself. Therefore, the Kremlin had no incentive to remove its troops from Hungary or any other part of Eastern Europe. In short, there seemed to be no genuine hope for positive change, either economically or politically, in Hungary.

The Soviets were willing to give Kádár some leeway since Hungary had been quiet since the uprising. Kádár had demonstrated his allegiance to the Kremlin for a decade, taking the Soviet line in every international dispute with the West. For example, he had firmly backed the USSR in its ideological rift with the People's Republic of China in the early 1960s. Similarly, Hungary had followed the Soviet lead in breaking diplomatic relations with Israel after the 1967 Arab-Israeli War. And, in 1968, Hungary had contributed a small contingent to the Eastern-bloc forces that invaded Czechoslovakia to halt the "Prague Spring" liberal reform movement in that country. The Kremlin's trust in Kádár explains why there was no strong Soviet objection to a rather revolutionary idea. Hungarian economists called it "capitalized socialism." To the West, it was "goulash communism." Kádár named it the "New Economic Mechanism."

Basically, the program used limited market mechanisms to revitalize Hungary's economy. Rigid central planning was to give way to flexible guidelines that would take into account the laws of supply and demand. State-owned companies would gain more power to set their own prices and wages. Companies could import from or export to the West with fewer bureaucratic restrictions. Taxes on the profits of money-making state-owned businesses would be lowered.

In a way, the New Economic Mechanism (NEM) was a kind of social contract. According to U.S. experts who studied the plan,

> The Hungarian reform program was designed as a tacit bargain between the government and the people, in which the leaders offered economic incentives and political concessions in return for public cooperation. The promise was that if the people did not actively challenge the political system or the Hungarian ties to the Soviet Union, the leadership would give priority to raising living standards and satisfying consumer needs. In addition, the government offered to relax internal controls and to reorient the country culturally toward the West, lifting barriers to Western travel and interaction. Citizens would no longer have to embrace the system to prosper, only to forswear active opposition.

The NEM was approved by the Central Committee of the Hungarian Socialist Workers' Party in 1966, and it took effect in 1968. One almost immediate result was that Hungary needed to borrow from the West in

order to get the capital it needed to begin modernizing its aging industries. Therefore, Hungary's foreign debt took a sharp upturn.

NEM's benefits were soon apparent. Hungarian companies had growing trade contact with the West, mainly Austria and West Germany.
Those deals brought consumer goods (televisions, refrigerators, automobiles, clothing, etc.) into the country.

Tourism increased dramatically. In 1970, about 6.3 million foreigners
visited Hungary. By 1982, the figure was 15.4 million (contributing about
4 percent of the country's foreign-exchange earnings). At the same time,
the government permitted about 4 million Hungarians each year to travel
abroad; 10 percent were allowed to visit Western countries. Hungary
became a favorite travel destination for visitors from the other Communist countries in Eastern Europe. Part of the reason was that consumer
goods that were scarce in their own nations could be found in Hungary.

Growth of national income rose to 6 percent in 1969 from 4.5 percent
in 1968. The value of Hungary's trade also rose by 14 percent. Some two-
thirds of Hungary's collective farms began to show a profit beginning in
1970. Real (inflation-adjusted) income rose steadily in the 1970s.

The benefits were real, but so too were the problems associated with
NEM. Hungarian companies increasingly had to borrow to get the hard
currency to import many Western goods because the postwar native currency, the forint, was inconvertible (it had no value outside of the closed
Communist economic sphere). The profits generated by the collective
farms were largely due to price increases; in actuality, collective farm production dropped. While real incomes were rising in the late 1970s, industrial productivity was flattening out. By the close of the 1970s, Hungary
was in a recession (a prolonged economic slowdown).

One obstacle to the success of the New Economic Mechanism was
that the program did not allow for privatization, or turning state-owned
enterprises into private companies. Nor did it allow for the private ownership of land. Therefore, the government still subsidized unprofitable
industries and state farms, which in turn did not reduce their workforces
or take other measures to cut costs.

A second obstacle was the oversized and unwieldy government
bureaucracy. Rather than cutting red tape, government economic rules,
decrees, and regulations increased under the NEM. For instance, the program allowed workers to form cooperatives to lease factory equipment

after normal working hours to produce their own goods. Workers could keep the profits derived from the sale of such goods. But the government monitored the process and required so much complicated paperwork that some workers did not feel it was worth the effort. Those who did, however, raised their income levels above those of ordinary employees.

Another obstacle to the NEM was Hungary's membership in the Council for Mutual Economic Assistance (Comecon), the Soviet-bloc trade alliance. All trade between Comecon nations was either barter (exchanging goods for goods) or denominated in the Soviet currency, the ruble. During the 1970s, up to 35 percent of all Hungarian trade was with the USSR. Also, Hungary was heavily dependent on Soviet oil to fuel its industries.

Transformation in the 1980s

The entire industrialized world endured a recession in the early 1980s, but the Western countries recovered at the mid-point of the decade. The Communist countries in Europe did not. The economic slowdown dragged through the entire decade. Hungary's economy was at a virtual standstill by 1985. Almost every economic indicator was flat, except for inflation. Real incomes could not keep up with rising prices.

The New Economic Mechanism had gone as far as it could go without radical changes backed by a daring political commitment. In order to revitalize its economy, Hungary would have to take steps to a true market economy like those in the Western nations. One West German writer in Hungary in the late 1980s doubted that the conservative Kádár or the party could go that far.

> A fossilized industrial structure can't be preserved. And that is precisely the regime's dilemma: economic reform is indispensible, but it can't be achieved without political costs. The managers are demanding a free hand, the workers need free unions. The Party would have to surrender a little bit of its power to each. As long as that thought is unthinkable, Hungarian reform will remain a chimera.

Kádár had attempted to meet some of the demands for change as the economy stagnated. For example, in 1981, Hungary had permitted its citizens to start private businesses of 30 or fewer employees. That gave Hungarians their first small taste of free enterprise under the Communists. In 1985, the government had given workers in 25 percent of state-owned industries the right to elect their own factory managers.

On the political front, Hungary in 1985 was the first Communist country in history to have multicandidate elections for office. Under the old system, there was only one person running for one office. Voters checked a "yes" or "no" box next to the candidate's name. Usually voters were required to show their marked ballot to a party official before the ballot went into a ballot box.

Granted, under the new voting system, all of the candidates either were once Communists or independents approved beforehand by the Socialist Workers' Party, and the races themselves were for local, not national, offices. Still, for the first time in nearly 40 years, Hungarians were given a choice on the ballot.

The government loosened censorship restrictions in the late 1980s. That opened Hungary to all kinds of literature, films, and plays from the Western nations, as well as works banned in other Communist countries. One such work was The Gulag Archipelago, a personal account of life in Soviet prison camps by exiled Russian writer Alexander Solzhenitsyn. No other Soviet-bloc nation allowed its people to read about oppression in the USSR. The government also had eased passport restrictions, making it much easier for Hungarians to travel abroad, including to the West.

In 1987, the government separated the country's five commercial banks from the National Bank of Hungary (the nation's central bank). The same year, the commercial banks were permitted to compete with the central bank in offering deposit accounts to state-owned companies. Hungary was the first Eastern-bloc nation to allow such competition in banking, which is one of the cornerstones of a market economy. Altogether, Hungary was by far the most politically and economically liberal Communist country in the world by the late 1980s.

Out with the Old, In with the New

The Soviet-bloc Communist parties were led typically by elderly men who found it difficult to deal with the idea of substantial change. In the

1980s, East Germany's ruler was the cold, rigid Erich Honecker. In Czechoslovakia, it was the scowling, inflexible Gustáv Husák. The Bulgarian leader was Marxist hard-liner Todor Zhivkov. In Romania, dictator Nicolae Ceauşescu reigned with almost God-like authority.

In comparison to his fellow Eastern-bloc leaders, Hungary's János Kádár was a liberal. At least, Kádár was willing to try daring approaches to solve his country's problems. The New Economic Mechanism and the personal freedoms allowed in Hungary were evidence that he was not quite like the other Eastern European party bosses.

Yet by 1988, Kádár reached the limit of his liberalism. He was 75 years old and simply could not go further toward reform than he already had without violating his lifelong principles. Younger members of the Socialist Workers' Party, people in their 40s and 50s, realized that Kádár was not the man to lead Hungary into the 1990s. The country's problems were too large.

At the end of 1987, Hungary's foreign debt stood at about $17 billion, the highest per capita (per person) in the Eastern bloc. According to offi-

Premier Károly Grösz speaks to János Kádár (right) at a special party conference in 1988. Grösz replaced Kádár as Hungary's Communist leader a few hours after the photo was taken. (AP/Wide World Photos)

cial government figures, 30,000 Hungarians were unemployed in early 1988, some 10,000 more than in 1987.

The Socialist Workers held a special party conference in May 1988 to discuss the problems and the party's future direction. Observers expected some personnel changes in the Politburo (the party's top policy-making body) because such changes were routine in Communist countries. What observers did not expect was that Kádár would be forced out as the party leader. That happened on May 22, the third and last day of the meeting. The 1,000 delegates—party officials, students, workers, and intellectuals—voted Kádár out of power. They handed the party leadership to Károly Grösz, who was then Hungary's premier.

Kádár had been party general secretary for 32 years, ever since he had betrayed Imre Nagy during the 1956 uprising. The delegates softened the blow somewhat by appointing Kádár to the presidency of the Socialist Workers' Party. However, that was largely a ceremonial position. He had no real authority.

The changeover to Grösz apparently came as a surprise to Kádár. There had been no prior indication he was ready or willing to step down. But he accepted his demotion with a sad grace.

Kádár's removal was not all. The delegates threw out 40 percent of the Central Committee (the large party parliament) and ousted seven Kádár allies from the Politburo on May 22.

Grösz, 57 at the time of the conference, was the first Hungarian Communist leader ever to spend most of his life under communism. He could barely remember when Hungary was not a Marxist country. However, he was not wedded to doctrine or ideology. If anything, Grösz (like Kádár in his younger years) was a pragmatist, a person willing to take whatever steps he deemed necessary.

If Grösz resembled any Communist political figure, it was Mikhail S. Gorbachev of the Soviet Union. Gorbachev had become the Soviet Communist Party leader in 1985, following to power a parade of sick old men. From the start, he dedicated himself to reforming the creaky, antiquated Soviet political and economic systems.

Like Gorbachev in the USSR, Grösz and his allies in the party leadership did not start out to transform Hungary into a capitalist democracy. And like Gorbachev, Grösz would find out that once certain political and economic forces were set in motion, they gathered their own momentum.

Both men seemed to believe that their reasonableness, moderation, and political savvy could somehow keep the forces in check.

There had been those in the Soviet Communist Party, like Moscow party chief Boris N. Yeltsin, who pushed Gorbachev to make faster and more radical reforms than Gorbachev wanted. (Yeltsin went on to become the president of Russia in June 1991.) In Hungary, the radical reformers were embodied in the so-called reform circles of the Socialist Workers' Party. The circles' most prominent figure was Minister of State Imre Pozsgay.

It was the reform circles that pushed Grösz and the party, in November 1988, into giving official status to independent political organizations like the Hungarian Democratic Union. The union described itself as a "democratic, intellectual, and political movement." It really was, in essence, a forerunner to the non-Communist opposition parties that would spring up in Hungary within a year.

By granting official status to the union and other such "movements," Grösz hoped to give Hungarians an outlet for political free expression without actually having the Communists give up their monopoly on political power. However, the move inevitably led to talk of a true multiparty system in Hungary. That is what the reform circles wanted.

The circles also wanted a Western-style market economy in Hungary. They wanted Hungary to be a neutral country, with no Soviet troops on its soil. They wanted an official reappraisal of the 1956 uprising, which, according to Hungary's history books, had been a revolt by "counterrevolutionary" traitors swayed by the West. Thanks in part to Gorbachev, the Hungarian radical reformers eventually would get everything they wanted.

Grösz and Gorbachev

In March 1989, Karoly Grösz visited the Soviet Union and held private discussions with Mikhail Gorbachev. According to Grösz, the Soviet leader promised that his country would not interfere with any political reforms in Hungary or elsewhere in Eastern Europe. The pledge was an explicit renunciation of the "Brezhnev doctrine" (named after former Soviet leader Leonid Brezhnev). The doctrine asserted the right of the Soviet Union to intervene militarily to preserve Communist regimes.

Brezhnev had formulated the doctrine to justify the Soviet-led 1968 invasion of Czechoslovakia.

Gorbachev in effect gave Grösz the green light to proceed with his reforms without fear of a repeat of the 1956 Soviet invasion. He also took away a major excuse Grösz and the Hungarian moderates might have used for blocking radical reforms.

In truth, reforms had been moving along in Hungary even before Grösz went to Moscow. But they had proceeded while everyone in Hungary glanced nervously eastward to see if there were any Soviet tanks on the horizon.

A month before Grösz's trip, the Central Committee of the Hungarian Socialist Workers' Party approved in principle the creation of a multiparty political system in Hungary. At the same time, a party historical committee announced that the 1956 revolt was a "popular uprising" against a dictatorial regime, rather than a counterrevolution.

The party removed János Kádár as its president in May 1989, explaining that he was no longer physically fit enough to hold the post. Kádár died of respiratory and circulatory problems on July 6, at age 77. He was given a state funeral eight days later that was attended by 10,000 people.

On June 16, 1989, an estimated 250,000 people gathered in Heroes Square in Budapest to view six flag-draped coffins. Five of the caskets contained the remains of Imre Nagy and four other leading figures of the 1956 uprising. The sixth coffin was empty; it symbolized all of the other dead freedom fighters. Nagy and his key associates—General Pál Maleter, József Szilagyi, Géza Losonczy, and Miklós Gimes—had been buried in an unmarked mass grave in Budapest. All but Losonczy, who died in prison while awaiting trial, were tried in secret and executed for treason. They were reburied with honors June 16 after the Budapest ceremony. Several speakers at the ceremony described the uprising as a revolution. Writer Tibor Meray made an emotional speech at Nagy's gravesite. He denounced the premier's executioners as "common criminals who are among us today," meaning men who still held high posts in the Communist Party. "But," Meray added, "we must not seek revenge. Their punishment is that they see what is happening today."

After reviewing their trials, Hungary's Supreme Court ruled in July 1989 that Nagy and his aides were unjustly accused of treason and illegally put on trial. At last, the heroes of 1956 were officially "rehabilitated."

The International Scene

The reform fever sweeping Hungary was not limited to domestic affairs. In May 1989, the country removed the barbed-wire fence that separated Hungary from neutral Austria. Thus, Hungary became the first Eastern-bloc nation to open a border with a non-Communist country.

U.S. president George H. W. Bush paid a state visit to Hungary on July 11, 1989, bringing with him a modest package of economic aid. Hungarians were elated by the visit. He was the first American president ever to set foot in the country.

Also in the summer of 1989, thousands of East German tourists in Hungary refused to return to their own country. At the time, East Germany was experiencing political turmoil, with masses of protesters in the streets demanding democratic reforms. East Germany had one of the most hard-line Communist regimes in the Soviet bloc.

Most of the East German vacationers in Hungary were young adults with children. They simply did not wish to go home. After initially trying to convince them to return to their country, the Hungarian government decided not to forcibly send them back. Instead, Hungary opened discussions with West Germany and Austria on the possibility of those two countries granting political asylum to the East Germans.

Between September 11, 1989, and October 1, 1989, Hungary allowed as many as 30,000 East Germans to cross the border into Austria. From Austria, they were taken to West Germany for political asylum. East Germany was furious. Under a 20-year-old agreement, Hungary was supposed to block any attempt by East Germans to reach the West. In effect, Hungary had thumbed its nose at its central European comrade.

Communists Dump Marxism–Leninism

The Socialist Workers' Party stunned the world on October 7, 1989, when it renounced Marxism-Leninism and adopted democratic socialism as its guiding principle. It also renamed itself the Hungarian Socialist Party.

It was also the first time in history that a ruling Communist party turned away from its fundamental ideology. Marxism, developed by 19th-century German social theorists Karl Marx and Friedrich Engels, espoused the belief that a natural process of economic class struggle would inevitably replace bourgeois (middle-class) capitalism with socialism (an economic system in which all property is held in common, eliminating class differences). V. I. Lenin, a Russian revolutionary, argued that the proletariat (working-class) masses of the world could gain political and economic power only through revolution.

Marxism-Leninism was the framework ideology of all of the Communist nations. In Hungary, the party entirely abandoned Leninism and backed away from such rigid Marxist concepts as "class struggle." A majority of members even refused to call themselves Marxists; they preferred the less historically weighted designation of "Socialists." At the same time, the party publicly committed itself to Western-style democracy.

The changes came at a special party congress (a high-level meeting) in Budapest. The gathering had been called to determine the direction of the party, and to fashion a new image for the party with national elections expected in 1990.

The shift to democratic socialism was guided by Rezso Nyers, the party president. It was a defeat for both the party's moderate Communists, under Károly Grösz, and its radical reformers, under Imre Pozsgay. Pozsgay wanted the party to turn liberal democratic (center-left on the political spectrum, to the right of Socialists). Grösz, who remained a faithful Marxist, was disgusted. He criticized the delegates for giving up unspecified "Communist values," and said he wanted nothing to do with the new Socialist Party.

Constitution Amended

On October 18, 1989, the National Assembly amended the country's 1949 constitution to pave the way for multiparty national elections. Among the changes, the deputies

- Eliminated the Socialist Workers' monopoly on political power, and removed all references in the charter to the party's "leading role" in Hungary;

- Stated: "Political parties may be freely established and may freely function";
- Renamed the country the Hungarian Republic. The Communist-era designation in use since 1949, the People's Republic of Hungary, was abandoned; and
- Codified civil liberties, such as freedom of speech, freedom of religion, freedom of association, and the right to peaceably assemble.

Hungarian Republic Proclaimed

An estimated 80,000 people gathered in front of the parliament building on October 23, 1989, to hear Acting President Mátyás Szuros proclaim Hungary a free republic. The event was nationally televised. The date marked the 33rd anniversary of the 1956 uprising. The building was decked with a giant portrait of Imre Nagy and a huge banner that read "Freedom, Independence."

Even though Hungary was still part of the Eastern bloc, and Soviet troops were still on Hungarian soil, the ceremony gave its people a heady sense that true freedom was close, indeed that it was an unstoppable process. October 23 would from that day on be celebrated as a national holiday.

The 1990 Elections

Hungary held its first free elections since the end of World War II in 1990. The voting was to fill the 386-seat National Assembly. The election was in two stages: the main voting on March 25, and runoff voting April 8 for races that had been left undecided.

An estimated 7 million Hungarians cast ballots. Some 1,600 candidates representing 54 political parties took part. When all the votes were tallied, the conservative Hungarian Democratic forum captured 42.7 percent of the votes, or 165 seats. That was more than any other party, but it was not an absolute majority. In other words, all of the other winning parties together held more seats than the forum.

The liberal Alliance of Free Democrats finished second, with 23.8 percent of the vote, or 92 seats. The Independent Smallholders' Party got 11.1 percent of the vote (43 seats). The ruling Socialists (former Communists) ended up fourth, with 8.5 percent, or 33 seats. The Christian Democrats came in fifth, with 5.4 percent, for 21 seats.

More than 80,000 people gather before the parliament building to hear Hungary proclaimed a free republic on October 23, 1989. (AP/Wide World Photos)

Because the Democratic Forum lacked an absolute majority, it formed a ruling coalition with the other major right-of-center parties, the Small-holders and the Christian Democrats. The Free Democrats and the Socialists made up the main parliamentary opposition.

The forum campaigned on a platform of ridding Hungary of the last vestiges of communism, but also of maintaining Hungary's links with existing Soviet-bloc organizations. (The Warsaw Pact military alliance and the Comecon trade alliance still existed, and Hungary still belonged to them.) However, the forum made no secret of its pro-Western orientation.

The elections were influenced by anti-Magyar riots in the Transylvania region of neighboring Romania. The forum, more than any other Hungarian party, capitalized on the strong anti-Romanian feelings in Hungary. Forum candidates hinted, but did not say outright, that Hungary should go to war with Romania to protect the lives of the ethnic Hungarians in Transylvania (see chapter 6).

Anti-Semitism, too, played a role in the election. The Free Democrats, a party with a high number of Jewish members, accused the forum of spurring anti-Jewish feelings among voters. The forum denied the accusation.

The forum's József Antall, a 58-year-old historian, became Hungary's first post-Communist premier on May 3, 1990. A new era moving toward democracy had begun.

NOTES
p. 60 "'He is said . . .'" Paul E. Zinner, *Revolution in Hungary* (New York: Columbia University Press, 1962), p. 114.

p. 62 "'. . . Invasion of privacy . . .'" Zinner, pp. 116–117.

p. 63 "'After 1950, . . .'" Joerg K. Hoensch, *A History of Modern Hungary: 1867–1986* (New York: Longman, 1988), p. 192.

pp. 64–65 "'Police interfered . . .'" Zinner, p. 115.

p. 71 "'Soviet tanks . . .'" Reg Gadney, *Cry Hungary! Uprising 1956* (New York: Atheneum, 1986), p. 53.

p. 71 "'Many officers . . .'" Gadney, p. 53.

p. 73 "'Within the hour . . .'" Gadney, p. 89.

p. 75 "'According to Lenin, . . .'" Zinner, p. 359.

p. 76 " 'The Hungarian reform program . . .' " Kerry Dumbaugh and Frances T. Miko, *Gorbachev's Reform Strategy: Comparisons with the Hungarian and Chinese Experience*, Congressional Research Service report number 87–813 F (Washington, D.C., 1987), p. 7.

p. 78 " 'A fossilized industrial structure . . .' " Hans Magnus Enzensberger, *Europa, Europa* (New York: Random House, 1989), p. 107.

PART II
Hungary Today

4

POLITICS AND
GOVERNMENT

Hungary, like most of the countries of Eastern Europe, has little experience with democracy. For most of the nation's history, it has been ruled by kings and emperors and by coercive governments of the right and left. The post-Communist era has encouraged the creation of many political parties, including ones on the political extremes. But, after four democratic national elections, power has been largely consolidated in three parties.

The Communist era to this day comes back to haunt Hungarians, nonetheless. Just ask the country's current premier, Péter Medgyessy, a quiet man with a once-secret past.

Parliamentary Democracy

Americans, particularly young Americans, are usually familiar with only one form of democratic government—the federal system used in the United States since its birth as a nation. But Hungary and most of the world's other democratic countries, new and old, use the parliamentary system.

Under the federal system, the executive branch (headed by the president) and the legislative branch (Congress) are separate parts of the government. The parliamentary system combines the executive and legislative branches.

Members of a parliament, or national legislature, are elected by the voters. The party that wins a clear-cut majority of seats (that is, its members can outvote members of all other parties represented in parliament combined) has the right to form a new government. If one party has a plurality—it holds a majority of seats, but can be outvoted by the other parties together—it might form a ruling coalition, or partnership, with one or more other parties in order to obtain a voting majority in parliament.

The majority party or coalition has the power to designate a premier (sometimes called a prime minister) to head the government. The premier, in turn, chooses a cabinet of officials (who are always fellow members of parliament) to head the government's major departments or ministries.

In the United States, the president is both the head of government and the head of state. In Hungary and the other parliamentary democracies, the premier is only the head of government. Hungary's president—who is picked by parliament—is the head of state, an official who embodies national unity but has mainly ceremonial powers and duties.

Members of Hungary's parliament, the 386-seat Országgyulés (National Assembly), are elected to four-year terms. At the end of the four years, new national elections must be held. But, in Hungary, as in countries with similar systems, the government (the premier and his or her cabinet) can be forced out of power at any time by a simple majority vote of the members of parliament. For that reason, frequent changes of government can be common in some parliamentary democracies.

The Death of a Leader

On December 12, 1993, Hungary's first post-Communist leader died quietly in a Budapest hospital. He was Premier József Antall, the man who had directed Hungary's initial steps in the transition from communism to democracy. Antall, 61, had taken office on May 3, 1990.

Antall's death came as no surprise, since he had been seriously ill for several years. Nevertheless, most Hungarians were stunned and saddened by the news of his passing. He had personally symbolized the emergence of a new era.

The premier died of non-Hodgkin's lymphoma, a type of cancer. In spite of his poor health, Antall had been known as a workaholic. He often arrived at his office before 8 A.M. and worked until late in the evening. He carried out a vigorous schedule of meetings, speeches, and official travel. Antall's energy, earnest manner, and strong conservative convictions gained him the respect of many Western leaders, including United States president George H. W. Bush.

The Hungarian press—which was not known for its gentle treatment of politicians—respected Antall's privacy so much that it declined to raise the issue of his health for as long as he was in power. Antall himself refused to discuss the matter in public. The government would not reveal the names of the premier's doctors or his course of treatment.

The premier's passing left the ruling Democratic Forum without a leader of Antall's stature. Hungarian president Árpád Göncz named Péter Boross, who had been the interior minister in Antall's cabinet, to the post of acting premier. Boross served as the head of government until the national elections in the spring of 1994.

The Ex-Communists Return

A jubilant crowd gathered at the Budapest former headquarters of the Communists on the night of May 29, 1994. They surrounded a slender, smiling middle-aged man. The celebrants wanted to slap the man on the back or hug him, but they could not. The center of attention, Gyula Horn, was wearing a head and neck brace. He had been in a car accident a few weeks earlier.

Horn was the leader of the Hungarian Socialist Party, which had once been the mighty Socialist Workers' (Communist) Party. The Socialists had just won the 1994 national elections, and Horn was poised to be Hungary's next premier. Horn, 62, had been a lifelong Communist and had served in an auxiliary police unit that had helped to put down the 1956 Hungarian uprising. But he had gone on to become an internationally respected foreign minister in the 1980s and had played a key role in opening Hungary borders in the late 1980s.

Horn had been one of the leaders of the reform wing of the Socialist Workers' Party.

Now that the ex-Communists were back in power, what could the nation expect? Horn took pains to calm any fears that his party would try to halt the advance of capitalism and democracy in Hungary. He spoke of "reconciliation," telling one observer, "Let us not deal with ideologies. Those with decent intentions have nothing to fear."

The 1994 national elections, held in two stages (May 8 and May 29), constituted the first nationwide vote since the 1990 balloting that had brought the Democratic Forum to power. The voting was to fill the 386-seat Országgyulés (National Assembly). Under the National Assembly system, the party with the most seats was empowered to form a government, with the party leaders as the nation's premier.

More than 60 percent of eligible voters cast ballots in each of the two stages. The Socialists captured a total of 209 seats, giving them a clear majority. The Alliance of Free Democrats finished second, with a total of 70 seats. The Democratic Forum ended up third, with 38 seats. The rest of the seats were divided mainly between the Independent Smallholders' and Civic Party, the Christian Democrats and the Alliance of Young Democrats.

Since the Socialists had an outright majority, they had no need to form a coalition government. Yet they invited the Free Democrats to be a coalition partner. The leader of the Free Democrats, Gabor Kuncze, initially rejected the offer. Less than a month later, he changed his mind and accepted.

From the Socialists' point of view, the coalition would give their party credibility and calm fears of a return to communism in Hungary. The Free Democrats gained power; they never before had been in a government. The two parties together could muster 279 votes in the National Assembly.

Several factors accounted for the sweeping Socialist victory. First, there was public disaffection with economic reform. Since the last elections, in 1990, Hungarians had seen an overall decline in their standard of living. Although wages had increased, high prices had eroded purchasing power. And tens of thousands of people were out of work. Many voters, especially blue-collar workers and the elderly on pensions, yearned for a return of the economic stability of the Communist era.

The ruling Democratic Forum, along with the Free Democrats, also had been implicated in a major scandal. It seems that the two parties in secret had sold office space that had been granted them by the government privatization (the selling of government-owned properties and industries to individuals and private businesses) agency, the State Property Agency. The transaction—which had not been reported in the parties' financial statements—had been revealed by two newspapers in 1993. Both parties claimed that they had not broken any laws. The national law on party financing apparently contained so many loopholes that the forum and Young Democrats could not be held accountable. The parties shrugged off the scandal, but it angered many voters. They viewed the two parties as self-serving pirates.

The Socialist–Free Democrat coalition was little more than a marriage of convenience. The two parties did not share the same philosophies, particularly on the matter of privatization. The Socialists appeared to be committed to slowing privatization, while the Free Democrats wanted it to continue apace.

A clash over economic reform was inevitable. It happened in 1995, when the Free Democrats threatened to quit the coalition over what they viewed as Premier Horn's political interference in the privatization process (see chapter 5).

Under pressure from the Free Democrats, the Horn government reversed its stand on privatization in 1996. The government accelerated the sale of state-owned companies, and opened the key sectors of banking, telecommunications, and energy to foreign ownership. In addition, the government created a special agency, the State Privatization and Holding Company (APV), to oversee the sale of state-owned properties.

Also, in March 1996, the government imposed a strict economic austerity program. The program froze social-welfare spending, raised taxes, and devalued the national currency, the forint, to make Hungary's exports cheaper for foreign customers. The austerity program remained in place until 1998, when the Socialists were ousted by the center-right coalition headed by Premier Viktor Orbán, who increased government spending.

The Socialist government was tainted by a major political scandal. In 1996, Premier Horn fired the industry and trade minister, Tamás Suchman, and the entire APV board when it was discovered that APV

had made millions of dollars in unauthorized payments to a private consultant. The consultant, Marta Tocsik, was paid exorbitant fees for nego-
tiating the sale of local government properties to private investors.

The Orbán Era

The center-right Fidesz–Hungarian Civic Party (formerly the Young
Democrats) came to power in 1998. Viktor Orbán, a 34-year-old lawyer,
led the party to victory and because the youngest premier in Hungarian
history.

Fidesz gained a total of 148 seats in the 386-seat National Assembly
in the two stages of the elections (held May 10 and May 24). The party
formed a governing coalition with the Independent Smallholders and the
Democratic Forum.

Fidesz had campaigned on a platform of fighting crime and corrup-
tion and promises to enact measures to aid middle-income families. The
party had also pledged to boost the nation's annual economic growth
rate to 7 percent from the 4.6 percent in the last year of the Socialist
government. (Annual growth of 3 percent is good; 7 percent growth
would be extraordinary.)

The Orbán government never hit its growth target, but the economy
did grow a very robust 5.5 percent in 2000. More important, Orbán
appointed respected free-market economists to his cabinet, including
Attila Chikan as his minister of economic affairs. Under Orbán, the government made the forint, the national currency, fully convertible with
other currencies. On the downside, the Orbán government continued the
trend of deficit spending. In 1998, the budget deficit was $2.3 billion,
more than double that of 1997.

The Orbán era may be best remembered for the premier himself. He
was youthful, dynamic, energetic, and charismatic. (Some observers
compared Orbán's style to that of U.S. president Bill Clinton and
British prime minister Tony Blair.) Since Hungarians were used to having older, rather dull leaders, Orbán was indeed a different breed of
premier.

During his tenure, on June 6, 2000, Hungary's parliament voted,
243–96, to elect Ferenc Mádl as the country's president. Mádl suc-

Viktor Orbán became Hungary's youngest premier in 1998. He lost his bid for reelection in 2002. (AP/Wide World Photos)

ceeded Árpád Göncz, who had been Hungary's head of state since 1990. (Presidents are limited to a maximum of two five-year terms in office.) Mádl, 69, was a conservative law-school professor and a former minister of education and culture.

Where Have All the Parties Gone?

The results of the 2002 national elections in Hungary were shocking. A virtual unknown, Péter Medgyessy, led the Socialist Party to an upset victory over the ruling Fidesz–Hungarian Civic Party and the incumbent leader, Premier Viktor Orbán. The Socialists, who had headed a coalition government from 1994 to 1998, were back in power.

The 2002 elections were held in two stages, on April 7 and April 21. In the overall popular vote, Fidesz actually beat the Socialists, 45 percent to 44 percent and gained more seats in the National Assembly: 188 to 178. But the Alliance of Free Democrats—the junior partner in the Socialists' last government—immediately pledged its 20 seats to the Socialists in 2002. This move allowed the new Socialist–Free Democrat coalition to outvote Fidesz, 198 to 188.

Perhaps a bigger shock to Hungarians was the fact that there were only three political parties represented in the Országgyulés. Such nationally familiar parties as the Democratic Forum, Christian Democrats, Independent Smallholders, and Justice and Life Party had all failed to send even a single member to the National Assembly in 2002. Their candi-

Premier-elect Péter Medgyessy (right) celebrates the Socialist Party victory in 2002. László Kovacs, the party's president, is at Medgyessy's right. (AP/ Wide World Photos)

dates as a whole had failed to meet the 5 percent minimum threshold in the first round's popular vote and therefore could not advance to the next round. The Smallholders' leader, József Torgyan, complained after the first round, "A two-party system was introduced to Hungary today, and this is a great loss to democracy."

Orbán, the defeated incumbent premier, was young (38 years old at the time of the elections) and charismatic, but he had made serious mistakes during the campaign. While addressing Hungarian farmers, he had frightened Western investors by repeatedly warning of the dangers of "big capital." Farmers in turn feared that foreign agricultural companies would buy up their land when Hungary joined the European Union. One Western diplomat commented during the campaign, "The last thing they [Fidesz] want to do is to be scaring foreign capital away. And that is what they're doing right now."

Perhaps Orbán's biggest error was flirting with the extreme right. Specifically, he publicly refused to rule out a Fidesz coalition with the ultranationalist Justice and Life Party. That position alarmed many of Fidesz's moderate supporters.

The new premier, Péter Medgyessy, was Orbán's opposite in almost every way. He was a 59-year-old banker with a quiet demeanor. Medgyessy was not well known at the start of the campaign, even though he had served as a finance minister (1987) and a deputy premier (1988–89) in the last Communist government.

The 2002 campaign was very divisive. There were loud, angry arguments over politics in Budapest's outdoor cafés. Husbands and wives at odds over the campaign stopped speaking to each other. The rancor contrasted sharply with the exhilaration felt by Hungarians during the first democratic campaign, in 1990.

Medgyessy, rather than match Orbán's aggressiveness, took a soft-spoken, conciliatory stance that many voters found refreshing. In the end, a combined 72 percent of Hungary's 8 million eligible voters went to the polls in the two stages—a record turnout for national elections.

Following the elections, Medgyessy told reporters, "We Hungarians depend very much on each other. The country divided into two camps and, after forming a new government, the country must begin to reconcile immediately. Instead of digging trenches, we need to reintroduce a normal, calm voice again."

Major Party Profiles

Hungary's major political parties have had their ups and downs in the years since the first post-Communist elections of 1990.

The Socialists have transformed themselves from a collection of reformed Communists into a true center-left social-democratic party. During their first reign, from 1994 to 1998, the Socialists surprised many Hungarians with their willingness to embrace free-market economics, even to the extent of limiting spending on the social safety net.

The Socialists' core support used to be the working class, particularly unionized workers. Now, it has much broader appeal, including among Hungarians who had been wary of the ex-Communists.

Fidesz–Hungarian Civic Party began in 1990 as the Young Democrats, an antiestablishment leftist party that resembled the Green parties of Western Europe. (Young people formed the Green parties in the 1980s on a proenvironment, antiwar platform.) The Young Democrats initially barred anyone over the age of 35 from joining their party. While the party received the support of young voters early on (they captured 20 and 21 seats in the 1990 and 1994 elections, respectively), relatively few Hungarians over the age of 40 took it seriously.

The party changed radically in 1993, when Viktor Orbán (one of the founders of the Young Democrats) won a bitter internal power struggle. Under Orbán, the Young Democrats restyled themselves as the Fidesz–Hungarian Civic Party and shifted to the center-right of the political spectrum. Fidesz's base constituency is the country's growing number of young urban professionals and entrepreneurs. Using that base, the party won the 1998 elections and ruled until 2002.

The liberal *Free Democrats* are the "bridesmaids" of Hungarian politics. The only real power the party has attained has been as a junior partner in ruling coalitions headed by the Socialists. Relations between the two partners have been strained at times.

The Free Democrats, led by Gabor Kuncze, come from the long tradition of Hungary's anticommunist intellectual left. Many of the party supporters are Jewish, and the party appears to have the financial backing of Hungary's Jewish community. However, the party is nondenominational and takes no stand on religion except to endorse freedom of worship.

The center-right *Democratic Forum* headed Hungary's first post-Communist government (1990–94). Since then, the party's popularity has slipped substantially, although it was part of the Fidesz-led coalition government (1998–2002). The party attracts older, conservative Hungarians. It advocates free-market capitalism, a strong military, Christian values, and Hungarian traditions. Following the 2002 elections, it had no representatives in parliament.

The Christian Democrats are an ally of the Democratic Forum but more conservative and more narrowly focused. The party's high point was in 1990–94, when it was a junior partner in the forum's ruling coalition. The party drew most of its support from Hungary's large Roman Catholic community. Following the 2002 elections, it had no representatives in parliament.

The Independent Smallholders are the self-proclaimed descendants of the same party that held power in Hungary briefly after World War II and before the Communist takeover. Their power base was originally among the farmers in rural Hungary, but support has expanded into the cities as well. The Smallholders are right-wing populists in that they advocate a farmer-worker alliance to achieve political parity.

The Smallholders were junior partners in the center-right governments of 1990–94 and 1998–2002. But in the 2002 campaign, Fidesz pointedly went after rural voters, effectively pushing aside its coalition partner, the Smallholders. Following the 2002 elections, the Smallholders had no representatives in parliament.

The ultranationalist *Justice and Life Party* of István Csurka is Hungary's most controversial, and most feared, political party. It is openly anti-Semitic, anti-immigrant, and antiglobalization. Justice and Life had modest electoral success in the period between 1994 and 2002, sending a total of 14 representatives to parliament. (None of Hungary's other extreme-right parties have achieved even that level of success.) No mainstream party has yet invited Justice and Life into a ruling coalition. Following the 2002 elections, it had no representatives in parliament.

The New Nazis

The fall of communism and the advent of economic transition have spurred the growth of extreme-right political parties and of neofascist skinhead movements in Hungary and elsewhere in Eastern Europe. The parties and movements attract people at the bottom of the economic ladder: jobless workers and working-class youths. They are people who do not see how they fit in with the new economic order.

Although the parties and movements differ in some respects, they all espouse radical nationalism. They hate Jews and foreigners and believe that Hungary has a right to take back the bordering lands it lost after World War I. They admire Ferenc Szálasi, the founder of Hungary's Fascist Arrow Cross movement. (Szálasi was executed in 1946.)

The growth of the extremists in many ways is a reflection of events on a higher political level. In August 1992, István Csurka, one of the leaders of the Democratic Forum, published a controversial essay in which he accused Jews and Communists of plotting against Hungary. He also suggested that Hungary expand its borders to include the lands it had once ruled. Premier Antall had been slow to criticize Csurka.

Csurka and some his followers were forced out of the Democratic Forum in 1993. They formed their own party, the Hungarian Justice and Life Party. In the 1998 election the party gained enough votes (4.4 percent) to send 14 representatives to parliament. It lost its seats in parliament after the 2002 election, in which it received only 4.4 percent of the vote.

Hungary has two registered political parties that are by all accounts neofascist. One is the Hungarian National Socialist Action Group, based in the city of Győr. The other is the World National Popular Rule Party (WNPRP), based in the working-class Angyalföld district of Budapest. The latter party is led by Albert Szábo, a Hungarian-born laborer who spent part of his life in Australia. According to one Western newspaper,

> Szabo described [the party's] goal as the protection of the interests of Hungarians, whom he considers culturally superior to all other nations. The WNPRP advocates restricting the number of minorities [Jews and Gypsies] at universities and at places of employment to their proportion in the population at large.

Skinheads, young neo-Nazis, first emerged in Hungary in the 1970s. Police estimated in the mid-1990s that there were 300–400 active skinheads in the country, with about 3,000 sympathizers. They were and are prone to violence. A knowledgeable observer of the skinhead scene reports:

> They blame Jews, Gypsies, and foreigners for Hungary's problems, and in recent years the number of incidents in which they have beaten up Asian and African students, Jews and Gypsies has increased, receiving great publicity. In the last few months, there have been a series of bomb threats against Jewish schools, and Jewish cemeteries and a synagogue were desecrated. Jewish leaders attributed the attacks to skinheads and expressed alarm that the movement was targeting Jewish institutions.

The Extreme Left

The fall of communism left Marxist hard-liners dazed and disheartened. They could not go along with the reformed Communists (today's Socialists), so they formed their own, new parties. The two best-known of the new extreme-left parties are the Labor Party (LP) and the Hungarian Socialist Workers' Party (the name of the former Communist Party). Of course, both parties oppose capitalism. Western reporter Edith Oltay sums up the Labor Party this way:

> The LP portrays itself as the only party in Hungary that represents the interests of workers and peasants. Defining the LP as "the party of the ordinary people," its leader, Gyula Thurmer, claims to speak in the name of those who failed to benefit from the change of regime—the unemployed, pensioners, and the young. The majority of the LP's supporters are elderly people who live in the provinces and have a low educational level. Most of its supporters are motivated by the feeling that "it was better in the old days. . . ."

Dealing with the Communist Past

The Communist past is never far away for Hungarians. An example occurred in June 2002, when the new premier, Péter Medgyessy, revealed that he had served as a counterintelligence officer from 1977 to 1982 inside the Communist-era finance ministry. Medgyessy made the admission to parliament on June 19. He had been prompted to do so by the Alliance of Free Democrats, who had threatened to withdraw from the ruling Socialist–Free Democrat coalition if Medgyessy failed to disclose his secret past.

Medgyessy claimed that he had worked within the finance ministry to prevent the KGB, the Soviet spy service, from discovering a covert attempt by Hungary to join the International Monetary Fund. (The Soviets in 1961 had blocked an effort by Hungary to become an IMF member.) Hungary eventually joined the international aid organization in 1982.

Following Medgyessy's admission, the Free Democrat's leader, Gabor Kuncze, reaffirmed his party's allegiance to the Medgyessy government, but the opposition Fidesz–Hungarian Civic Party repeatedly called for Medgyessy's resignation. The calls ended July 3, when the president of Fidesz, Zoltán Pokorni, resigned from his post amid press disclosures that his own father had been an informant for Hungary's Communist-era secret police.

Although some Hungarians have clamored for Communist-era officials to be put on trial, a majority of the country appears to be against the move. The opponents believe that such trials would needlessly reawaken hatreds over such issues as the use of ordinary citizens as secret-police informants.

As of the end of 2002, no Communist-era officials in Hungary had been prosecuted for major crimes. That is because in 1992 the Constitutional Court—the highest court in the country—overturned a new law that would have permitted Communist leaders to be brought to trial.

In 1991, the National Assembly passed a law lifting a Communist-era statute of limitations (a legal time limit on prosecutions) on such crimes as murder and treason if those crimes were committed in the name of Marxism. In other words, the Communists protected themselves from possible future prosecution.

By throwing out the statute of limitations, the Democratic Forum hoped to bring surviving Communists to justice for their past actions. President Árpád Göncz opposed the move. Göncz, who had been imprisoned by the Communists, believed that criminal trials would be vindictive and might divide the country.

The Constitutional Court criticized the 1991 law as "vague" and "unreliable." The court added:

We cannot judge a previous period of time from the point of view of the present. We must make laws in advance of a crime and not afterward.

In another development during 1992, the National Assembly passed a law voiding the convictions of all persons prosecuted by the Communists for political crimes between 1963 and 1989. The crimes included conspiracy, rebellion, and illegal emigration (leaving Hungary without official permission).

NOTES
p. 96 "reconciliation" and "'Let us not . . .'" *New York Times*, May 30, 1994, p. A3.
p. 101 "'A two-party system . . .'" *New York Times*, April 8, 2002, p. A3.
p. 101 "'The last thing . . .'" *New York Times*, April 21, 2002, Sec. 1, p. 8.
p. 101 "'We Hungarians . . .'" *New York Times*, April 22, 2002, p. A8.
p. 104 "'Szabo described . . .'" Edith Oltay, "Extremist Politics in Hungary," *RFE/RL Research Report*, April 22, 1994, p. 56.
p. 104 "'They blame Jews . . .'" Oltay, p. 57.
p. 105 "'The LP blames itself . . .'" Oltay, p. 60.
p. 107 "'We cannot judge . . .'" *Facts On File World News Digest*, March 19, 1992, p. 196A3.

5

ECONOMY AND TRADE

See if you can follow this. A Swiss energy company buys a Hungarian power-plant group from a U.S. company. A British energy group had built one of the power-plant group's three plants. Part of the overall sale involves an exchange of stock in a Czech power station and in the Czech subsidiary of a second Swiss company that is a partner in a German power-trading business. Got it?

This is a routine transaction in the age of globalization—the unrestricted exchange of capital, goods, services, and information around the world. Hungary these days is part of the global economy.

The seeds of Hungary's globalized economy were sown in the first half of the 1990s, when successive Hungarian governments welcomed foreign investors as partners and owners of businesses that had belonged to the state. Not long ago, Hungarians debated the role of foreigners in the economy; these days the debate is over how soon Hungary will be a member of the European Union.

The transformation was not painless. In the early years of economic restructuring, unscrupulous investors made a quick profit in Hungary and abandoned Hungarian workers. Hungarians as a whole struggled with declining standards of living. Now, following the turn of a new century, the country appears to have turned the corner.

The transaction mentioned above is real. In the fall of 2002, Aare-Tessin AG für Elekrizität (Atel) of Switzerland bought Hungary's Csepel Group from the U.S.-based Xcel Energy, Inc. The total deal was worth $517.7 million. Csepel Group supplies 7 percent of Hungary's electrical power.

An Overview: The Hungarian Path

Any discussion of Hungary's economy and trade must be preceded by an overview of the evolution of the free-market path on which the country was set in 1990–94. Simply put, the path was this: to place the Hungarian economy in private hands by opening all sectors to ownership by foreign investors.

The policy was the subject of heated debates in parliament, especially in the early post-Communist years. After more than 40 years of communism, with the government owning or controlling nearly every aspect of the economy, the idea of U.S.-style corporate capitalism filled many Hungarians with uncertainty. Also, Hungarians are a proud people, so the notion of foreigners taking over their major industries, newspapers, banks, and energy companies inspired opposition.

Something had to be done, however; the country had accumulated a huge foreign debt from borrowing to subsidize money-losing state-owned companies. Therefore, advocates reasoned, why not pump money into the economy by selling it off, piece by piece, to wealthy companies based in the United States, Western Europe, and Asia? This was known as privatization through foreign direct investment (FDI). Thus, Hungary set itself on the path to globalization before the concept of an integrated global economy was familiar to the average person.

The road has been bumpy, and there have been missteps and slight detours along the way. Keep in mind that the policies put in place in the first half of the 1990s did not really come to fruition until the end of that decade. For much of the 1990s, Hungarians had to endure high unemployment and soaring prices.

Through four post-Communist governments—the Democrat Forum, the Socialists, Fidesz–Hungarian Civic Party, and (as of April 2002) the Socialists—all of Hungary's governments have adhered to the basic path,

and all have seen to it that Hungary had a place in the international economic community. The Democratic Forum, under Premier Jozsef Antall,
took the first bold steps, even though the party opposed giving foreigners
access to the broadcast media. Hungary became an associate member of
the European Community, the forerunner of the European Union (EU),
in 1991.

The first Socialist government (1994–98), led by Premier Gyula
Horn, initially slowed the pace of privatization. It then suddenly reversed
course and threw open the banking, energy, and telecommunications
industries to FDI. In 1996, the Socialists launched a tough austerity program that even the conservative forum had not dared to undertake. The
Socialists capped spending on social-welfare programs, raised taxes, and
imposed a temporary 8 percent surcharge (tax) on imported goods. Under
Horn, Hungary joined the Organization for Economic Cooperation and
Development (OECD) economic research group in 1996.

The Fidesz government (1998–2002) of Premier Viktor Orbán took
an enormous step in 2001 by making the national currency, the forint,
fully convertible (interchangeable with other national currencies). Also
in 2001, the National Bank of Hungary announced an inflation-targeting
policy, the country's first, to counter what had been a persistent problem.
In 1997, the EU invited Hungary to begin formal membership negotiations with the aim of full membership by May 1, 2004. In a national referendum on April 13th, 2003, Hungarian voters approved of EU
membership.

The new Socialist government of Premier Péter Medgyessy is vocally
committed to keeping Hungary on the free-market path.

In the years 1997–2002, most of the economic indicators were upbeat.
(Many of the following economic terms will be further defined and discussed in greater detail in later sections of this chapter.)

- Foreign direct investment (FDI). FDI in Hungary reached a total of
  $23 billion by the year 2000. Since 1989, the country has attracted
  more than half of all foreign investment in post-Communist Eastern Europe.
- Privatization. In 1993, about 50 percent of Hungary's companies
  were privately owned. The figure had reached more than 80 percent by 1998. As of the year 2000, privately owned companies

accounted for more than 80 percent of Hungary's gross domestic product (the value of goods and services produced in a given year).

- Gross domestic product (GDP). Hungary's GDP in 2001 was $132.2 billion (using the purchase power parity method of calculation). In 1993, GDP had been about $27 billion.
- Real growth. This is the percentage of change in GDP when the negative effects of inflation are factored in. Hungary had real growth of 5.5 percent in 2000 and 3.8 percent in 2001. (Real growth of 3 percent or more is considered strong.) Note that Hungary had suffered a −18 percent growth rate from 1990 to 1993.
- Inflation. Inflation is a rise in consumer prices coupled with a corresponding loss of purchasing power. Hungary had an annual inflation rate of 6.8 percent in 2001, down from a high of 28.3 percent in 1995 and 23.6 percent in 1996.
- Unemployment. Some 5.8 percent of Hungarians were jobless nationwide in 2001, compared with a high of 14 percent in 1993.

Observing the Hungarian economic scene, a pair of Southern Illinois University professors commented in 2002:

One can conjecture that the upgrading of old technologies through foreign direct investment, increase in product quality and structure, decline in unit labor costs, and introduction of the post-95 measures have been some of the main driving forces of the increased output and decline in inflation in Hungary.

On the other hand, Hungary has some economic issues that remain a cause for great concern.

- Deficit spending. All of Hungary's post-Communist governments have spent more money than they have brought in. The budget deficit for the year 2000 was $1.4 billion (outlays of $114.4 billion on revenues of $113 billion). The 2000 deficit devoured 1.3 percent of the nation's GDP.
- Trade imbalance. Hungary continues to import more goods than it exports. In the year 2000, the country exported $25.2 billion in goods but imported $27.6 billion in goods.

- Foreign debt. Hungary's total foreign debt (including accumulated interest) stood at $29.6 billion in the year 2000, up from $23 billion in 1989. The good news is that the country by 2000 had repaid all of the money it owed the International Monetary Fund, more than $2 billion.
- Unfinished structural reforms. Hungary has not finished reforming its health care system (75 percent of the nation's medical costs are absorbed by the government), its tax system, or its pension system. It needs to restructure the formula of federal aid to local governments. In addition, it must radically change its system of agricultural subsidies to conform to EU standards.

Three Countries, Three Paths

Hungary chose to privatize its economy by selling state-owned companies to foreign investors. Other post-Communist countries in Eastern Europe had the same aim (privatization) but took different paths. A comparison of Hungary, Poland, and the Czech Republic, the three nations in the region with the largest economies, is most revealing.

The Czech Republic actually had further to go in privatization than either Hungary or Poland. When the Czechoslovak Communists were ousted in 1989, the government had owned *all* of the country's businesses. (Communist Hungary and even Communist Poland permitted some private enterprise.) One factor in favor of the Czech economy was that most of the unprofitable heavy industries in Czechoslovakia were in Slovakia. Thus, when Czechoslovakia divided into two countries at the start of 1993, Slovakia was stuck with the burden of those industries.

The Czechs, however, did not put their faith in privatization through foreign investment. Instead, Czech citizens were given preference in all sales of state-owned property. The Czech Republic created a voucher system that allows groups of its citizens to band together to purchase state properties. The Czechs, in 1997, were the first nation in the region to initiate "inflation-targeting," or having its national bank closely monitor price rises throughout the economy.

Of the three countries, the Czech Republic had the lowest inflation and unemployment rates in the 1990s, whereas Poland has the largest industrial and agricultural resources of the three. In 1990, the Poles launched a program of "shock therapy," or allowing prices to rise to their natural levels overnight by reducing or ending government subsidies to key sectors of the economy. Poland welcomed foreign investment, but the government was compelled to retain the two most troubled state-owned industries, mining and steel production. Both industries were unprofitable, badly in need of expensive modernization, and manned by workers in militant labor unions. As of 2002, the industries were still troubled and still state-owned.

Poland's combination of "shock therapy" and foreign investment led to high prices (inflation) and high unemployment but also to excellent real growth (GDP modified by inflation). Poland had the strongest sustained real growth in the 1990s of any of the three countries (an average of 5.5 percent from 1995 to 2000) but suffered a major downturn in 2001. Poland adopted inflation-targeting in 1999.

Hungary, Poland, and the Czech Republic Compared

ANNUAL SYSTEMATIC CHANGES IN EASTERN EUROPE

1993			
	INFLATION	REAL GROWTH	UNEMPLOYMENT
Hungary	21.1%	–1.5%	12.2%
Poland	37.6%	4.0%	15.7%
Czech Republic	18.2%	0.0%	3.5%

Source: *Reason,* April 1995

2001			
	INFLATION	REAL GROWTH	UNEMPLOYMENT
Hungary	6.8%	3.8%	5.8%
Poland	3.6%	1.1%	18.2%
Czech Republic	4.2%	3.6%	8.2%

Source: Organization for Economic Cooperation and Development, September 2002

The Wizard of Ózd

Picture a huge steel plant in Ózd, a small town in northeastern Hungary near the border with Slovakia. The complex has been in existence since 1804, when it manufactured brass military cannons. At its height, in the 1960s, the Ózd operation employed more than 14,000 steelworkers. Shifts worked around the clock amid searing blast furnaces and clanging machinery. The government-owned complex was one of the largest single employers in Hungary. And, it was a very profitable enterprise.

Now picture the same Ózd plant in 1994. The entire complex is deserted except for two sections. Nothing now emerges from the tall chimneys that used to belch black smoke 24 hours a day. Most of its machines are silent and rusting. Most of the workers have been laid off. In one of the only two operating sections of the complex, about 1,000 remaining workers are employed processing scrap steel for meager wages. But in the other section, about 700 well-paid employees are turning out clever, useful metal products for export all over Europe.

In a way, the Ózd plant is the story of Hungary's troubled transition from the "capitalized socialism" of the 1970s to the market economy of the 1990s. It is a story of both abject failure and daring success.

The steel complex, like most of Hungary's industries, had fallen on hard times in the late 1970s through the 1980s. That had been a period of recession (severe economic slowdown) and lagging productivity. During that time, the plant retained most of its workforce even though it was losing millions of dollars a year. Aging equipment and obsolete work rules had contributed to the problem. The plant no longer was competitive, even in the closed economic sphere of the Soviet bloc.

Then, in 1988, a savior of sorts appeared on the scene. He was János Petrenko, an ambitious former worker who had dreams of becoming an entrepreneur, or risk-taking business owner. This was a time when the reformed Communists were pushing the older, conservative Communists out of power. Petrenko used his charm and gift of gab to convince the government to sell him one section of the Ózd plant for about $2 million. A government-owned bank loaned him the money. Petrenko turned the small section into a private company, Peko Steel Industrial Works. He fired the entire management team of the section he had inherited from the government. At the same time he raised the number of workers in the section to 647 from 445. Among the new employees were creative people hired to design new products.

"If we were going to survive," he recalled in 1993, "we had to have new products. . . . The big problem with socialism was that people were embedded in tradition, old concepts, old ideas. I wanted fresh thinking."

In 1990, Petrenko was struggling to make enough money to pay his employees and to make his loan payments. That year, another apparent savior showed up. A German steel company purchased the rest of the Ózd complex (excluding Petrenko's company) in hopes of turning a quick profit. The Germans believed that they could use the cheap labor at the plant—Hungarian steelworkers earned much less than German steel-workers—to undercut the shaky steel markets in other parts of Eastern Europe. But they could not find any new markets in the region. And the Ózd workers could not adjust quickly to the rigid new work rules imposed by the Germans to increase efficiency. The plant continued to lose millions of dollars.

Peko Steel Industrial Works turned its first profit in 1991. Rather than trying to go head-to-head with the major steel manufacturers of Europe, Petrenko's company concentrated on finding niches ("vacuum areas" in his terminology) for metal products that no one else was turning out. One such product was an inexpensive portable stove that burned sawdust, cherry pits, and other waste materials. He focused initially on the Hungarian and Eastern European markets, setting the groundwork for exports to Western Europe as well.

Meanwhile, by the close of 1991, the Germans had decided to cut their losses on the Ózd facility. They declared bankruptcy and withdrew their remaining investments in the complex. More than 12,000 steel-workers lost their jobs. The relative handful of employees that were not laid off were left to eke out a living recycling scrap metal. One of the remaining workers, László Nagy, had worked at the complex for 25 years. Speaking with some bitterness, he told a reporter in 1994, "The Germans shut down the furnaces. They didn't do anything for us. Under the old system, we had security. Today we live from day to day."

Peko Steel experienced a downturn in 1992 but bounced back in 1993 to do an estimated $22 million in business. Petrenko increased and diversified his product line to include electronic motors and steel rims for buses and trucks. His company also created a retail division, opening several Western-style "superstores." Petrenko also incorporated a subsidiary, Peko Corporation, in the U.S. state of Wisconsin. By incorporating in the United States, Petrenko made it easier to export his products to America and to have access to American commercial technology. In addition, Petrenko cut a deal with Ukraine that gave Peko Steel 50 percent ownership of a steel plant in the Ukrainian capital of Kiev.

Hungary is full of new entrepreneurs like János Petrenko. They are men and women with the courage and insight to take advantage of the freedoms offered by the fledgling market economy. There is Péter Zwack, the head of Zwack Unicum Ltd., a leading distiller of alcoholic beverages. Zwack comes from an aristocratic family that fled Hungary in 1948. He returned in 1988 and started his company (in partnership with the German distiller Underberg Group) by selling a liqueur based on a secret recipe that had been in his family for generations. The liqueur, called Unicum, quickly became one of Hungary's favorite alcoholic drinks.

Gabor Szeles is another very successful entrepreneur. He is a former electrical engineer who founded Videoton, a private company that has become the largest consumer-electronics business in Eastern Europe. Szeless's rapid rise to the status of corporate mogul is legendary. Videoton is now entering the fields of computers and telecommunications equipment.

Hungarian-born George Lang, a world-famous restaurateur, forged yet another success story. Lang and a partner, Ronald S. Lauder, U.S. ambassador to Austria under President Ronald Reagan and son of Hungarian-American cosmetics magnate Estée Lauder, spent $10 million to buy and renovate a decrepit turn-of-the-century restaurant in Budapest. Today, the restaurant—named Gundel—is again one of the city's most exclusive, and expensive, dining places.

The lure of fortunes—or at least easy profits—turned Hungary into a kind of capitalist Old West in the late 1980s and early 1990s. The business atmosphere in the country was freewheeling, heady, and optimistic. Some of the entrepreneurs, such as Petrenko and Szeles, received government help to launch their private business empires. Others, like Zwack, entered into partnerships with foreign companies (such arrangements are known as joint ventures). Still others, like Lang and Lauder, were wealthy enough to use their own capital to finance their investments.

But by far most of the investment capital that flowed Hungary's way came from foreign companies that purchased all or part of Hungarian companies. For a while, Hungary was a foreign-investment paradise. Then things turned sour.

The Foreign-Investment Strategy

When we examine the current Hungarian economy, it is hard to believe that FDI was once a hotly debated topic. The list of foreign companies heavily invested in Hungary reads like a who's who of international business: automakers General Motors (U.S.A.), Ford (U.S.A.), Audi (Germany), and Suzuki (Japan); telecommunications giants Deutsche Telekom (Germany) and Ameritech and U.S. West (both U.S.A.); retailers Marks & Spencer (U.K.), Ikea (Sweden), Auchan (France), and Julius Meinl (Austria); aerospace titan Lockheed Martin (U.S.A.); U.S. industrial- and business-equipment manufacturers IBM, United Technologies, and General Electric; and American beverage and fast-food heavyweights such as Pepsico, Coca-Cola, McDonald's, Burger King, and Pizza Hut.

The *Access Hungary Commercial Guide*, produced by the U.S. embassy in Budapest, reported in 1998: "Foreign owners [in Hungary] produce 25% of the GDP and control 70% of financial institutions, 66% of industry, 90% of telecommunications, 60% of energy production, and 50% of the trading sector."

The reformed Communists of the Hungarian Socialist Workers' Party and their successors, the Hungarian Democratic Forum, believed initially that foreign investment would be the key to a successful transition to a market economy. The Communists encouraged joint ventures and began to remove legal barriers to foreign investment. When the Democratic Forum coalition took power, in 1990, it removed most remaining barriers and announced that virtually all state-owned companies would be for sale to foreigners.

The central package of laws easing curbs on foreign investment had been passed by the National Assembly in January 1989. The legislation gave tax breaks to foreign investors and allowed them 100 percent ownership of Hungarian companies.

Foreign direct investment (FDI) was the cornerstone of privatization, or the transfer of government-owned companies to private ownership. In order to get Hungary's economy in order, the country had to cut government spending. That spending could not be reduced as long as the state-owned companies—many of which were losing tens of millions of dollars a year—relied on government subsidies.

The Budapest Stock Exchange, the first such institution in post-Communist Eastern Europe, began trading in 1990. The plan was to issue shares of both private and state companies to anyone who wished to participate. But most of Hungary's politicians did not believe Hungarian citizens alone had enough investment capital (money to invest) or faith in the new system to buy up the state companies. That is why the foreign-investment strategy came about.

The very first Hungarian government-owned company to go on the trading block was IBUSZ, the national travel agency. Shares in IBUSZ went on sale both in Budapest and in Vienna, Austria, in June 1990. The agency was one-third privatized with the investments of some Austrians.

The foreign-investment strategy envisioned a stimulated national economy with only moderate inflation (an increase in currency or credit resulting in high prices) and only a temporary heavy loss of jobs in the state-owned sector. Both the Communists and the Democratic Forum thought that a growing private sector, awash with foreign investment, would soon absorb those workers displaced from the public sector. They believed that foreign investors would modernize and streamline the Hungarian economy with a minimum of hardship to the general public.

A key goal of the government's foreign-investment strategy was to avoid performing "shock therapy" on the Hungarian economy. Shock therapy—encouraged by some Western economists—is the practice of lifting controls on prices formerly controlled by the government in order to stimulate the production of scarce goods. The move can cause goods that were once affordable but in short supply to become unaffordable for a period of time. But the profit potential also encourages the growth of suppliers. Eventually, as more suppliers compete for consumers, the quantity of goods increases, and prices naturally fall to a point of affordability.

Shock therapy has been tried by two ex-Communist countries: Poland in 1990 and Russia in 1992. In Russia, for example, the price of smoked sausage rose to 50 rubles (45¢) a pound from 35 rubles (31¢) a pound. Big deal, you say? Keep in mind that the average Russian in 1992 earned the equivalent of only about $4 a month.

Unlike Poland or Russia, Hungary has never experienced routine shortages of goods. Even when the Communists were in power, Hungarian stores were usually well stocked. So the government saw no need for shock therapy as a tool of economic reform. Of course, Hungary had to lift its own price controls (beginning in January 1990), but it did so while playing the foreign-investment card.

No country in Eastern Europe attracted more foreign investment than Hungary between the years 1988 and the start of 1994: a total of $7 billion. In the period between 1990 and the start of 1994, the figure was $5.5 billion. In comparison, in 1990–93, Poland received about $3 billion in foreign investment; and the Czech Republic and Slovakia combined, about $2.4 billion.

Many heavyweight Western companies came to Hungary. America's General Electric Company paid $350 million to take over Tungsram, a state-owned maker of electric-light equipment. The Japanese automaker Suzuki invested $140 million in an auto plant (it was the largest Japanese investment ever in Eastern Europe). Audi, part of Germany's Volkswagen automakers, spent $200 million to open an automobile-manufacturing facility near the city of Gyo″r. Alitalia, Italy's national airline, invested $77 million for a 35 percent share of Malev, Hungary's national airline. Both General Motors Corporation and Ford Motor Company of the United States have established vehicle plants in Hungary.

The United States and Germany have led the way in foreign investment in Hungary. The largest single such deal came in December 1993, when a partnership of Deutsche Telekom (Germany's state-owned telephone company) and Ameritech Corporation of the United States bought 30.2 percent of Matav, Hungary's state-owned telephone company. The agreement was worth $875 million.

Like that of all the other countries of the former Soviet bloc, Hungary's telephone system was primitive compared to those of Western nations. Lack of capital and access to sophisticated Western technology had held Hungary back in the telecommunications area. The partial sale of Matav seems to have solved some of those problems. One Western publication detailed Matav's struggle to improve phone service:

> Despite major improvements in its telephone system over the past few years, Hungary still lags far behind the European average of thirty telephones per 100 people. (The U.S. average is more than fifty per 100.) In 1988, Hungary had fewer than ten main-line telephones per 100 inhabitants. During the past three years, Matav pursued an aggressive construction program that considerably enhanced telephone services and resulted in more than 300,000 new connections in the 1991–1992 period. By the end of 1992, the penetration rate had increased to 12.5 telephones per 100 of the population. Some 170,000 new lines were connected in 1993, resulting in a total capacity of 1.4 million main-line connections.

Hungary now is getting into advanced telecommunications. Westel, a U.S.-Hungarian joint venture, has set up the first mobile cellular-phone system in the country. And Matav has outbid Poland's state telephone company to provide an optical-cable link between Russia and Western Europe. Optical cables carry telephone signals in the form of light waves.

If everything had gone as planned by the government, an endless supply of foreign capital would have flowed into the Hungarian economy, the state sector would have disappeared, and every Hungarian would have a job. However, things did not go as planned. For every major multinational corporation that invested in Hungary for the long haul, there were many others that came in only to make a quick buck.

One problem, which began as early as 1988, was "hit-and-run" investment. That happened when foreigners bought up Hungarian companies, then broke up the companies and sold off the assets. Another problem was that some foreigners bought Hungarian companies simply to eliminate competitors for their own products. Some of the first foreigners to take advantage of the liberal investment rules in Hungary were Austrians, and they got a bad reputation around the country. According to the *New York Times*,

> When Austrian companies rushed in to buy up [Hungarian] retail businesses, they were looking for markets for their own products. The

Austrians pushed Hungarian goods out of the state-owned companies they bought and increased the prices for their better-produced imports. Now, families complain that food at the nationwide super-market chain acquired by Julius Meinl, an Austrian company, is unaffordable. Clothes imported by Kleiner Bauder, the new Austrian owners of a popular apparel chain, look better but are more expensive than the old Hungarian fashions.

Many foreign investors who came to Hungary committed to long-term investment were still surprised at how long it took them to become profitable. They had not anticipated the problems they encountered with Hungarian workers. The workers were not used to being pushed to work harder, and were suspicious of Western-style management methods. Under the Communists, even unproductive workers kept their jobs, but the Western managers were quick to reduce wages or fire workers to save money.

John Welch, the chairman of General Electric, in 1994 admitted that his company had not foreseen the difficulties it would encounter when it bought Tungsram in 1990. The company's production facilities were out of date, its financial records were in disorder, and its workforce was much larger than was needed. GE had to spend $200 million (in addition to the $350 million purchase price) to whip the company into shape. Tungsram only began to turn a profit in 1994. "We probably couldn't have been more naive four years ago," Welch noted.

The ruling Democratic Forum, which had staked its political fortunes on the foreign-investment strategy, was rocked by criticism when the benefits were not immediately apparent. Instead of a fast economic turn-around, workers were being laid off by the thousands and companies were being closed. In many towns where the local economies depended on one or two large factories, foreign investment meant that a majority of people were unemployed or facing unemployment. Opposition parties made a political issue of what they viewed as a foreign takeover of Hungary's economy.

In reaction to the criticism, in October 1992 the government pulled back from a plan to have 50 percent of the nation's state-owned companies fully privatized by the end of 1994. Instead, it announced that the government would retain sole or partial ownership of about 100 state companies in "strategic sectors." The sectors included such nationally important areas as communications, transportation, and energy. At the time of the policy change, about 8 percent of all of Hungary's companies were in foreign hands.

The policy change was a signal that foreign investment was no longer as welcome as it had been. Investors began to look elsewhere in Eastern Europe, such as Poland and the Czech Republic.

Even though foreign investment in Hungary had been a record $2.2 billion in 1993 (compared with $1.7 billion in 1992), that figure was swollen by the giant Malav deal. Without the telephone-company sale, actual foreign investment in 1993 would have been $1.3 billion, less than in 1992.

By 1994, nearly everyone was unssatisfied with the outcome of foreign investment. The government was backtracking. Opposition parties, as well as nationalists within the ruling Democratic Forum, were using the issue to hammer the government. Workers by and large distrusted it. And the investors themselves were wondering if their purchases were worth the money and headaches.

Direct foreign investment in Hungary amounted to only about $1 billion in 1994, a sure sign that the country was losing its attraction as an investment magnet. László Lengyel, the head of Financial Research, a Hungarian investment-advisory firm, summed up the 1994 picture this way:

> Hungary expected more results from these investments. The investors are also disappointed in the speed of the [economic] transition. They expected Hungary, as the most developed of the East European countries, to go through the changes in three years. Instead, we're in the fourth year, and there is negative growth, and we can't really see how it will stabilize.

The Socialist Party (the reformed Communists of the late 1980s) came to power in Hungary in the spring of 1994. The party's base of support was the working class, particularly Hungary's left-wing trade unions. The return of the reformed Communists concerned potential Western

Paprika and homemade baskets. Hungary was rocked by a scandal over tainted paprika powder in 1994. (Courtesy of David and Margaret Roberts)

foreign investors who were already worried about the course of investment policy.

The new premier, Gyula Horn, promised to continue economic reform. But he also promised to soften the impact of reform on workers and pensioners (retired people on fixed incomes). Horn slowed the privatization process and clashed over economic policy with key officials, including Finance Minister László Bekesi, Privatization Minister Ferenc Bartha, and the chairman of the National Bank of Hungary, Péter Akos Bod. The three officials—who were respected both by Western economists and aid donors—were committed to the policies of swift privatization and "tight money." Tight money means restricting the money supply and maintaining high interest rates in order to control inflation.

Bod, who had quarreled with Premier Horn over the tight money policy (Horn wanted interest rates eased), resigned under pressure in November 1994. Horn fired Bartha in January 1995 in an apparent power struggle over privatization policy. Bekesi quit his post soon after Bartha's

departure, complaining about what he considered Horn's political interference in the reform process.

Perhaps the most blatant example of political interference came in
January 1995, when Horn rejected an agreement to sell a 51 percent stake
in the state-owned HungarHotels chain to a U.S. company, American
General Hospitality. The sale price, approved by the State Property
Agency (the government office in charge of privatization), was to have
been $57.5 million. But Horn overruled the SPA, saying that the sale
price was too low. America Hospitality really was interested in acquiring
one of the 14 hotels in the chain—the aging riverfront Forum Hotel in
Budapest—but all 14 came as a package deal. Horn's reversal angered the
U.S. company, which declined to renegotiate the agreement and dropped
out of the sale.

Horn's actions created a political crisis in the country. The Socialists' junior partners in the ruling coalition, the Alliance of Free
Democrats, threatened to pull out of the coalition. And, as might be
expected, his actions also alarmed foreign investors. Ralph Gerson, the
head of the Hungary–United States Business Council, commented:
"I've heard a lot of concerns from companies interested in investing in
Hungary."

In an attempt to placate the Free Democrats and foreign investors,
Horn in February 1995 appointed Lajos Bakros as finance minister and
György Suranyi as chairman of the National Bank of Hungary. Both men,
respected experts in banking and finance, were admired in international
financial circles, and both appeared dedicated to a continuation of market reforms. The appointments bought some political peace and reassured
some investors, but doubts remained about Horn's commitment to a full
transition to a Western-style economy. However, his actions reflected the
attitudes of perhaps the majority of ordinary people. A telephone poll of
over 700 Hungarians, conducted by the newspaper *Magyar Hírlap* and
published February 14, 1995, found that 35 percent disapproved of foreign investment in Hungary. The same survey found that only about one-
third liked foreign investment, and that 28 percent believed it was "bad,
but necessary."

In March 1996, Horn made the stunning policy decisions to open virtually all sectors of the economy to foreign investment and to impose a
strict economic austerity program. Horn's successor, Viktor Orbán

(elected in 1998) eased the austerity plan. But Orbán and the following premier, Péter Medgyessy (elected in 2002) held firm on welcoming foreign investment.

The Growth of Private Enterprise

The debate over foreign-investment reflects only the big picture in Hungary. While the multinational corporations played a role in the country's economy, so did small- and medium-sized businesses started up by Hungarians themselves. The majority of new businesses have been in the service sector, rather than in the manufacturing sector. According to Western economics reporter Karoly Okolicsanyi,

> Service industries . . . have boomed; new accounting firms have been established; and new tax advisers seem to have multiplied. New office space is under construction, as are facilities such as gasoline stations, which were rare under the communist regime. New banking services [such as credit cards and automatic teller machines] are being provided that have long been commonplace in the West, but would have been unimaginable in Hungary until only recently.

Almos Kovacs, the vice president of the National Bank, in 1994 issued an economic assessment that noted the sharp increase in growth of private enterprise between 1990 and 1993. The assessment summarized

> The number of private enterprises had increased from 10,000 to almost 200,000, and [the number of] private entrepreneurs and proprietorships from 200,000 to 700,000 by the end of 1993. . . . The number of joint ventures had reached 21,485 by December of that year. The government had removed obstacles to entering the market and launching new businesses, and it had scrapped price and production subsidies [to businesses]. . . . Controls on wages and the flow of capital had been lifted. Revised laws on bankruptcy and the regulation of financial institutions had created conditions that had compelled more and more inefficient businesses to leave the market.

Kovacs noted that the private sector had accounted for between 45 percent and 50 percent of Hungary's GDP by the end of 1993. GDP is a key measure of a country's economic output based on the total value of goods produced by all sectors of the economy. A rise of 3 percent or more in GDP is universally considered a sign of a healthy, growing economy—provided that inflation is held in check and the growth is not being eaten away by government overspending. Hungary's GDP declined by 4.5 percent in 1992, and fell by 2 percent in 1993. But the GDP grew by at least 3 percent in 1994, reflecting a genuine economic turnaround.

Deficits have a negative effect on GDP. Thus, the 1993 Hungarian government budget deficit of 199.6 billion forints (about $2 billion) was approximately 7.5 percent of GDP. Roughly speaking, the government wiped out 7.5 percent of the national economic output by spending $2 billion more than it took in.

By 2001, Hungary's GDP was growing by a healthy 3.9 percent a year. The budget deficit for 2000 was 1.3 percent of GDP, indicating that the economy was growing and there was less overspending by the government. But the fact remains that no post-Communist government in the country has yet figured out how to balance the budget.

Land and Property Compensation

People whose property was confiscated by the Communists after 1949 were compensated under a law passed by the National Assembly in 1991. Each person with a valid claim to rural land was given the option of receiving up to 50 hectares (123 acres) or a government voucher. The voucher could be used to draw on a special compensation fund totaling $1.35 billion. As a result of the law, about one-half of the nation's arable (fit for cultivation) farmland was transferred from government ownership to private ownership.

Those with valid claims to urban property each received a government voucher worth up to $67,000. The vouchers could be used toward the purchase of privatized land, but not urban property. Urban real estate prices have soared, and $67,000 is far below the market value of most property in Budapest and other cities.

The law did not offer any relief to persons whose property had been taken away before 1949, thus excluding ethnic Germans, Jews, and Romany (Gypsies). Nor did it compensate the wealthy landowners who lost huge tracts when the Communists came to power.

However, in October 1996, Hungary's parliament approved the creation of a foundation to compensate Hungarian Jews for property seized by the government during World War II. Under an agreement with Jewish leaders, the government agreed to contribute $26 million to a compensation fund that would be managed by the foundation.

Currency and the Tight Money Policy

Hungary's national currency, the forint, has moved from being nonconvertible (in the Communist era) to being fully convertible in June 2001. The United States and the European Union in the 1990s jointly established a so-called forint fund to help make the currency convertible as the economy stabilized. The forint's value was determined when measured against the U.S. dollar along with the euro. (True hard currencies are measured individually against each other: for example, the dollar against the Japanese yen.)

The value of the forint is ridiculously low compared to the dollar. As of October 2002, 1 forint was worth .0040¢. Taken another way, if you went to a Hungarian bank, you could get 247 forints and change for each dollar you chose to exchange.

Hungarian governments are following a tight money policy. That means they are limiting the amount of currency in circulation and keeping bank interest rates high to discourage borrowing by companies or individuals. The policy is aimed at fighting inflation, or rising prices. More money in circulation, or more borrowing, means higher prices. As prices increase, workers demand higher salaries because their purchasing power has been cut. That is known as an "inflationary spiral." The Communists had held down inflation by simply imposing government controls on wages and prices. But that is not done in a free economy except in an extreme emergency.

Hungary also has battled inflation by periodically devaluating the forint when it feels the currency is becoming overvalued. Devaluation usually is made in steps of 1–3 percent against the U.S. dollar and euro. Hungary has had trouble with inflation, but the situation is improving. The annual inflation rate was 35 percent in 1991, 23 percent in 1993, below 19 percent in 1994, and just 6.8 percent in 2001.

Labor and Social Security

In the summer of 1990, the residents of Budapest began seeing something they had never before seen: large numbers of homeless people throughout the capital. There were indigent men sleeping under newspapers and panhandling near the city's tourist attractions. There were entire families, including small children, living in the city's train stations and parks. At that time, the government estimated that there were about 20,000 "hardcore" homeless people in Hungary. (The hardcore homeless were people who had no friends or relatives who could give them at least temporary shelter.) It was unclear how many of the 20,000 were in Budapest, but they appeared to number in the thousands.

Homelessness was a shocking indication of the downside of economic reform. Most of the homeless were men who had lost their jobs in the economic transition and were unable to pay their rent. Other factors impacted on the crisis, as well. For one thing, there had long been a shortage of housing in Hungary. For another, state-owned companies had been closing worker hostels (barracks-like living quarters maintained by the companies for their employees) as a cost-cutting measure. Also, some of the homeless men were immigrants from Romania and other neighboring countries who had hoped to find work in Hungary.

Under the Communists, joblessness and homelessness had been uncommon; anyone in good standing with the party could usually find a job and some form of housing, however meager. Without anticipating the problems ahead, Hungary entered its economic transition with no system of unemployment compensation or emergency housing.

By 2002, the homeless problem had eased considerably, though it had not disappeared. Hungary now has unemployment compensation, and both the public and private sectors have been building new housing. However, the new housing has not kept pace with the influx of tens of thousands of immigrant Magyars (ethnic Hungarians) from Romania and Serbia.

Unemployment was a persistent problem in Hungary in the 1990s as it was throughout the former Eastern bloc. In 1990, the official jobless rate had been 1.7 percent, or 79,521 people, but by early 1993, the figure was 14 percent, or 705,000 people. In the spring of 1994, about 12 percent of the workforce, or 593,000 people, were unemployed. The jobless rate had fallen to 5.8 percent by the end of 2001.

The worst-hit workers were those laid off from heavy industries, such as steel production. They generally lacked the skills to enter Hungary's flourishing service sector. And they do not have the knowledge or the capital to start their own businesses.

The average Hungarian worker took home the equivalent of $130 a month in 1990. By the end of 1995, the average monthly wage rose to about $350. However, wages failed to keep up with inflation in the 1990s. The national minimum wage, instituted in 1992, was about $112 a month.

The post-Communist law that governs management-employee relations came into effect July 1, 1992. By law, the standard work week is 40 hours, with employers required to pay overtime if their employees work on holidays or weekends. The law requires a minimum of 20 days paid vacation for all workers. If the employees of a business are unionized, then they have a right to collective bargaining. Unionized workers also have the right to strike.

Unlike Poland, which has experienced serious labor unrest during its transition to a market economy, Hungarian workers have been quiet for the most part. The worst labor disruption occurred in October 1990, when truck drivers and taxi drivers in Budapest blocked traffic for three days to protest a 65 percent hike in gasoline prices. The government partially gave in by lowering the price increase to 35 percent.

Those workers lucky enough to have jobs receive a generous package of benefits known in Hungary as "social security." It includes free (government paid) health care, free education, and guaranteed pensions upon retirement. The medical-insurance aspect of the program actually predates the Communist era: Hungary was one of the first countries in Europe to ensure that its workers had health coverage.

The Democratic Forum government not only left social-security benefits intact, it expanded them. In 1992, the Council for the Reconciliation of Interests—a body with representatives from the government, labor unions, and employers—had signed a "social contract." Under the agreement, the government vowed to increase pensions by 14 percent in return for union support for a new value-added tax (VAT). The VAT is a kind of national sales tax on goods and services. Hungary imposes levies of 6 percent or 25 percent, depending on the type of product or service. Food had at first been exempt from the VAT, but was later included at the 6 percent level.

It had appeared that no post-Communist government would tamper with the social safety net, but this was not so. The Socialists in 1996 froze social spending and raised taxes. Hungarians grumbled and tightened their belts, but there were no riots. The center-right government that succeeded the Socialists in 1998 was more generous than its predecessor. It hiked the minimum wage by 41 percent in 2001. Not surprisingly, the average wage of Hungarian workers soared, to about $460 a month, a 17 percent increase over the previous year.

Government Deficits

Uncontrolled government spending drains economic growth. Hungary has been deficit spending since the end of communism. That means that the government spends more money than it takes in.

In 1994, the central budget deficit was 321.7 billion forints (about $3.6 billion), while the general government deficit was 340 billion forints (about $4 billion). The central budget is the spending approved by the National Assembly. The general government figure included additional debts, including the costs of the government borrowing from the National Bank of Hungary. The central bank lends money to the government to make up for shortfalls in the central budget. Without such loans, the government would run out of money. The interest rate on government borrowing was 8.2 percent in 1994.

Unprofitable state-owned companies account for a large part of the deficit problem. First, the government has to spend money just to keep the companies in operation. Second, such companies are unable to pay their required corporate taxes or meet their mandated contributions to social-security programs. For example, in 1994, the government central budget had to pay about $1.8 billion to make up for the social-security obligations of MAV, the money-losing state-owned railroad.

Simply put, deficit spending erodes economic growth. In 1994, government deficit spending amounted to about 8 percent of Hungary's gross domestic product.

Counteracting this, however, the foreign direct investment strategy has paid off: By selling money-losing enterprises and taxing the new owners the government has slowly inched its way out of debt. The deficit for 2000 was $1.4 billion—troubling, yes, but nothing like what it would have been without FDI.

Foreign Debt

In 1989 foreign debt, the amount, including interest, that Hungary owes to other countries and to foreign commercial banks, was approximately $23 billion. By comparison, that was only about one-half of Poland's accumulated foreign debt in the same year. However, the Hungarian figure was—and continues to be—the highest per capita (per person) foreign debt in eastern Europe. Hungary has a population of less than 11 million. Poland's population is more than 38 million.

Between 1989 and 1993, Hungary paid $20.6 billion in principal and interest on its foreign debt, a huge sum for so small a country. Due to additional borrowing, Hungary's foreign debt has not gone down. In fact (over the last five years) it is has risen about $6 billion. But the country is proud of never having missed a debt payment. The excellent record of debt repayment explains the willingness of nations and banks to keep lending to Hungary.

Countries that rely on continuous borrowing to fuel their economies make foreign lenders and foreign investors nervous. Compare Hungary's situation to that of Mexico in February 1995. The Mexican government devalued the peso (the national currency), and panicky foreign investors (mainly Americans) began to withdraw their investments for fear of losing money. That precipitated a downward spiral in the Mexican economy. The value of shares on Mexico's stock market plunged, and the peso almost collapsed. U.S. president Bill Clinton decided to step in and bail out the peso with nearly $50 million in emergency aid.

Mexico, like Hungary, is heavily dependent on foreign loans to keep its economy going. At the time of the Mexican crisis, that country's foreign debt had been equal to 46 percent of its gross domestic product. Hungary's foreign debt in February 1995 had been equal to 67 percent of its GDP. In other words, Hungary's present economy—like that of Mexico and other struggling nations—is a precariously balanced house of cards. Hungary's total economic output is being eaten away by its large debt burden. Hungary's gross foreign debt stood at $29.6 billion in 2000. That figure seems small when compared with Poland's $64 billion foreign debt (in 2000) or Mexico's $191 billion foreign debt (in 2001). But keep in mind that Hungary is nowhere near the size of those countries in population. Hungary's foreign debt per person is enormous.

Aid and Trade

Hungary is getting outside help in the struggle to transform its economy. That help is aid from individual nations, groups of nations, and international financial institutions. Some of the aid is "free," in the sense that it does not have to be repaid. For example, the United States and some Western European nations have sent experts to Hungary to advise the government and the private sector on economic matters, business, and agriculture. There are U.S. Peace Corps volunteers in Hungary teaching English to the populace.

Most of the assistance is not free. Rather, it comes in the form of credit or loans with low interest—or no interest—and flexible, stretched out repayment schedules. One example of such aid came in 1990, when President George H.W. Bush granted $47.5 million in credits and loan guarantees so that Hungary could buy 500,000 tons of American grain. Hungary did not get the grain for nothing; it simply purchased it without having to pay for it immediately.

Groups of nations, including the G-7 (the top seven industrial countries) and the G-24 (the top 24 industrial nations), have given Hungary short-term loans over the last few years. But by far the largest amounts of aid have come from international financial institutions.

In 1990, when Hungary launched its full-scale effort toward a market economy, the central banks of the Western nations banded together to give the country a total of $280 million in short-term loans. And the Bank of International Settlements (BIS) granted Hungary $80 million in "bridge financing" (a loan to help pay off debts that are coming due). BIS is an arm of the European Union, the most important multinational economic partnership on the continent.

Hungary's most important potential aid donors are the International Monetary Fund and the IMF's affiliate institution, the World Bank. The IMF extends credit to member nations that need help transforming their economies or stabilizing their currencies. The World Bank (its official name is the International Bank for Reconstruction and Development) lends money to countries that normally would have trouble getting favorable terms from commercial banks. (The bank is known as the "lender of last resort.") The IMF and World Bank are associated with the United Nations. They are financed through contributions from UN member countries. Hungary became an IMF member in 1982.

IMF aid comes with strings attached. In order to get assistance, a country must meet strict limits on government spending and take prescribed steps toward a market economy. Hungary signed an agreement in February 1991 that would have given the country a total of $1.62 billion in stand-by credits. Such credits are a special fund available to a country over several years if that country chooses to use it. The IMF suspended Hungary's borrowing privileges (called "special drawing rights") in 1993 because of the government's inability to meet IMF-mandated annual budget targets. But Hungary was determined to meet its obligations. By 2002, all of the IMF debt had been paid back.

Imports and Exports

As of the year 2000, Germany and Austria were Hungary's most important trading partners. Germany receives 37 percent of Hungary's exports and provides 25 percent of Hungary's imports. Austria receives 9 percent of Hungary's exports and provides 7 percent of Hungary's imports. Hungary's other major trading partners are Italy, Russia, and the Netherlands. The United States is the sixth-largest market for Hungarian exports, but Hungary ranks only 72nd on the list of countries importing U.S. goods.

Hungary's main exports are heavy machinery, food, livestock, chemicals, natural gas, and raw materials (especially bauxite and coal). Agriculture exports have been hampered by changing government regulations, reduced government subsidies, legal disputes over land ownership, and scandals. One such scandal involved paprika, the spicy red-pepper powder that is a major export. Some dishonest paprika entrepreneurs were found to have mixed powdered copper with the spice in order to increase their inventories and hike their export sales.

Hungary's main imports are light machinery, transportation equipment, manufactured goods, and fuel. Hungary imports oil even though it has its own small oil reserves. Hungarian oil has a high sulfur content, meaning that it requires very expensive refining to remove its pollutants. Hungarian trade problems have less to do with bad government policies than with the fact that the country has had to completely reshape its trade structure. The fall of the Council for Mutual Economic Assistance (the Soviet-bloc trade organization) in 1991 had left Hungary in a hole. The Soviet Union had been its largest trading partner.

Hungarian exports declined by 50 percent in 1991, more than even the most pessimistic observers anticipated. The most positive event of the year in the area of trade was Hungary's signing of a European Community association agreement on December 16. The 10-year pact provided for the gradual entry of Hungary into the EC (now known as the European Union or EU). That meant that Hungary eventually would be a full partner in an economically integrated Europe.

The association agreement requires Hungary to structure its trade-related institutions and regulations to fit the prevailing standards of the EU nations. For example, EU countries subsidize some industries like dairy products and steel. In order to join the EU, Hungary's dairy and steel subsidies would have to conform to EU norms. The benefits of full membership would include reduced tariffs (taxes on imported goods) on the products Hungary exported to its EU partners. Without EU membership, Western Europe would remain partially closed to Hungarian trade.

The EU began to lift its barriers to Hungarian exports in 1992. Elsewhere, Hungary and its "Visegrad" colleagues (Poland, the Czech Republic, and Slovakia; see chapter 6) formulated plans in 1992 to create gradually a free-trade zone in Eastern Europe. The plan envisioned a time when there would be little or no barriers to trade among the four nations.

Trade with the West picked up in 1992, when Hungary exported $10.3 billion in goods. But there was a 13 percent drop ($8.9 billion) from the figure in 1993. The 1993 decline was in part due to a decrease in the nation's agricultural exports. (Agriculture output fell in 1993, when cuts in government farm subsidies forced changes in that sector of the economy.) Hungary exported about $7 billion in goods in 1994.

Hungary's exports have not kept up with its imports. In spite of periodic devaluations of the forint, which make Hungarian exports cheaper to buy and make imported products more expensive, Hungary has had a trade deficit every year since 1990. In 2002, the country imported about $33.9 billion worth of products, compared with $31.4 billion in exports.

NOTES

p. 112 "'One can conjecture . . .'" Selahattin Dibooglu and Ali M. Kutan, "Sources of Inflation and Output Fluctuations in Poland and Hungary: Implications for Full Membership in the European Union," Southern Illinois University Online, September 19, 2002, Chapter 4, p. 21.

p. 116 "'If we were . . .'" "Hungary: It's Unique!" *Fortune*, October 18, 1993.

p. 116 "'The Germans . . .'" *New York Times*, May 3, 1994, p. A12.

p. 118 "'Foreign owners . . .'" Embassy of the United States of America in Budapest, *Access Hungary Commercial Guide*, October 5, 2002.

p. 121 "'Despite major improvements . . .'" Karoly Okolicsanyi, "Hungarian Telephone's Landmark Privatization Deal," *RFE/RL Research Report*, February 11, 1994, p. 41.

pp. 121–122 "'When Austrian companies . . .'" *New York Times*, May 3, 1994, p. A12.

p. 122 "'We probably . . .'" *New York Times*, May 3, 1994, p. A12.

p. 123 "'Hungary expected . . .'" *New York Times*, May 3, 1994, p. A12.

p. 125 "'I've heard a lot . . .'" *New York Times*, February 21, 1995, p. D2.

p. 126 "'Service industries . . .'" Karoly Okolicsanyi, "Macroeconomic Changes in Hungary 1990–1994," *RFE/RL Research Report*, July 17, 1994, p. 25.

p. 126 "'The number of private . . .'" Okolicsanyi, July 17, 1994, pp. 22–23.

6

FOREIGN POLICY
AND DEFENSE

From the very beginning, Hungary's post-Communist governments have had two wishes. One wish was to have Hungary join the North Atlantic Treaty Organization (NATO). The other was to have Hungary admitted into what is now the European Union (EU).

The first wish came true in 1999, when Hungary became a member of NATO, and in early 2003, EU membership appeared to be within its grasp. Hungary was invited in 1997 to begin talks for membership, set for the spring of 2004. Now in a new century, a globalized Hungary is preparing to have an impact—however small—on the world scene.

Hungary Looks Westward

At the close of 1990, the Soviet bloc existed in name only. While it was true that the Soviet Union still existed and that the bloc's two most important international organizations, the Warsaw Pact military alliance and the Council for Mutual Economic Assistance (Comecon), were still operating, the USSR was losing its satellites in Eastern Europe. East Germany had disappeared in the reunification of Germany. Hungary, Poland, and Czechoslovakia all had pro-Western, non-Communist governments. Communist hard-liners were out of power in Romania and Bulgaria.

Visiting Hungarian premier József Antall (left) with U.S. president George H. W. Bush on the South Lawn of the White House in 1990. (AP/Wide World Photos)

Then, in the summer of 1991, both the Warsaw Pact and Comecon fell apart. With no organizations to bind it to the USSR, which itself would soon collapse, Hungary looked toward the West for new allies.

On October 18, 1991, Hungarian premier József Antall visited Washington, D.C., and held discussions with President George H. W. Bush and other top U.S. officials. The trip marked a turning point in relations between the two countries. Not only was Antall one of the first of Eastern Europe's post-Communist leaders to come to the United States, he was the first Hungarian leader to set foot in the country in more than 50 years.

Antall was treated to all the pomp and ceremony usually reserved for a visiting foreign dignitary. Bush, in welcoming the premier to the White House, praised Hungary's political transformation. "Hungary is no longer an emerging democracy," the president said. "Hungary is a democracy."

Bush did more than offer words of praise. He announced a program through which Hungary could buy $47.5 million worth of U.S. feed grain

(grain used to feed farm animals) on credit. Hungary needed the assistance because its own grain crop had been damaged in a severe drought during the summer of 1990. In the past, Hungary would have turned to the Soviet Union to supply the grain. Now it relied on America.

Antall's October trip to the United States was the second of two events that month that would set the course of Hungary's foreign policy. Earlier, on October 2, Hungary was admitted to the Council of Europe, an organization based in Strasbourg, France. The council is a forum for discussions on political and human-rights developments in Europe. Hungary was its 24th member and the first nation from post-Communist Eastern Europe to join the council.

Hungary is also an active participant in the Organization for Security and Cooperation in Europe (OSCE). The OSCE (formerly the Conference on Security and Cooperation in Europe, or CSCE) is a multinational organization that monitors human rights and security issues. Hungary hosted a CSCE summit in Budapest in December 1994 that was attended by many world leaders, including U.S. president Bill Clinton.

Taken together, the admission to the Council of Europe and Antall's trip to America showed the world early on that Hungary was forging a new foreign policy. The new foreign policy was based on friendship with the West as opposed to subordination to the Soviet Union. The military and economic ties that bound Eastern Europe to the Soviet Union completely unraveled in 1991. In the end, the Soviet Union itself shattered into 15 independent countries. But, months before the USSR's collapse, the Soviets had all but lost their empire in Eastern Europe.

First, the last Soviet troops based in Hungary left for the USSR on June 19, 1991. Next, Comecon—the Soviet-bloc trading organization—disbanded on June 28, at a meeting in Budapest. Then, on July 1, the Warsaw Pact disbanded at a summit of leaders in Prague, Czechoslovakia. Only the Soviet Union had wanted to keep the two organizations alive.

Hungary was finally free of the heavy hands of Soviet military and economic control. However, that did not mean that Moscow wished to see Hungary go its own way. Even before the demise of Comecon and the Warsaw Pact, Soviet leader Mikhail S. Gorbachev had pressured the new democracies of Eastern Europe to sign "friendship treaties" with the

USSR. Each such agreement would provide a framework for future diplomatic, cultural, and economic relations between the Soviet Union and the particular country. There was one major catch: Gorbachev demanded that Hungary, Poland, and the other nations not join any Western organizations that he regarded as hostile to the Soviet Union.

Romania, which was not especially pro-Western, signed a Soviet friendship pact in April 1991. But Hungary, Poland, and Czechoslovakia refused to sign. Their leaders regarded Gorbachev's demand as a Soviet ploy to maintain control of their countries' foreign policies. Besides, the three nations wanted to join the North Atlantic Treaty Organization (NATO), a military alliance created to counter the Soviet threat.

In the end, the resistance of the three countries forced Gorbachev to drop his demand. That cleared the way for the former Communist nations to have amicable relations with the Soviets and also be part of

Soviet troops withdrawing from Hungary in 1989. The last Soviet forces left in June 1991. (AP/Wide World Photos)

the new Europe. Gorbachev and Premier Antall signed a Soviet-Hungarian friendship treaty in Moscow on December 6, 1991. (Czechoslovakia and Poland also inked such agreements.) With the collapse of the Soviet Union at the end of 1991, Russia assumed responsibility for honoring the friendship pacts.

Russian president Boris Yeltsin paid a visit to Hungary in November 1992. Yeltsin was the first high-ranking Russian to come to Hungary since the downfall of the USSR. During the visit, Yeltsin laid flowers at the grave of Imre Nagy, the executed leader of the 1956 Hungarian uprising. Such a gesture by a Russian leader would have been unthinkable during the Communist era. Both governments were trying to end the friction between the two countries, friction that went all the way back to Russia's intervention in the Hungarian Revolution of 1848–49.

The Visegrad Summit

Hungary, Poland, the Czech Republic, and Slovakia are known as the Visegrad nations, having formed an unofficial alliance based on common foreign-policy and economic objectives.

The alliance dates back to a chilly day in February 1991, when the leaders of Hungary, Poland, and Czechoslovakia held a historic meeting in an ancient castle in Hungary on the banks of the Danube River. The meeting came to be known as the Visegrad Summit, after the castle's location, the town of Visegrad. The summit was hosted by Premier Antall and Hungarian president Árpád Göncz. Those in attendance included Polish president Lech Wałesa and Czech president Václav Havel.

The three nations were then—and are now—the most democratic and procapitalist to emerge from the Soviet bloc. The leaders agreed to future informal cooperation in reaching the goal of integrating their countries into (in President Havel's words) "the all-European building."

Stated simply, Hungary, Poland, and Czechoslovakia wanted to end their decades of isolation from the rest of Europe. With that goal in mind, the leaders vowed to create a united front in pursuit of their own countries' aims. The key aim, they agreed, was to have all three countries admitted to the European Community. The union, which includes most of the Western European countries, is moving toward an economically unified continent.

Following the summit, Hungary, Poland, and Czechoslovakia contin- ued to consult with each other on an informal basis as the "Visegrad Tri- angle," or "Visegrad Three." When, in 1993, Czechoslovakia divided into two countries—the Czech Republic and Slovakia—the unofficial group became the "Visegrad Quadrangle," or "Visegrad Four."

U.S. president Clinton met with Hungarian president Göncz and other leaders of the Visegrad nations in January 1994, during a visit to Prague, the capital of the Czech Republic. Clinton endorsed the objec- tives of the alliance and praised the spirit of cooperation among the four countries.

The true significance of the Visegrad alliance is that it gave the small, relatively powerless nations—no longer part of the Eastern bloc, but not yet part of the Western world—a sense that they could direct their own destinies if they spoke with one voice.

EU Membership: No Joke

There is a popular joke in Hungary. It goes like this: "Hungary is six years from European Union membership, and it always will be."

The EU is an economic-political alliance of nations. EU members benefit from low tariffs (taxes) on intra-alliance trade. The EU has a uni- fied currency, the euro. It even has an executive branch (the European Commission) and a parliament.

The joke stems from December 1997, when a summit of the 15 EU countries formally invited Hungary and five other nations to begin "nego- tiations" for membership. The other invitees were Poland, the Czech Republic, Estonia, Slovenia, and Cyprus.

What's so funny? Well, *negotiations* is a poor choice of words given that would-be members must transform their economic, monetary, immigra- tion, legal, and human-rights policies to conform to very strict EU stan- dards. Among its members, the EU has rules and regulations on everything from agricultural subsidies and workers' rights to government deficit spending and civil liberties.

The EU in December 2002 set a target date of May 1, 2004, for membership by Hungary and the other invitees. Hungary wants in, if only to help its trade situation. As a current nonmember, Hungary's exports to EU countries are being hit with high tariffs.

In June 2001, Hungary overcame one possible barrier to EU admission. If admitted to the alliance, Hungary pledged, it would delay the expected flow of Hungarian workers to other EU countries. The pledge eased fears that Hungarian workers would flood the richer EU nations in search of jobs that paid higher wages than they could earn in Hungary. (EU rules allow a free flow of labor among member states.)

Neighborly Relations

In 2001, Hungary's parliament passed a law that would give special benefits to the 5 million Magyars (ethnic Hungarians) who live in neighboring countries. Under the law, the Magyars were to receive a special document entitling them to state-funded jobs, health care, and education in Hungary. The governments of Ukraine, Slovenia, and Yugoslavia accepted the law. But the governments of Romania and Slovakia criticized the law as an illegal interference in their internal affairs.

Two issues, border guarantees and minorities, have long dominated Hungary's discussions with its neighbors. The neighbors have insisted that Hungary recognize the current borders and give up any claims to the lands that Hungary once ruled. On the other hand, Hungary has insisted that its neighbors assure the civil liberties of the Magyars who live outside Hungary.

Hungary, spurred by its desire to join NATO and the EU, signed friendship treaties with some of its neighbors in the mid-1990s, since neither NATO nor the EU would want an aggressive, nationalistic Hungary as a member. Following is a survey of the current state of relations between Hungary and its bordering countries.

The former Soviet republic of Ukraine borders Hungary on the northeast. Hungary once ruled the border region (known as Ruthenia), and today several thousand Magyars live on the Ukraine side of the border. In 1993, Hungary and Ukraine signed a friendship treaty guaranteeing the current border. The same pact guaranteed the civil liberties of the ethnic

Hungarians in Ukraine. The treaty would serve as a model for agreements between Hungary and other neighbors.

Slovakia is on Hungary's northern border. The Slovaks were under Magyar rule for nearly 1,000 years, and feelings of resentment continue. The Slovak majority at times has treated the 600,000 ethnic Hungarians in Slovakia like second-class citizens. Under Premier Vladimír Mečiar, for example, Slovakia insisted that Magyars adopt Slovak-sounding names. However, Slovakia also wants to join NATO and the EU, so Hungary and Slovakia signed a friendship treaty in May 1996.

Treaty or not, Slovakia was nervous about its Magyar minority. In July 1996, two months after the treaty was signed, ethnic Hungarians from throughout eastern Europe held a summit in Budapest. The final communiqué backed "autonomy" for all Magyars living outside Hungary. The Slovak president, Michal Kováč, criticized the document, saying that it "rouses mistrust."

On another matter, the International Court of Justice (World Court) in 1997 ruled that both Hungary and Slovakia had violated a 1977 agreement to build twin hydroelectric dams on the Danube River. Hungary had abandoned the project, while the Slovaks completed their end (a dam at Gabčikovo, Slovakia). The court ruled that Hungary should compensate Slovakia for having pulled out of the project and that Slovakia should compensate Hungary for the environmental damage to Hungarian wetlands caused by the Gabčikovo dam.

Austria, on Hungary's northwest border, is perhaps Hungary's best friend in Europe. Historic, cultural, and economic ties bind the two countries. Austria is Hungary's second most important trading partner, after Germany. Every year, thousands of Hungarian tourists visit Austria, and thousands of Austrians vacation in Hungary.

The tiny Alpine nation of Slovenia, once part of Yugoslavia, is on Hungary's western border. Slovenia has solid relations with Hungary in part because it was never under Hungarian domination. Hungary has never had any claims on Slovenian lands, and few Magyars live in Slovenia. Hungary recognized Slovenia's independence from Yugoslavia in 1992.

Croatia, also once part of Yugoslavia, borders Hungary on the southwest. Hungary once ruled northeastern Croatia, a border region known as Slavonia. Croats and Magyars historically have never gotten along, but

Hungary supported Croatia's break with Yugoslavia (recognizing Croatian independence in 1992) and gave refuge to thousands of Croats who fled the subsequent fighting in Croatia. At present, Hungary regards Croatia as a "strategic partner" (they share economic and security goals) in the region but not necessarily a friend.

The Republics of Serbia and Montenegro make up what is left of Yugoslavia. The Serbian province of Vojvodina borders Hungary on the south. Serbs and Magyars are traditional adversaries. Under the leadership of Slobodan Milošević (a hard-line Serb nationalist), the Yugoslav government curtailed the rights of the approximately 400,000 Vojvodina Magyars in the 1990s. In 1999, Hungary assisted the NATO war effort that resulted in Milošević's ouster. Now, with a more moderate element in power in Yugoslavia, the two nations have established a cautious

Foreign Minister Gyula Horn (right, with wire-cutters) helps remove a part of the barbed wire fence at the Austrian-Hungarian border in 1989. Horn would lead the Hungarian Socialist Party to victory in 1994. (AP/Wide World Photos)

relationship. The Yugoslav parliament in early 2003 voted to change the name of the country to Serbia and Montenegro.

Romania, to the east of Hungary, is another historic enemy of Hungary. The two countries nearly went to war in 1988–90 over the mistreatment of Magyars in Romania's Transylvania region (which used to belong to Hungary). According to Hungary, there are close to 2 million ethnic Hungarians in Romania, but Romania holds that the figure is less than 1 million. In 1992, the Romanian government reached an agreement with ethnic Hungarians in Transylvania to share power at the local level, but the pact fell apart in 1993.

Romania, too, is seeking NATO and EU membership; therefore, in September 1996, Hungary and Romania signed a friendship treaty. The two sides agreed that the pact could be interpreted in a manner that would allow a measure of local autonomy for the Magyars in Transylvania. In 1997, Hungarian president Árpád Göncz paid a historic visit to Romania. He was the first high-ranking Hungarian official to visit Romania in the post-Communist era.

The Hungary-Romania relationship remains edgy, at best. In February 2000, a large accidental spill of toxic cyanide in Romania flowed into the Tisza River in Hungary, killing fish and endangering drinking-water supplies. The cyanide originated in a gold mine half-owned by the Romanian government. When Hungary demanded compensation, the Romanian government flatly refused to pay.

A Lesson in Chess

In the game of chess, the most important squares are the eight squares in the center of the chessboard. The player who controls the center squares can move his or her pieces easily from one side of the board to the other. Hungary's role in the Warsaw Pact was roughly akin to that of the center squares. Hungary's military role in NATO is much the same as it was in the Warsaw Pact: to hold the center. Geographically, Hungary is in the center of eastern Europe. Its chief functions in the Soviet military alliance were to guard the Warsaw Pact's supply lines and ensure the uninterrupted passage of Warsaw Pact troops between north and south. If war had broken out on the southern front (in the area of Romania and

Bulgaria), for example, Warsaw Pact forces based in Czechoslovakia or Poland would have been able to move freely through Hungary to reach the front.

The Communist-era Hungarian People's Army had two principal tasks: defend Hungary (hold the center squares) and supply reserves for fighting north or south of Hungary. The Warsaw Pact never envisioned Hungary as a battleground in itself. The Soviet bloc had prepared for fighting NATO in either Germany (the northern front) or the Romania-Bulgaria southern region. The 50,000 or so Soviet troops based in Hungary were technically part of the Red Army's Southern Group.

The last Soviet troops quietly left Hungary, on June 19, 1991, with little fanfare. Soviet military bands played as the soldiers marched to rail depots around the country for the trip east. Some curious Hungarians watched them go, but the onlookers neither cheered nor booed. If there was any reaction among the Hungarians, it could be called a collective sigh of relief.

Less than a month later, on July 1, the Warsaw Pact disbanded. The two events meant that Hungary was truly free of foreign military domination for the first time in more than 40 years. But was the little country strong enough to defend its independence? The sad answer was no.

The Soviets not only had troops in Hungary, they may have had secret nuclear weapons there as well. In 1991 the former leader of Hungary's reformed Communists, Károly Grösz, claimed that the USSR had concealed nuclear arms in Hungary between 1956 and 1988. If true, it is most likely the weapons had been short-range (300 miles or less) "battlefield" armaments for use against concentrations of enemy troops or tanks. Grösz maintained that the Soviet leader Mikhail Gorbachev had withdrawn the weapons from Hungary in late 1988.

The Hungarian army did have some Soviet-built Scud-Bs and Frog-7s, which were medium-range ground-to-ground missiles. But those were believed to have had conventional (high-explosive) warheads, rather than nuclear warheads. Hungary began dismantling the missiles in 1990.

Hungary—unlike the Soviet Union, East Germany, Poland, Czechoslovakia, or Bulgaria—never developed a military-industrial complex. That is, it never had large-scale industries that produced sophisticated military equipment. Although Hungary manufactured some small arms and light military vehicles, it never built its own planes, tanks, or heavy artillery. Those weapons had been supplied by its Warsaw Pact partners, mainly the USSR. About 80 percent of all of Hungary's armaments and military equipment have come from the Soviet Union.

Defense spending was mostly secret during the Communist era. Experts believe that military expenditures hit a peak of 7.4 percent of the total government budget in 1963 and fell to about 4.8 percent of the budget by 1968. One thing is certain: Hungary's military spending—without a large military-industrial complex to feed—was relatively small compared to those of its Warsaw Pact allies.

Hungary may have had as many as 180,000 people on active duty in its army during the early 1960s, when cold war tensions were high. By 1989, with the reformed Communists in power, Hungary's armed forces consisted of about 155,700 on active duty and over 200,000 in the reserves.

The reformed Communists in 1989 decided that Hungary's military would have to be both scaled down and modernized. The scaling down was necessary to lessen the burden of defense spending on the country's weak economy. The modernization was necessary because a time was foreseen when Hungary would not be able to depend on its Warsaw Pact allies to come to its aid in time of war. The reshaping of the military was planned to continue over six years, to be completed by the end of 1995.

Hungary in NATO

In June 1999, Hungarian soldiers arrived in Kosovo, a province of the Republic of Serbia. The troops, 350 in all, were not in Kosovo to fight but to help keep the peace. Hungary was one of 25 nations that contributed soldiers to KFOR (Kosovo Force), the contingent of peacekeepers in Kosovo. Most of KFOR was made up of soldiers from the member states of NATO. The Western military alliance had gone to war in Kosovo to protect the province's predominantly ethnic Albanian population from mistreatment by Serb forces.

Hungary—along with Poland and the Czech Republic—formally had joined NATO in March 1999. (They were the first former Soviet-bloc nations to enter the organization.) NATO had invited the three into the alliance in July 1997. In November 1997, Hungary had sponsored a national referendum on NATO membership, with 85.3 percent of the voters voting "yes" on the question.

Following the 1991 collapse of the Warsaw Pact, the Soviet-led military alliance to which Hungary belonged, Hungary became the first Eastern European nation to seek openly NATO membership. But Hungary had to settle for 1994 membership in the "Partnership for Peace." The partnership, a compromise suggested by U.S. president Bill Clinton, allowed Hungary and other Eastern European countries to have high-level contacts with NATO without actually belonging to the alliance. From NATO's point of view, Hungary was not ready for full membership in the mid-1990s. For one thing, Hungary's relations with some its neighbors, such as Romania, were downright hostile. Under NATO's rules, the entire alliance might have been pulled into a war between Hungary and Romania if Hungary were a NATO member. Another factor was economic. NATO members are obligated to modernize their military forces. Hungary in the mid-1990s lacked the financial resources to bring its forces up to a NATO standard. But perhaps the most compelling reason for keeping the former Soviet bloc countries out of NATO was the opposition of Russia itself.

Hungary had to work hard to get into NATO. It signed friendship treaties with its neighbors, began to modernize its military, and maintained cordial relations with Russia. (Russia, convinced that NATO expansion posed no threat, eventually reversed its opposition.) Between 1991 and 1999, Hungary technically did not have any military allies. It was alone, a small country saddled with inadequate military forces and obsolete Soviet-made military equipment.

In the summer of 1991, Croatia, a neighbor of Hungary, broke away from Yugoslavia, precipitating a war. Hungary was neutral in that conflict, but Yugoslav warplanes violated Hungarian airspace with impunity during bombing raids on Croatia. A Yugoslav plane even accidentally dropped bombs near a Hungarian village on the Hungary-Croatia border. Hungary was helpless to do anything about the actions of Yugoslavia because it was no match militarily for Yugoslavia.

Hungary was officially neutral in the 1995 conflict in Bosnia-Herzegovina, a breakaway province of Yugoslavia. But, when the fighting ended, Hungary allowed U.S. troops in the NATO peacekeeping force—known as IFOR, or Implementation Force—to use the village of Taszar, in south-central Hungary, as a key staging area. (The people of Taszar welcomed the U.S. "invasion." One café owner spent his life savings to stock up on American cigarettes, whiskey, and kitchen equipment to cook pizzas and hamburgers.)

While Hungary had no role in the Bosnia conflict, the 1999 Kosovo conflict was a different matter. Hungary, now a NATO member, did not send any troops to fight in Kosovo, but it did allow NATO warplanes to conduct bombing raids from a Hungarian military airbase.

Hungary did not take part in the fighting in Afghanistan in 2001–2, either. The Hungarian government vocally supports U.S. president George W. Bush's international war on terrorism, however.

Reshaping the Military

Hungary's federal expenditures for the year 2000 totaled $114 billion. Of that figure, $1.1 billion went to the military. That was 1.2 percent of the total expenditures and 1.8 percent of the national gross domestic product (the sum value of goods and services produced in a given year).

Priorities have changed. The nation spent almost $100 million more on the military in 2000 than it did in 1992, when the government's aim was to cut defense spending. Now, with NATO membership, Hungary must spend more on defense and actually increase the number of its active-duty forces.

All Hungarian males ages 18 to 49 are subject to military draft and must serve a minimum of 18 months on active duty. At the end of 1992, Hungary's armed forces had a total of about 100,000 people on active duty. By the end of 1993, the figure had been reduced to 78,000 (60,500 in the army, and 17,500 in the air force). That made Hungary's military one of the smallest in Europe. The goal of the early reorganization was to have approximately 75,000 troops on active duty by 1996. The goal was met—and then some. By the end of 1998, Hungary's armed forces totaled 43,500. But by then, NATO loomed on the horizon. Hungary simply had to spend more money on modernizing its forces and buying new weapons and equipment to replace its aging Soviet-made gear.

As of the year 2000, Hungary's armed forces stood at 64,000. Hungary's approximately 9,000 armed border guards are not counted in that figure. Under the Communists, the guards worked for the Interior Ministry and their main duty was to keep Hungarians from leaving the country without permission. Today, the guards are part of the Transportation Ministry, and they prevent illegal immigration and smuggling. The guards can be pressed into service as a defense force in the event of war.

Hungary's forces are now better trained than ever. Today, Hungarian officers are training in the United States, Canada, Great Britain, and France, and Hungarian soldiers are getting better equipment because their country can purchase advanced gear from its NATO partners. The United States provided millions of dollars in aid in 2000 and 2001 to help Hungary buy new military equipment.

Hungary and the Iraq War

On March 19, 2003, the first U.S. missiles fell on Baghdad, the capital of the Middle East country of Iraq. It was the beginning of the war between Iraq and the U.S.-led "coalition of the willing," a term coined by U.S. president George W. Bush. The coalition was a group of about 40 countries that, according to Bush, fully supported America's effort to disarm Iraq by force. Bush regarded Hungary as a member of the coalition, but Hungary flatly refused to take an active role in the war.

The war had been preceded by months of bitter international debate over whether or not Iraq possessed weapons of mass destruction (chemical, biological, or nuclear armaments) in violation of restrictions set by the United Nations following the 1991 Gulf War. UN weapons inspectors had failed to find any substantial evidence of Iraqi violations. The United States insisted that Iraq was hiding the banned arms and argued that the country should be disarmed by force, with or without UN approval. On the other side, a group of nations that included France, Russia, Germany, and China pushed for continued weapons inspections, and argued that force should be used only with explicit UN approval.

The U.S. position had received welcome support on January 30, 2003, when the leaders of eight nations published an open letter in the *Wall Street Journal* and several European newspapers. The letter praised the "trans-Atlantic bond" (the historic relationship between the United States and Europe) and urged the world community to take a united stand against Iraq. Hungary was one of the signatories, along with Great Britain, Spain, Poland, the Czech Republic, Italy, Portugal, and Denmark.

French president Jacques Chirac regarded the letter as a slap in the face from the former Communist nations. France had supported the expansion of the European Union to include Hungary, Poland, the Czech Republic, and now those three countries were siding with the United States against France. Speaking at a press conference in Belgium on February 18, 2003, Chirac angrily told reporters that the eastern European nations had "missed an opportunity to keep quiet" on the Iraq issue. He called their support of the United States on the matter "dangerous." The French leader hinted—but did not say outright—that France might delay the entry into the EU of the candidate nations. Hungary, Poland, and the Czech Republic were set to join the EU in 2004.

From the start of the war, American and British forces did by far the bulk of the fighting against the Iraqis. But less-powerful members of the "coalition of the willing" also actively participated. For example, Poland contributed a unit of commandos, and the Czech Republic sent a small contingent of military chemical-arms experts.

Hungary's participation was limited to granting permission to the United States to use the airbase at Taszar, Hungary, to train up to 3,000 Iraqi exiles in noncombat roles. The exiles, who began their training in February 2003, were to act as translators, police officers, teachers, and civil administrators upon a U.S. overthrow of the Iraqi regime.

The war was a touchy political issue in Hungary. Public-opinion polls indicated that a majority of Hungarians opposed the war. Former premier Viktor Orbán publicly urged Hungarian neutrality. Orbán's Fidesz-Hungarian Civic Party took a strong antiwar stance in parliament.

Hungarian premier Péter Medgyessy, reacting to the pressure, announced on March 20, 2003, "Hungary is not part of the armed conflict, it is not at war, and is not going to be. The Hungarian government will not send troops to Iraq."

In addition, Hungary's Foreign Ministry politely rejected a U.S. request to expel all the Iraqi diplomats in Budapest. The United States had made a similar request to all of the members of the coalition.

NOTES

p. 138 "'Hungary is no longer . . .'" *Facts On File World News Digest,* October 26, 1990, p. 800C2.

p. 141 "'the all-European building.'" *Facts On File World News Digest,* February 21, 1991, p. 120C2.

p. 152 "'missed an opportunity to keep quiet'" and "dangerous" *New York Times,* February 19, 2003, p. A1.

p. 152 "'Hungary is not . . .'" Eszter Balazs, *Budapest Sun Online,* March 27, 2003.

7

ARTS AND MEDIA

The fall of communism ushered in a new era of free expression in Hungary. No longer does the government censor the arts, bar Western films, or control the print media. Today, Hungarians can watch American (and American-inspired) programs on their televisions, pick up foreign magazines devoted to any subject on virtually any newsstand, and attend plays that were once banned by the authorities.

But the new freedom comes with a price tag. While Hungarian publishers can choose what they print, many are struggling to survive in difficult economic times. The country's tiny film industry has had only an equally small impact on the international film market. Much of television and radio is foreign-owned. Art theft has become a major problem.

Literature: A Day at the Budapest Book Fair

Visitors to the 1994 Budapest Book Fair, held outdoors in Vorosmarty Square in late May, were able to browse through books at colorfully decorated booths sponsored by various publishing houses. Classical music wafted through the air, played by strategically located string quartets. Clowns and magicians put on shows for children.

Even though it was the 65th annual book fair, there was something different about this one. It was not simply the presence of a wide variety of books from North America and Western Europe. Selected books from those regions had been available in Hungary since the early 1980s, when the Communists had loosened some restrictions on foreign publications. No, the difference was that there was evidence of a revival of Hungary's robust literary tradition.

Writers

Few Hungarian writers have gained worldwide recognition, although the country has produced talented novelists, essayists, poets, and playwrights. That anonymity ended on October 10, 2002, when novelist Imre Kertesz won the Nobel Prize in literature. Kertesz, 72, was Hungary's first Nobel laureate in the literary arts.

Kertesz had not been a well-known author, even in Hungary. As of 2002, only two of his several books, *Fateless* and *Kaddish for a Child Not Born*, had been translated into English. *Fateless*, published in 1965, is a novel about a Hungarian Jewish teenager sent to the Nazi German concentration camp of Auschwitz in 1944. The book is autobiographical; Kertesz survived horrendous conditions in Auschwitz and Buchenwald in 1944–45.

In the 1950s, the Hungarian government blocked Kertesz's budding career as a journalist because he refused to join the official, Communist-approved Writer's Association. He wound up making a living in Budapest as a translator of German literature. Kertesz, in a 2001 interview, described his writing as "a form of commitment to myself, to memory and to humanity."

Most of Hungary's major novelists, essayists, and poets have not been well known outside of the country, or at least outside of central Europe. This was due in part to the fact that they wrote in a language that was rarely translated for the purpose of reaching large foreign audiences. Although some of the key literary figures' works were translated into German and the Slavic languages during the era of the Austro-Hungarian Empire, there were few translations into English, French, Spanish, or Italian.

Much of Hungarian writing in the pre-Communist days was passionate and rebellious in spirit. At the heart of the most important literary works was an abiding faith in native Hungarian traditions and values as a refuge in a hostile world.

Hungary's first great literary era came in 1840–60, the heyday of rebellion against Austrian rule. It was during that period that Sándor Petőfi (1823–49) wrote fiery poems urging revolution against the aristocracy and foreign domination. Other leading writers of the period included János Arany (1817–82) and József Eötvöes (1813–71).

A second great literary period occurred at the turn of the 20th century, spurred by a group of young intellectuals associated with a prodemocracy Budapest newspaper, *Nyugat* (The West). The *Nyugat* circle included poet Endre Ady (1877–1919), writer Gyula Juhasz (1883–1937), and novelist Zsigmond Móricz (1879–1942). Ady was known for giving new life to the lyrical form of poetry. While lyrical poems were usually deeply personal, Ady used the form for political comment in the revolutionary spirit of Petoefi.

Following World War I and through the 1930s, Hungary's right-wing governments harassed the left-wing "village writers," or intellectuals who supported the peasants in their demands for land reform. Two of the best known social-protest works by the village writers were *The Silent Revolution* by Imre Kovacs (1913–80) and *Thunderstorms* by Géza Feja. Both works were banned by the authorities, and their authors were imprisoned on charges of inciting revolution.

Ferenc Molnár (1878–1952) perhaps Hungary's most highly regarded playwright, also emerged in the period between the two world wars. Molnár was best known for his comedies, but he, too, was affected by the repressive political atmosphere. A Jew, he immigrated to the United States in the 1930s in the face of rising anti-Semitism in Hungary.

Two major literary figures openly sympathetic to Marxism emerged during the pre-Communist days. They were poet Attila József (1905–37) and essayist/literary critic György Lukacs (1885–1971). József's poetry featured gritty portrayals of working-class life. Lukács gained fame for his innovative application of Marxist-Leninist social theory to literary criticism. The writings of both men were suppressed before the Communists came to power.

Several writers—including Lukács, poets Gyula Illyes (1902–83) and Ferenc Juhasz (b. 1926), and novelist George Konrad (b. 1933)—rose to prominence under the Communists. They were subsidized by the

A young woman selling books at a street stand in Budapest. Once-banned works such as The Gulag Archipelago *(lower center) now are freely available. Note* Rambo *(left center).* (AP/Wide World Photos)

government and their careers were promoted by the ruling Hungarian Socialist Workers' Party. Of course, the work of those favored by the authorities was expected to be enthusiastically Marxist, or at least apolitical.

Most of the writers in good standing with Communist rulers were careful to remain so. But a few major literary figures eventually rebelled against the Communists. Lukacs was appalled by the police-state tactics of the party, became a reformist, and fell into political disfavor following the 1956 Hungarian uprising. Konrad, author of *The Visitor* and *The Founder of the State*—two novels widely hailed in Hungary—incurred the wrath of the authorities by coauthoring a study accusing the Marxist intellectual elite of being power-hungry.

A few who remained in government favor gained a measure of notoriety outside of Hungary. A lyrical poem by Juhasz, titled "The Boy Changed into a Stag Cries Out at the Gate of Secrets," was praised by the world-famous British poet W. H. Auden as one of the most remarkable poems of the post–World War II period. The poem was a mixture of dreamlike fantasy and Hungarian peasant legend.

Writers who quietly opposed the government, such as poet György Petri (b. 1943) and film scriptwriter Sándor Csoori (b. 1930), found their careers blocked at almost every turn. The Ministry of Culture in 1986 accused dissident writer István Csurka of "distorting history" and banned all of his works. (Csurka went on to become a leading right-wing politician in the 1990s.)

Some Hungarian writers risked fines or jail by contributing (usually under false names) articles to dissident publications. One of the best known of the underground publications was *Beszelo*, a journal started in 1979. Some above-ground magazines, like the daring literary journal *Tiszataj*, tested the limits of the censorship and lost. The government shut down *Tiszataj* in 1986 for publishing the works of banned writers.

In the late 1980s, Hungary loosened its censorship of domestic books and magazines, and began permitting some Western publications into the country. In the freer climate, cultural journals such as *Elet es Irodalom* (Life and literature) and *Mozgo Vilag* (World in action) flourished thanks to a growing audience of younger Hungarians. Articles in the journals, while not openly anticommunist, discussed the need for social and political reforms in ways that had not been permitted by the authorities a few years earlier.

The transition from Marxist socialism to capitalist democracy, beginning in 1989, was accompanied by lifting of the restraints on free speech. The result was an almost obsessive examination, in fiction, poems, and essays, of the change. Politics and economics were the subjects of the vast majority of the works published in Hungary. While the examination was to be expected, and probably was necessary, observers reached a sad conclusion: much of what was being published was downright shallow. A key exception was the work of journalist Péter Esterházy (b. 1950), who dissected the confusing post-Communist political scene in a series of acclaimed newspaper essays. But, on the whole, it was as if the years of repression had robbed Hungary's writers of their flair for innovation and rebelliousness.

A new air of optimism was evident at the 1994 Budapest Book Fair. First, there was range of new work by Hungarian writers on a variety of subjects and in a variety of styles. Second, there was strong presence at the fair of small, privately owned Hungarian publishing houses.

Browsers were treated to a fresh collection of political essays by Esterházy, *Egy Kekharisnya Feljegyzesey* (Notes from an intelligent whore), published by Helikon, one of the country's oldest publishing houses. Abovo, a small publishing house, offered a collection of short stories, titled *Horroar*, by György Spiro, one of the new generation of Hungarian authors. As well, there was a Hungarian translation of *Under the Frog*, a novel by Tibor Fischer, a British-born writer of Hungarian heritage. *Under the Frog*, set in Hungary between World War II and the 1956 uprising, was a finalist for the 1993 Booker Prize (Great Britain's highest literary award).

Abovo was founded in 1991 by novelist Miklós Vamos. Vamos expressed some bitterness over the problems of Abovo and other small Hungarian publishers. The small houses, he said, struggled to make a profit while the large, well-established houses used their political connections to get government subsidies. "I hope the big publishing houses go bankrupt as soon as possible. The state grants go to publishers who are the favorite children of the government. The next government won't like me because I won't support them, either."

Hungarians love to read, but the publishing market is limited because of the country's small population. Through the 1990s, only a handful of contemporary Hungarian writers—Imre Kertesz, Péter Esterházy, and George Konrad among them—had their works translated into other languages. And few contemporary Hungarian writers have garnered attention in the United States. But that may be changing.

Novelist Péter Nádás (b. 1942), who is regarded highly in Hungary, attracted glowing reviews when his works reached the United States in the late 1990s. (Some critics have compared him favorably to the French writer Marcel Proust for his use of memory to evoke emotions.) Nádás has had three of his works translated into English, *A Book of Memories* (1997), *The End of a Family Story* (1998), and *A Lovely Tale of Photography* (1999).

And American literary critics finally have "discovered" Sándor Marai (1900–89), one of Hungary's best-known authors of the 1930s and 1940s. Marai's 1942 novel *Embers*, about the travails of a middle-class family in pre–World War II Hungary, was published in the United States in 2002. It was his first work to be translated into English, and others are set to follow. Some U.S. reviewers have compared Marai to John Updike, the American author famed for his fictional portrayals of middle-class life.

"The Vig" Reopens

On a cool October evening, the cream of Budapest society gathered at an ornate theater for a gala performance of a musical, *Ossztanc* (Let's dance together). Some of the theatergoers arrived in chauffeured limousines, while others drove up in high-priced sedans. The men were dressed in formal attire, the women in expensive evening gowns from top French and Italian designers. A mood of quiet excitement filled the air.

A scene from the opulent pre-Communist past? No, this was 1994, and the occasion was the reopening of the restored Vigszinhas, one of Budapest's most famous theaters. The event signaled nothing less than the reawakening of theater in Hungary.

Vigszinhas roughly translates to "house of comedy." To the people of Budapest, it has always been known as "the Vig." The theater, designed by two German architects, first opened in 1896, during the period of the Austro-Hungarian Empire. It became the creative home of Hungary's most renowned playwright, Ferenc Molnár. Molnár was best known for his comedies and social satires. His very first play, *The Doctor*, had debuted at the Vig in 1902. His lone dramatic play, *Lilliom* (the basis of the American musical *Carousel*), premiered at the Vig in 1909. Molnár was the theater's resident playwright until the 1930s, when he left Hungary in fear of the country's growing Fascist movement.

In its prime, the Vigszinhas was a symbol of the golden age of Hungarian culture, the late 19th century and the early years of the 20th century. Its interior was one of the most splendid examples of baroque architecture in central Europe. The baroque style, which dominated European art, architecture, and music from the 17th century until the mid-18th century, was defined by its dynamism and extravagance. The original Vig had inlaid-marble floors, gold-trimmed fixtures, crystal chandeliers, and seats padded in red velvet.

The Vigszinhas was badly damaged in the 1944 bombing of Budapest during World War II. The Communists rebuilt the theater and reopened it under a new name in 1951, as part of a Hungarian celebration of the birthday of Soviet leader Joseph Stalin. Needless to say, they got rid of the theater's glittering baroque elegance, which Marxists viewed as a signature of a decadent era. Under the Communists, the renamed Vig presented mainly boring dramas about the struggle of the working class. As a *New York Times* reporter observed:

> Officially called the Hungarian Popular Army Theater, it was for decades a beacon of Stalinist social realism, with boxes that were far from plush, military motifs on the walls and lighting that consisted of bare bulbs, not chandeliers.

In the 1960s, when the Communists took the first cautious steps toward easing the heavy hand of censorship, a few works by Molnár were allowed to be presented at the Vig, as well as selected plays by foreign writers like Germany's Bertolt Brecht and America's Arthur Miller. But the theater itself remained a musty shadow of its former self. Ironically, by the close of the 1980s—when most censorship had been lifted—the Vig itself had fallen into disrepair.

With the end of communism in 1990, the government made a decision to restore the Vigszinhas to its baroque splendor at an eventual cost of $20 million. The effort was spearheaded by Budapest's mayor, Gábor Demszky, and the Vig's director, László Marton. Even as the building was being renovated, Marton set a new creative direction for the theater. He presented plays by young Hungarian writers and staged popular foreign productions, such as the American musical *West Side Story*.

The renovation of the Vig coincided with a government drive to clean up and restore many of the old, neglected public buildings in the Hungarian capital. However, it was the reopening of the restored Vigszinhas that most symbolized a national cultural reemergence. "This [opening night] production gives us all a chance to send a very special message," said Marton. "Theater is back."

Classical Music: The Next Generation

In the fall of 1996, Hungary became the permanent home of a unique institution, the European Mozart Foundation. The foundation is a special school for young adults gifted in classical music. Each year since the early 1990s, about 50 students are chosen by a panel of experts to attend the school under full scholarship. The students are given a one-year intensive course in such areas as instrumentation, voice, composing, and conducting.

The students come from both Eastern and Western Europe. But the foundation places particular emphasis on molding students from the former Communist countries into budding classical artists. One American newspaper noted: "The Mozart Foundation is an academy devoted to the notion that more attention should be paid to the arts in Eastern Europe."

From the 1930s through the 1950s, hundreds of classical musicians, composers, and conducters left Eastern Europe to escape the Nazis, World War II, and then the Communists. (Among the émigrés had been Hungary's own George Szell [1897–1970], one of the world's great conductors. Already well established in Europe before World War II, Szell settled in the United States and gained further renown as the head of the Cleveland Symphony Orchestra.) As a result of the migration, Eastern Europe lost generations of talented musicians who could have passed down their knowledge and expertise to young people.

The first temporary home of the Mozart Foundation had been Dobris Castle, near Prague, the capital of the Czech Republic. In 1994, the foundation moved it to a site in Kraków, Poland. Currently its next and permanent location is to be Esterházy Castle in western Hungary. The castle is under renovation.

Esterházy Castle has an honored place in Hungarian history. It was the principal estate of the Esterházys, one of wealthiest and most politically powerful families in Austrian-ruled Hungary. Between 1760 and 1790, the Esterházys were the patrons of the great Austrian composer Franz Joseph Haydn (1732–1809), who lived and worked at Esterházy Castle for most of those years. (A patron is a wealthy sponsor of an artist, composer, or writer.)

Haydn was born in Rohrau, Austria, about 30 miles from the Hungarian border. Some of his compositions were influenced by the Hungarian peasant and Gypsy folk music he heard as a boy.

Hungarians are proud of their country's connection to Haydn. But they idolize three homegrown composers: Franz Liszt (1811–86), Béla Bartók (1881–1945), and Zoltán Kodály (1882–1967). To Hungarians, Liszt is known as Ferenc (the Magyar version of his first name), not Franz. He was the most talented pianist of his era, and achieved a popularity throughout Europe akin to that of a modern rock star. (Women were known to faint from excitement during his concerts.) He elevated the rhapsody, a romantic and free-flowing musical style, to a serious art form. His Hungarian Rhapsodies, a collection of 20 works written over several years, incorporated melodies from his homeland. Other famous compositions by Liszt include the Sonata in B Minor, the *Faust* Symphony, and Transcendental Studies (Douze Études d'execution transcendante). Liszt founded Hungary's National Academy of Music, in Budapest. A statue of the composer stands outside the academy.

Bartók—who once taught at the National Academy—is widely regarded as one of the 20th century's finest composers. He was a devotee of Hungarian regional folk music and used the varying rhythms and melodies throughout his orchestral works. Bartók's compositions include piano works such as *Mikrokosmos,* the opera *Duke Bluebeard's Castle,* and the ballet *The Wooden Prince.*

Bartók left Hungary for the United States in 1940 and died in New York City five years later. In 1988, his remains were transported to Hungary, where he was buried in Budapest with state honors. Bartók's remains passed through three countries—Great Britain, France, and Germany—en route to Hungary. All three nations held concerts of his music in his memory.

Kodály was a renowned composer and innovative music educator. Like Bartók, he studied Hungarian folk music and melded that music into his compositions. He specialized in the suite, a form made up of a succession of short musical pieces. His best-known works include *Psalmus Hungaricus* and *Hary János.* The Kodály Institute, one of nation's top music schools, is located in the central Hungarian city of Kecskemét.

Composer Zoltán Kodály was heavily influenced by Hungarian folk music.
(Library of Congress)

Béla Bartók, pictured here in 1941, was one of the finest composers of the 20th century. (Library of Congress)

Hungarians love classical music. Among the nation's classical ensembles, the Budapest String Quartet has enjoyed an international reputation for excellence for more than 50 years. The city of Budapest, the national cultural capital, holds a spring music festival every year.

The festival features concerts, operas, music-theater productions, and open air performances.

Festivals aside, some ensembles have run into money troubles in the wake of drastically reduced government subsidies for the arts. The Hungarian Symphony Orchestra in 1993 found an unusual way to ease its money woes. It formed a special partnership with one of the foreign companies in Hungary, International Business Machines (IBM) of the United States. IBM sponsored some of the symphony's concerts in return for the right to advertise by placing the IBM emblem on the concert programs and tickets.

Looting as an Art Form

Hungarian art dealers, both public and private, for centuries were ardent collectors of works from all over Europe. The Hungarian National Museum contains the largest collection of Spanish art, including masterpieces by Goya and El Greco, outside of Spain itself. But how secure are these works? The theft of art, antiquities, rare books, and religious objects is a growing problem in Hungary and the rest of Eastern Europe.

The problem was illustrated in December 1993, when thieves broke into the Budapest Jewish Museum and took 200 religious artifacts. The value of the stolen objects, some dating back to the 17th century, was estimated to be in the millions of dollars. Police said they had few clues in the case, but they believed the crime was committed by a professional gang.

Under communism, when the crime rate was low, most of Hungary's museums, ancient churches, and historical sites lacked sophisticated security. Now, thievery is much more common, but security has continued to lag behind the sophisticated safeguards afforded valuable art works in the West. Art thieves today can easily cross borders that were once closed by communism. And they have found that they can sell their stolen goods to dishonest art dealers and private collectors in Western Europe and the United States.

Constance Lowenthal, the executive director of the International Foundation for Art Research, in New York City, regretted the impact of art theft on Hungary and the rest of Eastern Europe: "These countries are hemorrhaging their heritage. The hard currency, and a ready and unscrupulous market in the West, makes for a recipe for cultural disaster." Lowenthal said that Eastern Europe was further disadvantaged because art collections in the region were poorly cataloged, making it difficult to trace them when they were stolen.

The break-in at the Jewish Museum was the largest single theft of its kind thus far in Eastern Europe. But art theft on a large scale is not new to the continent. During World War II, the Germans looted museums and private collections in every country they conquered. As Soviet forces were throwing back the Germans, they too pillaged European art. When the war ended, more than 2 million works of art and rare objects had vanished from Europe.

The Hungarian crown jewels—including the precious Crown of St. Stephen—vanished at the close of World War II. It turned out that the Nazis had removed them from Hungary to keep them from falling into the hands of the advancing Russian army. Then the jewels disappeared from Germany. Decades later, they turned up in a private art collection in America. U.S. president Jimmy Carter returned them to Hungary in 1978.

One of the great mysteries in Hungarian art history was the disappearance at the close of the war of 130 paintings in the private collections of two wealthy Hungarian families, the Herzogs and Hatvanys. The paintings are probably worth tens of millions of dollars at today's art prices because they were the works of such masters as Spain's El Greco and France's Edouard Manet and Pierre-Auguste Renoir.

The answer to the mystery came in January 1994, when Russian officials revealed that the 130 missing works were at an art-restoration center in Moscow. The Russians did not disclose how the paintings had gotten into their possession. Nor did they promise to return the works to their rightful owners.

Lights, Camera, Action

Hungary's tiny, but persistent, film industry took another small step in March 1995. That is when a new movie, A *Light-Sensitive Story*, debuted at the New Directors/New Films forum at the Museum of Modern Art in New York City.

A *Light-Sensitive Story* is the first post-Communist Hungarian film to get significant attention outside of Hungary. The film, directed by Pál Erdoss, concerns a young photographer (played by actress Erika Ozsda) who is struggling to make a living in 1994 Budapest. One scene depicts a newspaper editor rejecting her shots of people lined up outside an unemployment office. In a sly comment on the new capitalism, he tells her he will buy only photographs of frivolous subjects.

Hungarian movies usually get only limited distribution in Europe, and rarely make it to the United States. Unlike some other countries in Eastern Europe—most notably Poland and Russia—Hungarians never made many films. The Communists did not put much money into the industry. Today, with government subsidies lacking, Hungarian filmmakers have to scramble for private funding. Because motion-picture costs are high—and the Hungarian audience is small—films must have international distribution in order to make a profit.

Few Hungarian-language films have captured international attention. *The Revolt of Job* (1984), codirected by Imre Gyongyossy and Barna Kabay, is set in 1943 and concerns an elderly Jewish couple who take in an orphaned Christian child. *Naplo* (1983) and *Diary for My Children* (1984) are both anti-Stalinist—and subtly anti-Soviet—films by director Marta Meszaros. *Naplo* won the third-place award at the 1984 Cannes Film Festival in France.

Hungary's most acclaimed director is István Szábo. His earliest films were in his native language and won him a following in Hungary. They include *Father* (1966) and *25, Firemen's Street* (1973). But Szábo had to go outside of Hungary to get the financing and artistic freedom that brought him worldwide fame.

Szábo's *Mephisto* (1981), *Colonel Redl* (1985), and *Hanussen* (1989) are historical dramas largely financed by German investors and made in the German language. All three movies star Austrian actor Klaus Maria Brandauer. *Mephisto*, about a fictional German actor who boosts his career by collaborating with the Nazis, won the 1981 Academy Award for best foreign-language film. In spite of the German and Austrian participation, *Mephisto* was a Hungarian production, and the Oscar was Hungary's first.

Several Hungarians gained movie fame in the United States and Great Britain. They include actress Vilma Banky (real name Vilma

Lonchit), a Hollywood silent-film star in the 1920s; actor Béla Lugosi, the screen's most famous Dracula; the Gabor sisters (entertainers Zsa Zsa, Eva, and Magda); and 1950s Hollywood director Laslo Benedek. Sir Alexander Korda (born Sándor László Korda), a producer-director of popular movies in the 1930s and 1940s, was the first filmmaker ever to receive a British knighthood, in 1942. The highest-paid screenwriter in America in the 1990s was Hungarian-born Joe Eszterhas (*Flashdance, Basic Instinct, Showgirls*).

What kind of movies do Hungarians love? Big-budget Hollywood comedies and action films are favorites. American author Benjamin R. Barber, a critic of globalization, laments in his book *Jihad vs. McWorld:*

> The Hungarian film industry, traditionally Eastern Europe's most fecund market and still active in the financially pinched post-Communist era, has discovered that Hungarian audiences will not support local filmmakers. Dozens of domestic films are made but only a handful are shown in a few small "art" houses in Budapest; the main screens in the large houses are entirely devoted to American product; hence, in Hungary the top eight grossing films of 1991 (as in the proceeding several years) were all American.

Barber notes that Hungarians in 1991 filled movie theaters to watch *Look Who's Talking 2, Terminator 2, Kindergarten Cop, Hot Shots!, Naked Gun 2 ½, Dances with Wolves, Home Alone,* and *Oscar.* All of the films were made in the United States.

Hungarians continue to enjoy American films, but the Hungarian film industry is far from dead. Hungarian studios released a total of 44 new films—most of them low budget—in 2002.

"Reality" Comes to Hungarian TV

Hungarian television broadcasting marked a milestone of sorts in September 2002, when two "reality" programs debuted in prime time, the first such shows ever produced in Hungary. The program *Big Brother* was launched on September 1 on the TV2 channel. A rival show, *Valo Vilag* (Real world) aired on the RTL Klub channel eight days later.

TV2 is one of Hungary's two government-owned nationwide broadcast television channels. It is financed by revenue derived from commercial advertising. (The other government broadcast channel, TV1, is tax supported and specializes in news and public affairs programming.) RTL Klub, created in the mid-1990s, is a nationwide independent commercial channel. It is owned by RTL Group, a company based in Luxembourg.

Does *Big Brother* sound familiar? The show is a Hungarian version of the popular American "reality" program of the same name. TV2 went to the expense of purchasing European production rights to the U.S.-produced *Big Brother*, giving the channel a licensed use of the name for its homegrown Hungarian version.

Valo Vilag has a format similar to the Hungarian *Big Brother*. RTL Klub, it appears, simply borrowed the bickering-contestants-in-a-house premise and gave it a different name. According to the *Budapest Business Journal*:

> Although both stations are keen to emphasize fundamental differences between the shows, they share many characteristics. Contestants are isolated from the world in a luxury building, supervised by cameras 24 hours a day. Both teams—made up of fairly average Hungarians—must perform various tasks and sustain themselves without outside aid. One member is cast out every two weeks by a combination of votes from the other participants and from the audience at home. The last one left standing in each game receives a hefty cash prize.

There are 5 million television sets in Hungary (about one set for every two people). TV2 and RLT Klub are competing for the most coveted TV audience: viewers in the 18–49 age group. Hungarians between these ages have the most disposable income, or money to spend on nonessential products. They have the money for leisure clothes, music CDs, fast foods, soft drinks, entertainment magazines, movies, and a variety of recreation products. Advertisers in Hungary, as elsewhere, specifically target this group.

Hence, Hungary got two TV shows—both laden with slick commercials—created for a youthful audience. When it debuted on a Sunday evening, Hungary's *Big Brother* attracted a 53.4 percent nationwide share of viewers ages 18 to 49. *Valo Vilag*, a Monday night program, did not do as well; its opening show was watched by 23.2 percent of younger Hungarian TV watchers.

Some Hungarian observers attributed the initial success of *Big Brother* to its spicy content. (Viewers considered *Valo Vilag* tame in comparison.) In terms of nudity and blunt language, Hungarian primetime broadcast TV—like television in other parts of Europe—resembles U.S. cable TV.

The landscape of Hungarian broadcasting has changed enormously in the years following the end of communism. Under the Communists, all legal TV and radio stations in the country were under government control. That made it easy to censor or slant the news in favor of the government's agenda. As a result, Hungarians received only the news the Communists wanted them to receive. And, for the most part, the people viewed or heard only programs the authorities approved. (An exception was the anticommunist radio broadcasts beamed into Hungary by Radio Free Europe in the 1950s through the 1980s. Radio Free Europe was a U.S.-sponsored organization that broadcast to Eastern Europe from London.)

In 1989, with communism on the way out, parliament lifted virtually all government restrictions on media ownership. However, the law did not require the government to sell off (privatize) any of the state-owned radio or TV stations. With the Communists out of power, the Constitutional Court—Hungary's highest court—in 1992 overturned a Marxist-era law giving the government the power to supervise public (state-owned) broadcasting. But the court said that the Communist law should remain in effect until a parliament passed comprehensive rules on broadcasting ownership and the distribution of broadcast frequencies.

The Democratic Forum, the senior party in Hungary's first post-Communist government, firmly opposed foreign ownership of the nation's broadcasting media. As a result, Hungarians were free to buy or start TV and radio stations, but most lacked the money to produce sophisticated original programming. In the TV sphere, many stations relied on reruns of old American and Western European programs, dubbed in the Magyar language, to satisfy viewers hungry for entertainment. That explains why, in the early 1990s, the most popular TV program in Hungary was *Dallas*. Picture this: Every Friday night, millions of Hungarians gathered around their TV sets to watch reruns of a 1970s TV show from the United States about a conniving, filthy-rich Texas oil family. Who shot J.R.? Hungarians wanted to know.

In April 1994, with the ruling Democratic Forum in disfavor, parliament rewrote the broadcasting laws to allow foreign ownership. RTL Group, a Western European broadcasting conglomerate, quickly established the independent, nationwide RTL Klub channel in Hungary, creating heated competition with the government's own TV2 commercial channel. Other foreign investors rushed to invest in, or buy outright, Hungarian local TV and radio stations. In turn, the stations benefited from rising advertising revenues as foreign companies and foreign goods flooded the Hungarian market. Today, there are almost as many McDonald's commercials on Hungarian television—featuring Hungarian actors chomping happily on Big Macs—as there are on U.S. television.

These days, most of Hungary's TV shows are domestically produced. Western European and American programs and films account for the rest. Whereas earlier Hungarian programming emphasized the country's history and culture, more recent shows, like *Big Brother,* have a worldly, urban flavor.

Foreign television-production companies like to use Hungary for location shooting. The nation offers a wide variety of architecture (both ancient and modern) and terrain, so it can double for almost any country at almost any period of history. Another key factor, of course, is that labor and related production costs are cheaper in Hungary than in Western Europe. Such costs probably will rise when Hungary enters the European Union.

Today, almost all of Hungary's broadcasting media is in private hands. The government owns two TV channels and three radio stations. The networks are grouped into two quasi-independent public-broadcasting agencies, designated Magyar Television and Magyar Radio.

Public broadcasting in any country is vulnerable to partisan political influence unless carefully shielded. Over the years, the degree of such shielding in Hungary has been questionable. In 1993, the government forced the resignations of the chairmen of both Magyar Radio and Magyar Television and replaced them with men close to the ruling Democratic Forum. Over the next year, the Democratic Forum government fired more than 100 reporters from the public-broadcasting networks. The government claimed that the reporters were holdover

Communists who were biased against the government. The main opposition parties—the Free Democrats, Young Democrats, and Socialists (reformed Communists)—charged that the firings were part of a move by the Democratic Forum to use the broadcasting monopoly to keep its grip on political power. A large part of the Hungarian populace agreed with the opposition complaints; the 1993–94 firings spurred large protests in Budapest and other cities.

The dispute over public broadcasting was one of the reasons cited by political analysts for the defeat of the Democratic Forum in the national elections in the spring of 1994. But the issue of political bias in public broadcasting has not gone away. Following the defeat of the ruling Fidesz–Hungarian Civic Party in 2002, the defeated premier, Viktor Orbán, accused TV1 of slanting its coverage of his reelection campaign.

Murder, Mayhem, and the Press

In the summer of 2002, a 48-year-old taxicab driver was shot to death in the sleepy southwestern village of Totujfalu. The murder sparked a feeding frenzy among Hungary's tabloid newspapers. Why? Because the chief suspect was the victim's pretty, blond 14-year-old stepdaughter. She was reported to have told the press that her stepfather had been abusing her.

For two consecutive weeks, the tabloids ran front-page stories that detailed every lurid aspect of the case. The newspapers were filled with photos of the young suspect. She eagerly gave interviews, dazzled by all the attention. "According to the tabloids, said she 'felt like she was Britney Spears.'"

The tabloids appall serious journalists in Hungary, but the fact is, the tabloid press is the most profitable sector of the country's print media. Violent crime, celebrity news, gossip, sexy scandals, and sensationalism sell newspapers. With the end of communism, Hungary lifted all restrictions on foreign ownership of the print media. Western publishers rushed in to buy stakes in Hungary's newspapers and magazines. Australian-born media mogul Rupert Murdoch purchased 50 percent of two Hungarian tabloids, *Reform* and *Mai Nap*, in 1990, making him the first Westerner to have substantial ownership in newspapers in post-Marxist eastern Europe. Other major Western investors followed, including the late

British magnate Robert Maxwell, French publisher Robert Hersant, and the German publishing conglomerate Bertelsmann.

As of 1993, Western investors owned about 80 percent of the capital assets in the Hungarian print media. Foreigners own virtually all of the country's daily newspapers—Hungary had 40 dailies with a total circulation of nearly 2 million in the late 1990s—totally or in part. For example, three of the largest dailies, *Nepszabadsag* (People's freedom), the tabloid *Blikk*, and the sports-oriented paper *Nemzeti Sport*, are published by Swiss-owned Ringier Rt. *Nepszabadsag*, one of the most influential newspapers in Hungary today, used to be the official publication of the Socialist Workers' Party.

There is one big problem, however, for the print media: there are not enough readers in Hungary to support a growing newspaper market. And advertisers, a prime source of income for the papers, are choosing increasingly to sell their wares on television, where they can reach a larger audience:

> The circulations of dailies is heading downhill slowly but steadily, according to figures from Hungary's print media auditor, the Hungarian Distribution Monitoring Association (Matesz). With the exception of some tabloids and niche publications, the print run of Hungary's dailies drops a few percent each year.
>
> "In the case of dailies, the tendency is a declining one," [according to János Peto of the Association of Hungarian Newspaper Publishers.] "Look at *Nepszabadsag*'s circulation: from 300,000 five years ago, it went down by some 100,000."
>
> At the same time, the share of the print media is shrinking as the largest advertisers prefer to direct their spending towards television. While in 2001, daily newspapers accounted for 14% of total ad spending and magazines for 15%, in the first six months of 2002, these shares sunk to 13% and 12% respectively, according to the media research firm Mediagnozis.

Some major newspaper publishers, in order to save money by streamlining their operations, are buying stakes in independent printing companies. In September 2002, for example, Ringier Rt signed an agreement to take over part of Szikra Printing House Rt, Hungary's largest printer.

Polls in Hungary indicate that the people want factual, objective reporting in the press, which is hard to come by. Hungarian journalists tend to view issues in political terms, and they take sides openly. According to one Western reporter: "Most Hungarian journalists still have difficulty separating news from comment, and seem obliged to play a political role by supporting the group of their choice. A change of attitude inside the profession in order to meet Western criteria of objectivity and timeliness is likely to be slow and painful, since the Hungarian media in general are still staffed by journalists and reporters who for decades were accustomed to toe the line of one single party."

The debates over press objectivity and broadcast-media ownership may linger, but there is little doubt that Hungary's press and arts are more free than those of most other former Communist countries of Europe. Of the ex-Communist countries, only Poland and the Czech Republic rival Hungary for freedom of expression.

NOTES

p. 156 "'a form of commitment . . .'" *New York Times,* October 11, 2002, p. A8.

p. 160 "'I hope . . .'" *New York Times,* June 7, 1994, p. C15.

p. 162 "'Officially called . . .'" *New York Times,* October 27, 1994, p. C15.

p. 163 "'This [opening night] production . . .'" *New York Times,* October 27, 1994, p. C17.

p. 163 "'The Mozart Foundation . . .'" *New York Times,* October 13, 1994, p. C15.

pp. 167–168 "'These countries . . .'" *New York Times,* April 12, 1994, p. C15.

p. 170 "'The Hungarian film industry . . .'" Benjamin R. Barber, *Jihad vs. McWorld* (New York: Ballantine Books, 1995), p. 90.

p. 171 "'Although both . . .'" Ágnes Csonka, Budapest Business Journal, September 16, 2002. URL: www.bbj.hu. Downloaded October 2002.

p. 174 "'According to the tabloids . . .'" Tamás S. Kiss, "Girl, 14, Prime Suspect in Shooting," Budapest Sun Online, September 19, 2002. Availabe on-line. URL: www.budapestsun.com. Downloaded October 2002.

p. 175 "'The circulations . . .'" Csonka, September 16, 2002.

p. 176 "'Most Hungarian journalists . . .'" Edith Oltay, "Hungarian Radio and Television under Fire," RFE/RL Research Report, September 24, 1993, p. 53.

8

SNAPSHOTS:
PEOPLE AND PLACES

Return of a Favorite Son

In late September 1995, a 14-car motorcade stopped in a small, poor village in northeastern Hungary. A tall, well-dressed man got out of one of the vehicles and was nearly mobbed by crowds of cheering, grinning villagers. The visitor was George Pataki, the governor of New York State.

The village, Aranyosapati, is the home of Pataki's grandparents on his father's side. He came to Hungary in part to meet distant relatives he had never before met. The visit was sponsored by the Hungarian government and Hungarian companies in hopes of promoting business ties between the country and New York State.

Pataki is the most prominent politician of Hungarian descent in the United States. As such, his trip to his grandparents' homeland was front-page news in Hungary. Hungarian television news crews accompanied him wherever he went.

The people of Aranyosapati—several of whom introduced themselves as the governor's distant cousins—gave him a hero's welcome. Pataki could not resist sounding like a politician on the campaign trail. "It's just extremely moving to look around at the crowd, and see the faces, and know so many of you are relatives of mine," he told the villagers. "I can tell because the women are beautiful and the men are all handsome."

School Days

A turn-of-the-century brick building in Hungary's capital houses a daring experiment in education, the Budapest Alternative High School for Economics. Here, most of the teachers are in their 20s and 30s. Everyone, including the chief administrator (who has the title of "coordinator," not principal) wears jeans, T-shirts or work shirts, and athletic shoes. Classes are small, sometimes as few as nine students. And even though the school has plenty of desks, the teachers enjoy sitting with their students in intimate circles on the floor to create an informal atmosphere.

The Alternative High School has about 400 students. It opened in 1990 as an experiment in education reform. Even before the Communists came to power, Hungarian schools were both academically demanding and strictly regimented. The one major choice offered students was in language classes. (The national curriculum demanded fluency in at least one language other than Magyar. Most students opted to study German. Under communism, the curriculum required the study of Russian.) Even though the school receives a government subsidy, each student has to pay a tuition of $370 a year. In the 1990s that was slightly more than the average monthly earnings of a Hungarian worker.

The mission of the Budapest school is excellence without regimentation. Although economics is its main focus, the school gives its students broad leeway in elective courses and in how many classroom hours per week they wish to devote to each course. Foreign languages, especially English, are very popular. Orsolya Gosztony, a 26-year-old English teacher, told a visitor, "They realize they can't do anything without languages. No one in the world speaks Hungarian except Hungarians, and the students know it."

Even the economics classes are geared more to the practical—for example, how to run a business—than the theoretical. More students talk about becoming entrepreneurs than professors of economics. In the post-Communist atmosphere, they want to make Western-style big money. One 18-year-old, András Danko, said of his future plans, "I would like to work for an international company and then own my own company."

Hungary has a long history of excellence in education, particularly in the sciences. Today the nation claims a 99 percent literacy rate. Students are required to attend school until they are 16. Admission to the country's best schools is through competitive examinations. Hungarian youngsters are introduced to such subjects as chemistry, physics, geometry, and trigonometry in the elementary grades.

Products of the Hungarian education system have included Leo Szilard, the chief physicist on the Manhattan Project (the project that developed the U.S. atomic bomb), and Dennis Gabor, who won a 1971 Nobel Prize for pioneering laser holography. Hungarian-educated mathematician John von Neumann was one of the early pioneers in computer technology. Hungarian born and educated physicist Edward Teller is known as the "father" of the hydrogen bomb.

In the 1980s, an organization called the International Association for Educational Achievement tested more than 200,000 students at 7,581 schools in 24 countries. One of the findings: Hungarian 14-year-olds were ahead of every other nationality in scientific literacy. Japanese and Dutch students at that age level finished second and third, respectively. U.S. students finished 15th.

The high academic performance of Hungarian students comes with a drawback: parents and teachers put a lot of stress on the youngsters. One recent Hungarian émigré to the United States, a mother with adolescent children, surprised an acquaintance by disclosing that she was happy to have her children in an ordinary American public school. Why? Because, she explained, her youngsters are free from the academic pressure they had been under in Hungary.

The Road to Trouble

Beside a busy highway in western Hungary, near the industrial city of Győr, several young women stroll about in halters, miniskirts, or tight shorts. Once in a while a truck or car pulls over and a young woman gets in. She will be back in the same spot in 15 minutes or so, richer by a few more forints or German marks.

This is prostitution in post-Communist Hungary. With the economic dislocation and joblessness caused by the transition to a free market, more and more young women are being drawn into this dangerous profession. One young woman, an 18-year-old high school dropout who works the

Győr highway, revealed that she earned about $80 a day by selling herself. That is nearly the equivalent of an average Hungarian's weekly wage.

Hungary is a major transit point for trucking throughout central Europe. Although the incidence of HIV infection and AIDS is relatively low in Hungary, there is an increasing risk that infected foreign drivers will boost the spread of AIDS in Hungary through contact with Hungarian prostitutes.

The 18-year-old prostitute, named Tunde, shrugged off the danger. "There's no AIDS in Hungary," she insisted. "AIDS is only outside Hungary." Not true. According to the government, as of fall of 1993, there were 350 reported cases of HIV infection and 131 cases of patients diagnosed with AIDS. At the close of 1999, there were 2,500 Hungarians living with HIV/AIDS. A total of 100 Hungarians died of the disease that year.

Prostitution was banned by the Communists, but now it is legal. However, there are laws against profiting from prostitution, so it is illegal to be a panderer in Hungary. However, Hungarian newspapers have reported incidents of young Hungarian women being lured into prostitution in Western Europe by firms promising them high-paying regular jobs in that part of the continent.

Hungary is a major transit point for illegal drugs entering Europe from Asia and Africa. In 1994, Hungarian customs agents seized almost 1,600 pounds of heroin. Most of it had been shipped from Turkey, destined for Western Europe.

Hungarian officials are concerned about other kinds of smuggling, too. First, there is a growing traffic in central Europe of uranium and other nuclear materials from the former Soviet states. In April 1995, Slovak agents found 37.4 pounds of uranium in a car bound for Hungary. The car carried Hungarian license plates, and three Hungarians were among nine Eastern Europeans subsequently arrested by the Slovaks.

Human smuggling is also a problem. An undetermined number of cars and trucks traveling through Hungary carry hidden cargoes of illegal immigrants trying to get to Western Europe. Many are from Turkey, the Middle East, Africa, and Asia. Hungary's border guards arrested close to 15,000 illegal immigrants in 1994. The guards' spokesman, Colonel Attila Krisan, told a Western reporter, "It's like drugs—there are routes."

In 2000, Hungarian officials estimated that 9,000 to 10,000 illegal immigrants attempted to pass through the country every year. The officials claimed that about 70 percent of the undocumented aliens were caught each year.

Just as in other parts of post-Communist Europe, organized crime appears to be growing in Hungary. According to one unconfirmed figure, at least 20,000 cars were stolen in Hungary every year in the early 1990s, most by organized car-theft rings. Most of the vehicles are shipped to other parts of Europe. Car thefts began to drop in the late 1990s thanks to better policing. (Hungarians love automobiles. They bought 88,000 cars in 1994. Germany sells more BMWs in Hungary than in any other country in Europe, excluding itself.)

Hungarians tend to believe either the Romany, or Gypsies, or the "Russian Mafia" are behind organized crime in Hungary. However, that accusation may have as much to do with anti-Gypsy and anti-Russian prejudices in Hungary than with the actual involvement of those ethnic groups in criminal activities.

The Funeral Cortege

A horse-drawn carriage winds its way along a 138-mile route between the Austrian border and the Hungarian town of Esztergom, the traditional seat of the country's Roman Catholic Church. The carriage carries a coffin with the remains of József Cardinal Mindszenty, once the Catholic primate of Hungary. As many as 50,000 Hungarians walk in somber silence behind the carriage in a line that stretches for miles. It is May 1991, and the cardinal has come home.

Mindszenty was jailed for opposing the Communists. He was released by the freedom fighters during the 1956 uprising. Then he was forced to take refuge in the U.S. embassy in Budapest when the revolt was crushed. He stayed at the embassy for 15 years, until the Communists allowed him to leave without the threat of arrest. He died in Austria in 1975. His last wish was to be reburied in Hungary when the nation was no longer Communist.

József Antall, Hungary's first post-Communist premier, spoke at Mindszenty's burial in the basilica in Esztergom, praising the cardinal for his bravery and staunch faith.

Hungary has freedom of religion, but unlike the United States it does not have a concept of separation of church and state. The government grants small subsidies to officially registered religions. Seven million Hungarians, or about 67 percent of the population, are Roman Catholics. The Reformed (Calvinist) Church claims 2 million members, or 20 percent of the nation. Lutherans make up 4 percent of the country, or about 430,000 people. The center of Protestantism in Hungary is the city of Debrecen, once called the "Calvinist Rome" for its citizens' staunch resistance to Catholicism.

Some Hungarians object to the government giving subsidies to controversial religious groups, such as the Church of Scientology and the Unification Church. Whatever the outcome of the debate, there is no doubt that Hungary has a colorful variety of religions, sects, and cults. As one observer noted:

> [Since 1989,] the number of officially registered small denominations has grown from twenty-nine to forty-seven. Among the religious groups now registered as churches is, for example, the Federation of Hungarian Witches. It is estimated that at least thirty more sects or cults exist that are not officially registered; these include such obscure sects as the Satanists. . . . The number of believers belonging to small churches or denominations, including sects, is estimated to be 120,000.

Nightlife in Budapest

Budapest had a very lively nightlife even when the Communists were in power. The city still has no rival in central Europe when it comes to late-night partying.

Kozgaz Pinceklub, an underground disco, is a favorite hangout of college students. Sophisticated singles like to dance and flirt at the Bahnhof Music Club. Those seeking "adults-only" entertainment gravitate to the E-Klub. There is a nightspot for nearly every musical taste, be it jazz (Fat Mo's Music Club), salsa (Trocadero), hip-hop (Club 11), or techno/house (Club Colosseum).

Casino gambling is legal in Budapest. The city has more than a dozen casinos, most of them requiring formal evening dress. Two of the capital's best hotels, the Budapest Hilton and the Hyatt Regency, have casinos on their premises.

Hungary's Horsemen

In the eastern part of Hungary is the endless grassland known as the Great Plain. Here is where you find the Hungarian equivalent of the American cowboy. They are the most direct descendants of the old Magyar warriors who terrorized Europe in the ninth and early 10th centuries.

Today's Hungarian horsemen are peaceful folk, but—like their ancestors—they adore their steeds. A favorite herding trick is for one of them to stand on the back of a horse and gather the reins of several other horses and ride without falling.

The horseshoe is a good luck charm in Hungary (as in other parts of the world), but particularly so in the Great Plain region. North of the Great Plain, in the Danube Bend region, the town of Visegrad holds a Palace Festival every year that features horse tournaments and historical plays performed on horseback.

It's in the Blood

It is easy to forget that Dracula, the bloodthirsty vampire of popular myth and entertainment, is not Hungarian in origin, but Romanian. It is true that the vampire's legendary hunting ground was Transylvania, once part of Hungary. It is also true that filmdom's most famous Dracula was a Hungarian actor, Béla Lugosi. But the historical model for Dracula was Vlad Tepes, a brutal 15th-century Romanian prince.

Hungary, however, does have its own legendary vampire-like figure in Countess Elizabeth Báthory (1560–1614). It is said that the beautiful aristocrat kept herself youthful by bathing regularly in blood drained from the bodies of hundreds of young peasant girls murdered by her henchmen. Báthory died at the age of 54 (an advanced age by 17th-century standards), and witnesses claim that she retained an eerie loveliness up until the time of her death.

Death in Hungary

Why is the death rate in Hungary so high? Hungarian women live, on average, 76.5 years. Hungarian men live an average 67.5 years. Those are some of the lowest such figures in Europe. Hungary's mortality rate, 13.09 per 1,000 people, is one of the highest among developed countries.

Experts attribute the high death rate and relatively short life spans to several factors, including deteriorating living conditions, stress, high alcohol consumption, heavy smoking, and pollution.

Hungary also has a stunning suicide rate: 26.2 per 10,000. That is the highest rate in the world. No one has yet come up with an explanation of why so many Hungarians choose to kill themselves.

Customs, Traditions, and Diversions

Hungary is a tiny nation, but it is also a fascinating mosaic of places, customs, and pastimes. Here are a few that make this country unique.

Budapest has thousands of cafés and coffee shops. In these establishments, city residents have a long tradition of passing the hours gossiping, arguing over politics, or playing chess while sipping coffee. However, young people are increasingly gravitating to the many U.S. fast-food restaurants in the capital. Unlike the cafés and coffee shops, a McDonald's, Pizza Hut, or Burger King has no waiters. Therefore, teenagers can hang out for hours in those establishments without being pestered to either order something or leave.

At Easter time, tradition-minded Hungarian women undertake the painstaking decoration of eggs. The painted eggs are usually exchanged between family members. In rural areas, if an unmarried young woman gives such an egg to an unmarried young man, then they are betrothed. Similarly, if an unattached young man sprays perfume on an unattached young women, they are as good as engaged.

If invited to a Hungarian house for dinner, tradition dictates that the guest bring gifts to the host and hostess. What kind of gifts? A bottle of wine for the host, and flowers for the hostess. To appear at their doorstep without gifts is considered an insult.

A Hungarian girl, dressed in traditional folk garb, paints Easter eggs. (Courtesy Free Library of Philadelphia)

Western Hungary, the Transdanubia region, features the Busojaras mask festival every year. It is a medieval tradition in which craftspeople compete to make the most frightening mask to scare away evil spirits. The festival attracts many tourists. Transdanubia also features Siklos Castle, one of Hungary's favorite destinations. The castle was built in the 13th century and is one of the best-preserved ancient structures in the country.

Traditional folk costumes like these are handed down from mother to daughter for many generations. (Courtesy Free Library of Philadelphia)

Thousands of people from all over the country travel to the Lake Balaton region to bathe in the spring waters of Heviz Lake, Europe's largest hot-water lake. The waters have legendary medicinal powers. Hungarians say their healing properties derive from the mildly radioactive mud at the bottom of the lake.

Eger, in northeastern Hungary, is the source of a deep red wine called Bull's Blood, and the site of a castle in which 2,000 Magyars are said to have held off 100,000 attacking Turks in the year 1552. Legend has it that the defenders (led by folk hero István Dobo) sustained themselves by drinking a then-unnamed wine, which stained their beards. The Turks were so impressed by the Magyars' toughness, that they believed the defenders were drinking the blood of bulls. Hungary's other most famous wine is Tokaj (Americans call it Tokay), a sweet beverage from the town of Tokaj.

NOTES

p. 177 "'It's just . . .'" *New York Times*, September 25, 1995, p. B1.

p. 178 "'They realize . . .'" *New York Times*, May 25, 1994, p. B9.

p. 178 "'I would like . . .'" *New York Times*, May 25, 1994, p. B9.

p. 180 "'There's no AIDS . . .'" *New York Times*, September 14, 1993, p. A4.

p. 180 "'It's like drugs . . .'" *New York Times*, June 14, 1995, p. A12.

p. 182 "'[Since 1989,] the number . . .'" Edith Oltay, "Religious Sects at the Center of Controversy in Hungary," *RFE/RL Research Report*, July 16, 1993, p. 37.

CONCLUSION:
INTO THE FUTURE

In the mid-1990s, a cynic could be forgiven for doubting the probable success of the efforts of the newly liberated countries to throw off the legacy of communism. One such doubter, author Benjamin R. Barber, wrote in his 1995 book *Jihad vs. McWorld*:

> Lithuania, Belarus, the Ukraine, Poland, Hungary, Serbia, Croatia, Bulgaria, and Mongolia are among the countries where frustrated citizens in the second wave of free elections elected "new" governments composed of old Communists wedded to nationalist and ethnic doctrines of one kind or another. Where even they are too moderate, radical right nationalists and anti-Semites—like István Csurka in Hungary and those in the Romanian parliament who recently voted to honor Romania's wartime fascist leader Ion Antonescu—stalk both the moderates and their parliamentary system as Hitler once stalked Weimar. They wait for popular impatience to overcome frail and unrooted political institutions, often because there is no civil society to root and secure them.

Barber uses the word *jihad* to describe a retreat by frustrated people into religious fundamentalism or extreme nationalism. In his book he goes on to say:

> There is no country in Eastern and Central Europe or the republics of the old Soviet Union that has proved immune to Jihad's contagion,

and that has not suffered politically and economically for it. Spawned by fear and insecurity and driven by the failure of clumsy and foolhardy attempts to impose Western economic and political institutions wholesale on societies wholly unprepared to accommodate them, a variety of small but toxic Jihads have flourished, leaving the region with no really convincing success stories.

Perhaps Hungary could not be viewed as a "success story" in 1995. But the architects of the democratic and economic reforms adopted by the country from 1989 through the early 1990s never expected everything to be rosy by the middle of the decade. And, by the way, Hungarians did not have "Western economic and political institutions" imposed on them; they chose the institutions and continue to do so.

Hungary's "old Communists" have been in the forefront of free-market restructuring. In fact, it was they, not the conservatives, who accelerated privatization by eliminating the last barriers to foreign participation in the economy.

Hungary gave right-wing nationalists like Csurka a democratic safety valve. Any adult Hungarian can vote for candidates of Csurka's Justice and Life Party (and a minority of Hungarians do support the party). If nationalism is rising in popularity, it was not reflected at the polls in 2002; no Justice and Life candidate got past even the first round of the national elections.

Economic restructuring did cause much discomfort—persistent inflation, slow economic growth, and high unemployment—in Hungary during the 1990s. But, as of 2002, things look much better. Inflation and unemployment are relatively low. The economy is growing steadily. Hungary's currency is now fully convertible.

Hungary is a member of the North Atlantic Treaty Organization and is poised to join the European Union. It has taken steps to repair relations with neighboring countries. It has democratically elected four post-Communist governments. It has welcomed with open arms foreign participation in its economy. In short, the country is now a full-fledged, functioning member of the capitalist, democratic community of nations. Hungary has been globalized.

Yes, there are ongoing problems. Hungarian governments continue deficit spending. The country's foreign debt is huge. Some Hungarians are uncomfortable with having so much of the economy and media in foreign hands. And not all Hungarians have enjoyed the benefits of the free market.

Regardless of the ultimate destination, Hungary's path into the future is as unique as the Magyar people themselves. There will be no turning back.

NOTES

p. 189 "'Lithuania, Belarus, . . .'" Benjamin R. Barber, *Jihad vs. McWorld* (New York: Ballantine Books, 1995), p. 197.

pp. 189–190 "'There is no country . . .'" Barber, p. 198.

CHRONOLOGY

The Magyars

895–896
Magyars under chieftain Árpád invade Carpathian Basin, subjugate Slavs

896–955
Magyars conduct raids throughout Europe

955
Germans defeat Magyars at Battle of Augsburg

1000
Magyar ruler Stephen crowned Christian king and holy apostle

1038
Stephen dies, elevated to Roman Catholic sainthood

1222
Vatican mediation ends absolute rule of Magyar kings over Magyar nobles

1241
Mongols invade, slay half of Hungary's population

1301
Last king descended from Árpád dies. Reign of non-Magyars begins in Hungary

1377
Turkish invaders turned back at Battle of Belgrade

1458–1490
Reign of King Matthias Corvinus. Hungary is richest kingdom in central Europe

1514
Peasant revolt put down with large loss of life

Hapsburg Rule

1526
Turks destroy Hungarian army at Battle of Mohács. Most of Hungary occupied for 150 years. Free portion, "Royal Hungary," dominated by Austria's Hapsburg dynasty

1697
Austria defeats Turks

1740
Empress Maria Theresa of Austria assumes Hungarian crown

1843
Hungarians force Magyar culture on non-Magyars living in lands ruled by Hungary

1847
Austria grants Hungary limited autonomy

1848
Francis Joseph becomes Austria's emperor

1848–1849
Hungary revolts against Austria. Francis Joseph gets Russian help to crush rebellion

1849–1867

Period of Hapsburg absolute rule in Hungary

The Dual Monarchy

1867

Austro-Hungarian Empire formed. Emperor Francis Joseph, an Austrian, is also crowned king of Hungary

1914

Austrian archduke Francis Ferdinand assassinated, triggering World War I

1914–1918

Austria-Hungary and chief ally, Germany, defeated. Empire breaks up. Hungary proclaims itself a republic

Before Communism

1919–1920

Marxist Béla Kun proclaims short-lived Hungarian Communist state. Bloody right-wing counterrevolution follows. Period of Horthy regency begins

1920

June 24: Treaty of Trianon forces Hungary to give up 87,748 square miles of territory and 13.2 million subjects. More than 3 million Magyars in lost lands come under Slavic or Romanian rule

1930–1935

Hungary draws closer to Nazi Germany and Fascist Italy

1938

November 2: Germany and Italy "award" Hungary a small portion of its lost lands

1939
World War II begins

1940–1943
Hungary formally joins Germany and other Axis powers. Hungary regains more lost territories, but its forces are routed on Russian front

1944
German troops aid fascist takeover of Hungarian government. Hundreds of thousands of Hungarian Jews deported to Nazi death camps

1945
February 13: Soviet Red Army captures Budapest, nearly destroying city
November 7: Free elections held. Communists finish second to Independent Smallholders

1946–1948
Communists under Stalinist Mátyás Rákosi infiltrate government agencies, the military, opposition political parties, and labor unions

1949
"People's Republic of Hungary" proclaimed after the Communists merge with the ruling Social Democrats. No effective political opposition remains in country

Under Communism
1949–1956
Rakosi turns Hungary into a police state. Attempts at rapid industrialization fail. Hungary joins Soviet-led Warsaw Pact military alliance

1956

October 23–November 4: Anti-Soviet protests in Budapest turn into bloody, full-scale uprising. Premier Imre Nagy attempts to break country from Soviet hold. Red Army smashes revolt. Tens of thousands flee Hungary

1958

Nagy and key aides executed for treason

1968–1988

Communist leader János Kádár institutes New Economic Mechanism. Censorship and travel restrictions eased. Hungary becomes the most liberal nation in Soviet bloc

1988

May 22: Kádár ousted by reformed Communists. Károly Grösz assumes party leadership

August: Relations with Romania sour over persecution of rural Magyars

Transitions

1989

March: Soviet leader Mikhail S. Gorbachev vows noninterference in Hungarian political and economic reforms

May: Hungary opens its border with Austria

June 16: Nagy and other executed heroes of the '56 uprising are reburied with honors

July 6: Former Communist leader Kádár dies

July 11: U.S. president George H. W. Bush visits Hungary

September–October: Hungary allows thousands of East German tourists to receive political asylum in West Germany

October 7: Hungarian Communists renounce Marxism-Leninism and adopt democratic socialism

October 18: National constitution amended to allow multiparty elections. Communist political monopoly ended

October 23: Free republic proclaimed

1990

January: Budapest Stock Exchange begins trading. Government begins lifting state subsidies in many sectors of the economy

March 19–20: Anti-Magyar riots in Transylvania further strain Hungarian-Romanian relations

March–April: First truly free national elections held since 1945. Center-right coalition takes power. József Antall becomes first post-Communist premier

June: First state-owned company, IBUSZ, privatized

October 26–28: Gasoline price hike sparks major protests in Budapest

November 19: Conventional Forces in Europe (CFE) treaty signed, formally ending cold war

1991

February 15: "Visegrad" partnership formed with Poland and Czechoslovakia

February 21: International Monetary Fund aid pact signed

April 24: National Assembly passes property-compensation law

June 19: Last Soviet troops leave Hungary

June 28: Soviet-led trading organization Comecon folds

July 1: Warsaw Pact military alliance collapses

October: Hungary joins Council of Europe. Premier Antall visits United States. Hungary and Yugoslavia at odds over military aircraft incursions

December 1: Banking system reformed

December 6: Russian friendship treaty signed

December 16: European Community association agreement signed

1992

October: Government begins to pull back on privatizing state industries

November 11: Russian president Boris Yeltsin visits and honors Nagy

1993

December 12: Premier Antall dies. Péter Boross heads government

1994

January: Western military alliance NATO rejects membership. "Partnership for Peace" joined instead
May: Socialists (reformed Communists) win in national elections, form coalition government with Free Democrats. Socialist Gyula Horn becomes premier
December: Hungary hosts CSCE human rights/security summit

1995

January–February: Socialists and Free Democrats clash over privatization, threatening political coalition

1996

January: U.S. troops begin using Hungary as key staging area en route to peace-enforcement duties in Bosnia
March: Government launches strict austerity program. Banking, other economic sectors, opened to foreign ownership
March 29: Hungary joins Organization for Economic Cooperation and Development
May 15: Hungary and Slovakia sign friendship treaty
July 4–5: Eastern Europe Magyars hold Budapest summit, support "autonomy" for those outside Hungary
September 16: Hungary and Romania sign friendship treaty
October 15: Parliament votes to compensate Hungarian Jews for World War II property

1997

May 26: Hungarian president Árpád Göncz pays historic visit to Romania
July 8: Hungary invited to join the North Atlantic Treaty Organization
September 25: World Court rules on Hungary-Slovakia dam dispute
November 16: National referendum backs NATO membership
December 13: European Union formally invites Hungary to begin membership talks

1998

May: Fidesz–Hungarian Civic Party wins in national elections and forms coalition with the Smallholders and the Democratic Forum. Viktor Orbán becomes premier

1999

March 12: Hungary joins NATO

April 27: Hungary agrees to base NATO aircraft in Yugoslavia bombing campaign

June: Hungarians join NATO peacekeepers in Kosovo

2000

February: Romanian cyanide spill contaminates Hungary's Tisza River

June 6: Ferenc Madl succeeds Árpád Göncz as Hungarian president

2001

June 16: Forint becomes fully convertible. National Bank adopts inflation-targeting policy

June 19: Parliament passes law granting benefits to Magyars in neighboring countries

2002

April: Socialists win in national elections and form coalition with Free Democrats. Péter Medgyessy becomes premier

June 19: Medgyessy admits role as Communist-era counterintelligence officer

October 10: Novelist Imre Kertesz awarded Nobel Prize in literature

December 12: EU sets May 1, 2004, target date for Hungary membership

2003

January 30: Hungary sides with United States in dispute over Iraq disarmament

March 20: Medgyessy bars Hungarian combat role in Iraq war

April 13: Hungarian voters approve of EU membership in a referendum

FURTHER READING

BOOKS

Barber, Benjamin R., *Jihad vs. McWorld*. New York: Ballantine Books, 1995.

Blitzer, Charles, *The Age of Kings*. New York: Time, 1967.

Carter, Rowlinson, *Insight Guides: Eastern Europe*. Singapore: APA Publications, 1993.

CIS and Eastern Europe On File. New York: Facts On File, 1993.

Corey, Melinda, and Ochoa, George, *Facts about the 20th Century*. New York: H. W. Wilson, 2001.

Croteau, Maureen, and Worchester, Wayne, eds., *The Essential Researcher*. New York, HarperPerennial, 1993.

Crystal, David, ed., *The Cambridge Factfinder*. Cambridge, U.K.: Cambridge University Press, 1993.

Dumbaugh, Kerry, and Miko, Frances T., *Gorbachev's Reform Strategy: Comparisons with the Hungarian and Chinese Experience*. Washington, D.C.: Congressional Research Service (Report No. 87–813F), 1987.

Elisseefe, Vadime; Naudou, Jean; Wiet, Gaston; and Wolff, Phillippe, *The Great Medieval Civilizations*. Vol. 3 of *The History of Mankind*. New York: Harper & Row, 1975.

Enzensberger, Hans Magnus, *Europe, Europe: Forays into a Continent*. New York: Pantheon Books, 1989.

Finch, David E., *The Business Handbook to Hungary*. Budapest: Budapest Week, 1993.

Fodor's Europe 58th Edition. Toronto: Fodor's Travel Publications, 2002.

Gadney, Reg, *Cry Hungary! Uprising 1956*. New York: Atheneum, 1986.

Grun, Bernard, *The Timetables of History*. New York: Simon & Schuster/Touchstone, 1991.

Hoensch, Joerg K., *A History of Modern Hungary, 1867–1986*. New York: Longman, 1988.

Hungary: Essential Facts, Figures & Pictures. Budapest: MTI Corporation, 1997.

The Hutchinson Guide to the World, New Edition. Phoenix: The Oryx Press, 1998.

Lands and Peoples Europe Index, Volume 4. Danbury, Conn.: Grolier, 2001.

Meras, Phyllis, *Eastern Europe: A Traveler's Guide*. Boston: Houghton Mifflin, 1991.
The World Almanac and Book of Facts, 1994. New York: World Almanac, 1993.
The World Reference Atlas. New York: Dorling Kindersley, 1994.

NEWSPAPERS, PERIODICALS, AND SPECIAL PUBLICATIONS
Facts On File World News Digest, selected issues, 1975–2002. Hazlett, Thomas W. "The Czech Miracle." *Reason*, April 1995.
Hungaria, Hungarian Tourist Board (tourism booklets), 1994–95.
Hungarian Commercial Counselor's Office business/investment guides and government economic reports, 1994–95.
"Hungary: It's Unique!" *Fortune* (special advertising supplement), October 18, 1993.
New York Times, selected editions, 1993–2003.
RFE/RL (Radio Free Europe/Radio Liberty) Report, selected issues, 1993–95.

INTERNET SOURCES
Allan, Fraser, "Hungary Marks September 11," Budapest Sun Online. Available on-line. URL: http://www.budapestsun.com. Posted September 19, 2002.
American Chamber of Commerce in Hungary, "Shooting in the Dark: National Bank Moves to Inflation-Targeting," *Business Hungary* (July 2001). Available on-line. URL: http://www.amcham.hu. Downloaded October 2, 2002.
Budapest Sun Online, "Csepel Group Sold." Available on-line. URL: http://www.budapestsun.com. Posted September 19, 2002.
Central Intelligence Agency, U.S. *The World Factbook 2002*. Available on-line. URL: http://www.cia.gov/cia/publications/factbook.index.html. Updated December 9, 2002.
Csonka, Ágnes, "National Dailies Wake to Benefits of Buying Own Press," Budapest Business Journal. Available on-line. URL: http://www.bbj.hu. Posted September 16, 2002.
———, "Sex, Timing Keep TV2 Ahead in 'Real Life' Race with RTL," Budapest Business Journal. Available on-line. URL: http://www.bbj.hu. Posted September 16, 2002.
Dibooglu, Selahattin, and Kutan, Ali M., "Sources of Inflation and Output Fluctuations in Poland and Hungary: Implications for Full Membership in the European Union," Southern Illinois University Online, Department of Economics. Available on-line. URL:http://www.siu.edu/econ/. Updated September 19, 2002.
Embassy of the United States of America in Budapest, Commercial Section, Access Hungary Commercial Guide. Available on-line. URL:http://www.access-hungary.hu. Downloaded October 5, 2002.

Hungarian Central Statistical Office, "Economic and Financial Data." Available on-line. URL: http://www.ksh.hu/pls/ksh/docs/index eng.html. Downloaded February 11, 2003.

Hungarian Government Portal, "Key Data." Available on-line. URL: http://www.ekormanyzat.hu/english/. Updated February 11, 2003.

Kiss, Tamás S., "Girl, 14, Prime Suspect in Shooting," Budapest Sun Online. Available on-line. URL: http://www.budapestsun.com. Posted September 19, 2002.

Kirsch, Adam, "Lost Time," Boston Phoenix Online. Available on-line. URL: http://www.bostonphoenix.com/arts/books. Posted November 30, 1998.

Martelle, Scott, "After Death, a Literary Rebirth," Los Angeles Times Online. Available on-line. URL: http://www.latimes.com. Posted January 15, 2002.

Organization for Economic Cooperation and Development, "OECD Economic and Social Data Rankings," European Institute of Japanese Studies. Available on-line. URL:http://www.hhs.se/personal/suzuki/default.htm. Updated January 1, 2003.

Talking Cities, "Budapest Nightlife Introduction." Available on-line. URL: http://www.talkingcities.co.uk/budapest pages/entertainment nightlife.htm. Downloaded April 5, 2003.

INDEX

Page numbers followed by *m* indicate maps, those followed by *i* indicate illustrations, and those followed by *c* indicate an item in the chronology.

A

Aare-Tessin AG für Elekrizität (Atel) 110
Academy Awards 169
Access Hungary Commercial Guide 118
advertising 167, 171, 175
Ady, Endre 20, 157
Afghanistan 150
agriculture *see* farming
AIDS *see* HIV/AIDS
alcohol and alcoholism 117, 150, 184, 187
Alitalia (airline) 120
Alliance of Free Democrats. *See* Free Democrats, Alliance of
Allied Control Commission 55
Allied powers. *See* World War I; World War II
American General Hospitality Corp. 125
Ameritech Corp. (telecommunications company) 118
András II (king of Hungary) 10
András III (king of Hungary) 11, 193c
Antall, József 88, 94, 104, 111, 141, 181, 198c
  in U.S. 138–139, 138i, 198c
anti-Semitism 33, 40, 42, 46i, 65, 88, 103, 104–105, 157, 189 *see also* Jews
Antonescu, Ion 189
Arabs 4
Arany, János 157
Aranyosapati (village) 177

armed forces *see also* Magyars; military reorganization
  under Austrian rule 16, 17–19, 20i
  under communism 65, 66, 71, 72i, 74, 146–148, 196c
  in current military 150–151, 152, 200c
  in World War I 21, 23–27, 24i, 195c
  in World War II 45, 47–49, 50–51, 196c
  between World Wars 29, 32–33, 35, 37, 38, 40, 43
Árpád (Magyar king) 4, 5, 9, 11, 193c
Arrow Cross Party/Hungarist Movement 43, 46, 49, 104
art 11, 155, 167–168
Art Research, International Foundation for 167
Attila (leader of the Huns) 7
Auchan (retailer) 118
Auden, W. H. 159
Audi (automaker) 118
Augsburg, Battle of (955) 8, 193c
Auschwitz (Nazi death camp) 156
Austria and Austrians vim, viii, 5, 6, 12, 27, 43, 66, 74, 77, 84, 163, 181. *See also* Austro-Hungarian Empire; Hapsburg dynasty
  border opening 84, 145i, 197c
  current Hungary relations 144
  Dual Monarchy 17–22, 26, 27–28, 195c
  as Germanic state 8
  Hungarian revolt 16, 16i, 194c

investments in Hungary 118, 121–122, 169
  trade data 134
  under Hapsburgs 12–17, 194c–195c
Austro-Hungarian Empire vim, 16i, 18i 156
  in World War I 21, 23–27, 24i, 195c
automobiles 77, 118, 120
  thefts 181
Avars 5
AVH (Allamvedelmi Hatosag; State Security Authority) 63, 68
AVO (Allamvedelmi Osztaly; State Security Department) 56, 63, 65, 72–73, 72i
Axis powers *see* World War II

B

Bach, Alexander 17
Bahnhof Music Club (Budapest nightspot) 182
Bakros, Lajos 125
Balaton, Lake vim, viii, 187
Balkan region 21
Balkan Wars (1912–13) 21
Bank of International Settlements (BIS) (of European Union) 134
banks and banking *see* economy; market economy, transition to
Banky, Vilma (Vilma Lonchit) 169
Barber, Benjamin R. 170, 189–190
Bárdossy, László 47–48, 58
barley viii
Bartha, Ferenc 124
Bartók, Béla 20, 164, 166i
Basic Instinct (film) 170
Báthory, Elizabeth 183

baths, social 13, 13*i*
Batthányi, Lajos 15, 16
bauxite ix, 135
Bavaria *see* Germany
Bekeshi, László 124
Béla IV (king of Hungary) 10
Belarus 189
Belgium 24
Belgrade, Battle of (1377) 11
Benedek, Laslo 170
Berinkey, Denes 29
Beszelo (journal) 159
Bethlen, István 37, 38–40, 41
Big Brother (TV show) 170–172
Black Sea 4
Blair, Tony 98
Blikk (newspaper) 175
Bod, Péter Akos 124
Bohemia *see* Czech Republic
Bolshevik Revolution (1917) 28
Book of Memories, A (Péter Nádás) 161
Boross, Péter 95, 198*c*
Borszormeny, Zoltán 42
Bosnia-Herzegovina 12, 21, 150, 199*c*
"Boy Changed into a Stag Cries Out at the Gate of Secrets" (Ferenc Juhasz) 159
Brandauer, Klaus Maria 169
Brezhnev, Leonid 83
Brezhnev doctrine 82
Buchenwald (Nazi death camp) 156
Buda (town) *see* Budapest
Buda Castle (Budapest) 50, 51
Budapest (city) v*im*, viii, x, x–xii, 20, 26, 27, 46*i*, 65, 104, 129, 158*i*, 167, 177
  1956 uprising 69, 70*i*,71–74, 72*i*, 197*c*
  cafes, restaurants and nightspots 101, 117, 182–183, 184
  September 11, 2001 anniversary vii
Budapest Hilton (hotel) 183
Budapest Jewish Museum 167
Budapest String Quartet 166
Bulgaria and Bulgarian peoples x, 10, 21, 45, 80, 137, 189
  military issues 147
Burger King (fast-food chain) 118, 184
Bush, George H. W. 84, 95, 133, 138*i*, 197*c*
Bush, George W. 150, 151

C

cafes and restaurants 101, 117, 184
Calvinist (Reformed) Church x, 182
Canada xii, 45, 151
Carousel (musical) 161
Carpathian Basin 3–5, 6, 8, 10
Carpathian Mountains 3–5, 24
Carter, Jimmy (James Earl) 168
Carter, Rowlinson 7, 10
Caspian Sea 4–5
Ceauşescu, Nicolae 80
Celts 5
Central Powers. *See* World War I
Charlemagne (Emperor of the West) 7–8
Charles I. *See* Charles IV
Charles IV (king of Hungary)
  abdication 27
  as emperor of Austria 25
  monarchy debate 35
  return and exile 38
  in World War I 25
chemicals 135
China and Chinese people vii, 45, 76, 151
Christianity 6, 7–9, 10, 38, 42, 103
Christian Democratic Party
  in 1990 elections 88, 198*c*
  in 1994 elections 96
  in 2002 elections 100
  profile of 103
Christian Social Party. *See* Unity Party
Ciano, Galeazzo 44
cities and towns v*im*, x, 19
  largest in Hungary xii
Chain Bridge (Budapest) 27
Chikan, Attila 98
Chirac, Jacques 152
Cleveland Symphony Orchestra 163
climate and weather viii,
Clinton, Bill (William Jefferson) 98, 132, 139, 142, 149
clothing 4, 17, 20*i*, 77, 122, 171, 183, 185*i*, 186*i*
Club 11 (Budapest nightspot) 182
Club Colosseum (Budapest nightspot) 182
coal ix, 135

Coca-Cola Co, (beverage company) 118
cold war (1945–90) viii
Colonel Redl (film) 169
communism. *See* specific organizations (e.g., Socialist Workers' Party)
Communist Information Bureau (Cominform) 59
Communist Party, Hungarian 28, 39, 54, 55
  merger with Social Democrats 60, 196*c*
computers vii, 67, 179
constitution, Hungarian
  freedom amendments 85–86, 197*c*
copper ix, 135
corn viii
Corvinus. *See* Matthias Corvinus
Council for Mutual Economic Assistance (Comecon) 78, 88, 135, 137–139, 198*c*
Council of Europe 139, 198*c*
courts 17, 31, 33, 58, 62, 63, 106–107
crime xii, 40, 53, 98, 105, 106–107, 167–168, 174, 180–181. *See also* drug abuse and trafficking; prostitution
Croatia and Croats vii, viii, x, 5, 6, 8, 14, 15, 16, 18–19, 21, 36, 189
  current Hungary relations 144–145
  in Yugoslav civil war 145, 149, 198*c*
crown jewels 9–10, 168
Crown of St. Stephen. *See* crown jewels
Csaky, István 44, 47
Csepel Group 110
Csoori, Sándor 159
Csurka, István 103, 104, 159, 189, 190
currency 10, 37, 39, 40, 53, 78, 97, 111, 128–129, 132, 135, 142, 168, 190. *See also* economy
  forint convertibility 98, 128, 200*c*
customs and traditions, Hungarian 5, 12–13, 13*i*, 103, 183, 184–187, 186*i*
  Easter traditions 184, 185*i*
Cyprus 142

Czech Republic and Czechs 6,
12, 17, 26–27, 32, 36, 46i,
109, 142, 149, 152, 163, 176.
See also Czechoslovakia;
Visegrad alliance
Hungary, Poland economic
comparison 113–114, 114i,
120
Czechoslovakia 36, 40, 43–44,
54, 74, 76, 80, 83, 137, 139,
141–142, 198c. See also
Czech Republic; Slovakia
military issues 147
Russia "friendship treaty"
140–141

D
Dallas (TV show) 172
Dálnoki-Miklós, Béla 54
Dances with Wolves (film) 170
Danko, András 178
Danube (Duna) River vim, viii,
x, xi, 9, 10, 53, 144, 199c
Darányi, Kálmán 43
Deák, Ferenc 17
Debrecen (city) vim, xii, 66,
182
debt, foreign see foreign debt
democracy, transition to xii, 93,
103, 106, 189–190
1990 elections 86–88, 198c
1994 elections 95–96, 199c
1998 elections 98, 200c
2002 elections 99–101, 200c
constitution amendments
85–86, 197c
as free republic 86, 87i, 197c
major party profiles 102–103
media ownership debate
111, 172–173
Democratic Forum, Hungarian
104, 106, 173
in 1990 elections 86–88,
198c
in 1994 elections 96
in 1994 elections 98, 200c
in 2002 elections 100
profile of 103
Antall death 95, 198c
economic reform policies 97,
110–111, 118, 122–123,
130, 172–173
Demszky, Gábor 162
Denmark 152
Deutsche Telekom (telecommunications company) 118, 120
Diary for My Children (film)
169

Dinnyés, Lajós 59
Distribution Monitoring Associ-
ation (Matesz) 175
Dobi, István 59
Dobo, István 187
Dobri Castle 163
drug abuse and trafficking 180
Duke Bluebeard's Castle (Béla
Bartók) 164

E
Eastern bloc see Soviet Union
Eastern Orthodox Church 8
East Germany 80, 84, 137, 147,
197c see also Germany and
Germanic peoples
Economic Cooperation and
Development, Organization
for (OECD) 111
economy xii, 19–20, 25, 28, 31,
35, 37, 39, 40–41, 43, 45, 46i,
48–49, 51, 53, 55, 58, 62, 64,
65, 65i, 66–68, 79, 81, 196c
see also currency; foreign
investment; market economy,
transition to; New Economic
Mechanism
education 10, 11, 15, 17, 20,
31, 40, 46i, 62, 66, 69, 71, 99,
104, 130, 163, 178–179
Educational Achievement,
International Association for
179
Eger (town) vim, 5, 187
Egy Kekharisnya Feljegyzesey
(Notes from an intelligent
whore) (Péter Esterhazy) 160
E-Klub (Budapest nightspot)
182
Elet es Irodalom (Life and literature) (journal) 159
Embers (Sándor Marai) 161
employment and unemployment
see economy; industries;
strikes
End of a Family Secret, The
(Péter Nádás) 161
energy 109–110, 111, 118, 144,
199c
Engels, Friedrich 28, 85, 197c
English language x, 66, 161,
178
environment 102, 135, 144,
146, 184, 199c, 200c
Eötvös, József 157
Erdoss, Pál 169
Esterházy, Péter 160
Esterházy Castle 163

Estonia 3, 142
Estonian language x, 3
Esztergom (town) vim, 10, 181
Eszterhas, Joe 170
European Community (EC) see
European Union
European Mozart Foundation
163
European Union (EU) (formerly
European Community) xii,
134, 141, 146, 173
Hungary association pact
111, 135, 198c
Hungary membership devel-
opments 101, 111, 113,
137, 142–143, 152, 190,
200c
Hungary referendum 111,
200c
Export-Import Bank, U.S. 67

F
farming viii, 4, 10, 19, 24
29–31, 32, 35, 37, 38i, 40, 45,
53, 55, 56i, 64–65 65, 68, 101,
103, 113, 142
foreign trade data 135, 136
under New Economic Mech-
anism 77, 197c
fascism 37, 41, 43, 46, 46i, 54,
55, 74, 103, 189, 195c
Fateless (Imre Kertesz) 156
Father (film) 169
Fat Mo's Music Club (Budapest
nightspot) 182
Faust Symphony (Franz Liszt)
164
Feja, Géza 157
Felsopeteny Castle (Budapest)
73
Ferdinand I (emperor of Austria) 15
feudalism 8, 14, 15. See also
land reform; peasants
Fidesz–Hungarian Civic Party
see also Young Democrats,
Alliance of 106, 152
in 1998 elections 98, 99i,
200c
in 2002 elections 99i,100,
174
economic reform policies
110, 111
profile of 102
films and filmmaking 79, 155,
168–170, 171, 197c
Financial Research (investment–advisory firm) 123

Finland 3
Finnish language 3
Fischer, Tibor 160
Flashdance (film) 170
Florida 66
food and cooking xi, xii, 13, 25, 33, 118, 120, 122, 124*i*, 135, 150, 171, 173, 184, 185*i*
Ford Motor Co. (automaker) 118, 120
foreign aid 84, 106, 133–134, 138
foreign debt xii, 39, 40, 41, 43, 80, 110, 113, 132–133, 190
foreign investment 101, 109–110, 110–111, 112, 113–114, 118–126, 190–191
foreign trade 17, 39, 43, 78, 97, 111, 112, 118, 134–136, 137–139, 142–143, 144, 177, 198*c*, 200*c*
48 Party. *See* Independence Party
Forum Hotel (Budapest) 125
Founder of the State (George Konrad) 159
France and French people 6, 11, 13, 17, 21, 23–24, 28, 32, 36, 40, 42, 45, 74, 139, 151, 164
    investments in Hungary 118, 175
    Iraq war dispute 151–152, 200*c*
Francis Ferdinand (archduke of Austria) 21
Francis Joseph (emperor of Austria and king of Hungary) 18*i*, 21
    as Austrian ruler 15, 194*c*
    crowned king of Hungary 17, 195*c*
    death 25
    on ethnic manipulation 19
    and Hungary revolt 16, 194*c*
Free Democrats, Alliance of 39, 106, 174
    in 1990 elections 87, 88, 198*c*
    in 1994 elections 96, 199*c*
    in 2002 elections 100, 200*c*
    profile of 102
    economic reform policies 125
French Revolution (1789) 15

G

Gabčikovo dam (Slovakia) 144, 199*c*
Gabor, Dennis 179
Gabor, Eva 170
Gabor, Magda 170
Gabor, Peter 63
Gabor, Zsa Zsa 170
Gadney, Reg 71
gambling 183
Garbai, Sándor 31
gasoline 71, 126
    price-hike protest 130, 198*c*
General Electric Co. 118, 120, 122
General Motors Corp. (automaker) 118, 120
geography vi*m*, viii
Gerard (Gellert) (Catholic bishop and saint) 9
German language x
Germany and Germanic peoples vii, x, 5, 6, 7–9, 10, 13, 14, 17, 28, 37, 40, 42, 43–44, 84, 128, 137, 151, 164, 179, 181, 195*c*, 197*c*. *See also* East Germany; Holy Roman Empire; West Germany
    East bloc military issues investments in Hungary 116, 118, 120, 169
    trade data 134
    as World War I ally 21, 23–27, 195*c*
    as World War II ally 37, 45–51, 60, 168, 196*c*
"goulash communism" xii, 76
Gerő, Ernő 54, 69, 71
Géza (Magyar king) 9
Gimes, Miklós 83–84, 197*c*
globalization xii, 103, 109, 137, 170 *see also* foreign investment; foreign trade
gold ix, 7, 146
Gömbös de Jafka, Gyula 29, 38–39, 41, 42
Göncz, Árpád 99, 106, 141, 142, 146, 199*c*, 200*c*
Gorbachev, Mikhail S. 81–83, 139, 147
Görgey, Artur 16
Gosztony, Orsolya 178
goulash (*gulyas leves*) (stew) xiii*i*, xii
goulash communism xiv, 76
government, post-communist. *See also* democracy, transition to 177

amendments to constitution 85–86, 197*c*
    elections 86–88, 95–96, 98, 99*i*, 99–101, 198*c*, 199*c*, 200*c*
    on parliamentary system 93
    republic proclamation 86, 87*i*, 197*c*
Goya, Francisco 167
grains 133, 138. *See also specific types* (e.g., barley)
Great Britain 21, 23–24, 32, 42, 45, 49, 74, 98, 109, 151, 152, 160, 164, 170
    investments in Hungary 118, 175
Great Depression 40–41
Great Plain (region) 5, 12, 183
Great Powers (World War I victors) 35, 40
Greco, El (Domenikos Theotokopoulos) 167, 168
Greece and Greeks 21
Grösz, Károly 80*i*, 81–82, 85, 147, 197*c*
Group of Seven (G-7) 133
Group of Twenty-four (G-24) 133
Gulag Archipelago, The (Alexander Solzhenitsyn) 79, 158*i*
Gundel (Budapest restaurant) 117
Gyongyossy, Imre 169
Győr (city) vi*m*, xii, 72, 104, 120, 179
Gypsies (Romany) x, 104, 105, 128, 164, 181

H

Hadik, János 27
Hadyn, Franz Joseph 163
Hapsburg dynasty 12–17, 16*i*, 25, 35, 194*c*–195*c*. *See also* Austria; Austro-Hungarian Empire; specific figures (e.g., Maria Theresa)
Hary János (Zoltán Kodály) 164
Havel, Václav 141
health issues 95, 113, 130, 180, 184, 187. *See also* HIV/AIDS; mental health
Hegedüs, András 70
Hersant, Robert 175
Heviz Lake 187
Hitler, Adolf 41, 43, 49, 50, 189
HIV/AIDS 180

Hoensch, Joerg K. 50, 63
holidays 86, 184, 185i. See also customs and traditions
Holy Roman Empire 7–9, 12. See also Germany
Home Alone (film) 170
Honecker, Erich 80
Horn, Gyula 95, 145i, 199c
privatization dispute 97, 111, 124–126, 199c
Horroar (György Spiro) 160
horses 3–4, 6, 7, 9, 14, 181, 183
Horthy de Nagybánya, Miklós 33, 34i
as regent 35, 37, 38, 47, 49, 50, 51, 195c
hotels 125, 183
Hot Shots! (film) 170
housing 53, 64, 75, 129, 171, 184
HungarHotels (hotel chain) 125
Hungarian National Museum 167–168
Hungarian News Agency (MTI Corporation) x
Hungarian Newspaper Publishers, Association of 175
Hungarian Revolution (1848-49) 15–16, 16i, 194c
Hungarian Royal Guard 20i
Hungarian Symphony Orchestra 167
Hungarian uprising (1956) xii, 67, 70–75, 70i, 72i, 81, 82, 86, 95, 181, 197c, 198c
Hungarian Witches, Federation of 182
Huns 4–5, 7
Hanussen (film) 169
Husák, Gustáv 80
Hyatt Regency (Budapest hotel) 183

I
IBUSZ (national travel agency) 119, 198c
Illinois viii
Illyés, Gyula 157
Ikea (retailer) 118
immigration and immigrants 10, 36, 45, 46i, 66, 74, 75, 103, 104, 107, 129, 143, 145, 145i, 151
Hungarians in U.S. vii, xii, 66–67, 163
smuggling issue 180–181
Imrédy, Béla 43, 44, 58,

Independence Party 19, 25, 26
Independent Smallholders' Party 41, 49, 54, 55, 58–59
in 1990 elections 87, 198c
in 1994 elections 96
in 1998 elections 98, 200c
in 2002 elections 100
profile of 103
Indiana viii
industries 19, 24, 29, 31, 32, 40, 64, 65i, 66–68, 118, 126–127, 196c
International Business Machines (IBM) 118, 167
International Court of Justice (World Court) 144, 199c
International Monetary Fund (IMF) 106, 134
Internet see computers
Iraq war (2003) 151–153, 200c
Ireland and Irish people vii
iron ix, 45, 58, 64
Islam 10, 12
Italy and Italians vii, 6, 9, 17, 19, 23, 27, 41, 43–44, 45, 46, 134, 151, 195c
investments in Hungary 120

J
Japan 45, 179
investments in Hungary 118, 120
Jews 10, 39–40, 42, 44, 46i, 65, 88, 102, 104, 128, 156, 157, 167, 169
as early middle class 19, 46i
"White Terror" plight 33
World War II plight 46i, 48i, 49–50, 51, 156
Jihad vs. McWorld (Benjamin R. Barber) 170, 189–190
Joseph II (emperor of Austria) 14
József, Attila 157
Juhasz, Ferenc 157–158
Juhasz, Gyula 157
Julius Meinl (retailer) 118, 122
Justice and Life Party, Hungarian 100, 101, 104, 190
in 1994–2002 elections 103, 104, 190
profile 103

K
Kabay, Barna 169
Kádár, János 60
death 83, 197c

1956 uprising role 71–72, 74, 81, 197c
New Economic Mechanism 75–76, 78, 80, 197c
party leadership loss 80–81, 80i, 197c
Kaddish for a Child Not Born (Imre Kertesz) 156
Kállai, Gyula 75
Kállay, Miklós 48
Karolyi, Gyula 41
Károlyi, Mihály 25–27, 28–29, 31
Kerekes, Tibor vii
Kertesz, Imre 156, 160, 200c
Khazars 4
Khrushchev, Nikita 69
Kindergarten Cop (film) 170
Kleiner Bauder (store chain) 122
Kodály Institute (Kecskemet, Hungary)
Kodály, Zoltán 20, 164, 165i
Kohn, Hans 42
Konrad, George 157–158, 160
Korda, Alexander 170
Kossuth, Lajos 15–16, 19
Kovac, Michal 144
Kovacs, Almos 126–127
Kovacs, Imre 157
Kovacs, László 100i
Kozgaz Pinceklub (Budapest nightspot) 182
Krisan, Attila 180
Kun, Béla 28, 31, 46i
Kuncze, Gabor 96, 102, 106

L
labor see economy; industries; strikes
Labor Party 105
Lakatos, Géza 50
lakes vim, viii, 187
land reform 29–31, 32, 35, 37, 40, 55, 64–65, 68, see also farming; peasants
Lang, George 117
languages, study of x, 66, 156, 178 see also Magyars
Lauder, Estée 117
Lauder, Ronald S. 117
League of Nations 39
Lechfeld, Battle of see Augsburg, Battle of
Lengyel, László 123
Lenin, V. I. 28, 32, 75, 85, 197c
Libenyi, János 17
Liberal Party 19

Light-Sensitive Story, A (film) 168–169
Lilliom (Ferenc Molnár) 161
Liszt, Franz 20, 164
literature 16i, 20, 79, 155, 156–161, 158i, 197c
Lithuania 189
livestock 4, 7, 53, 56i, 68, 135, 139
Lockheed Martin Corp. (aerospace company) 118
Look Who's Talking 2 (film) 170
Losonczy, Géza 83–84, 197c
Louis I (Louis of Anjou, king of Hungary) 11
Louis (Lajos) II (king of Hungary) 12
Lovely Tale of Photography, A (Peter Nadas) 161
Lowenthal, Constance 167
Lugosi, Béla 170, 183
Lukács, György 157–158
Lutheran Church 182
Luxembourg 171

M

machinery 53, 67, 77, 135
Magyar, Joseph
   interview with 66–67
Magyar Hirlap (newspaper) 125
Magyarovar (town) 72–73
Magyars. *See also* customs and traditions; nationalism
   early description of 4
   Christian conversion 9–10, 193c
   culture and language x, 3, 7, 12–13, 14–15, 16i, 17, 20, 42, 43, 46i, 47, 103, 178, 183, 184–187, 185i, 186i, 194c, 195c
   as majority in Hungary x
   migrations x, 3–5, 36, 129, 193c, 195c
   as minority in neighboring states 36, 44, 47, 143–146, 195c, 199c, 200c
   raiding period 6–7, 193c
Mádl, Ferenc vii, 98, 200c
Mai Nap (newspaper) 174
Malenkov, Georgi 68
Maleter, Pál 74–75, 83–84, 197c
Malev (Hungarian airline) 120, 123
Manet, Edouard 168
Manfred Weiss Steel Company 65i

Marai, Sándor 161
Maria Theresa (empress of Austria) 13, 194c
market economy, transition to xii, 96, 98, 102, 103, 112, 148, 177, 179, 190–191. *See also* currency; economy; foreign investment; foreign debt
   Budapest Stock Exchange 119, 198c
   Czech, Poland comparison 113–114, 114i
   foreign investment strategy 109, 110–111, 118–126, 132,
   government deficits 98, 112, 131–132, 142, 190
   housing shortage 129
   inflation-targeting policy 111, 200c
   land compensation 127–128
   military spending 150
   private enterprise, growth of 102, 111, 117–118, 126–127
   privatization start 119, 198c
   "tight-money" policy 124, 128–129
   unemployment problem 96, 104, 105, 110, 112, 113–114, 114i, 115, 122, 129–131, 169
Marks and Spencer (retailer) 118
Marton, László 162
Marx, Karl 28, 85, 197c
Marxism-Leninism 28, 54, 81, 84–85, 105, 106, 157, 159, 197c
Matav (Hungarian telephone company) 120
Matthias Corvinus (king of Hungary) 11, 194c
Mátyás Hunyadi (king of Hungary) 11
MAV (Hungarian railroad) 132
Maxwell, Robert 175
McDonald's (fast-food chain) 118, 173, 184
Meciar, Vladimir 144
Medgyessy, Péter vii, 99, 100i, 101, 111, 126, 200c
   hidden past revealed 93, 105, 200c
   Iraq war stand 152, 200c
   on national reconciliation 101
mental health 184

Mephisto (film) 169
Meras, Phyllis 9
Meray, Tibor 83
Meszaros, Marta 169
Mexico 132–133
Mikoyan, Anastas 71
Mikrokosmos (Béla Bartók) 164
military reorganization. *See also* armed forces; North Atlantic Treaty Organization
   arms control 147
   budget issues 148, 150
   foreign assistance 151
Milošević, Slobodan 145
Mindszenty, József Cardinal 64, 73, 74
   funeral cortege 181
mines and mineral resources ix, 24, 29, 31, 45, 114
Miskolc (city) viim, xii, 72
Mohács, Battle of (1526) 12, 194c
Mohi, Battle of (1241) 10
Molnár, Ferenc 20, 46i, 157, 161
Molotov, Vyacheslav 71
Mongolia and Mongols 10–11, 189, 193c
Montenegrins. *See* Serbia and Montenegro
Moravia. *See* Czech Republic
Móricz, Zsigmond 20, 157
Mozgo Vilag (World in action) (journal) 159
Munich Agreement (1938) 43
Murdoch, Rupert 174
Museum of Modern Art (New York City) 168
music 20, 163–167, 171,182
Mussolini, Benito 41, 43

N

Nádás, Péter 160–161
Nador, Livia 48i
Nagy, Ferenc 54, 58, 59
Nagy, Imre 56, 57i, 68–69. *See also* Hungarian uprising (1956)
   honored 83–84, 86, 197c
   1956 uprising role 71–75, 197c
   Yeltsin at grave 141, 198c
Nagy, László 116
Naked Gun 2 ½ (film) 170
Naplo (film) 169
National Bourgeois–Democratic Party 39, 54

nationalism and nationalists
xii, 15, 17, 19, 20, 41–42, 43,
189–190, 195c. *See also* Mag-
yars
National Peasants Party 54
National Smallholders' Party 35
National Socialist Action
Group, Hungarian 104
National Socialist Hungarian
Party 43
NATO. *See* North Atlantic
Treaty Organization (NATO)
natural gas 135
natural resources ix
Nemzeti Sport (newspaper) 175
Nepszabadsag (People's freedom)
(newspaper) 175
Netherlands 134, 179
Neumann, John von 179
New Economic Mechanism
75–79, 80 197c
New York City 168
September 11, 2001,
anniversary vii
New York State 177
nightclubs 182
Nobel Prize 156, 179, 200c
North Atlantic Treaty Organiza-
tion (NATO) 145, 146
Hungary membership 137,
140, 143–144, 148,
150–151, 190, 200c
Hungary referendum 149,
199c
Partnership for Peace 149,
199c
Nyers, Rezso 85
Nyugat (The West) (newspaper)
157

O

Obuda (town) *see* Budapest
oil 45, 46, 78, 135
Okolicsanyi, Karoly 126
Oltay, Edith 105
Onogur *see* Magyars
Orbán, Viktor 97, 98, 99i, 102,
111, 125, 152, 174, 200c
Organization for Security and
Cooperation in Europe
(OSCE) 139, 199c
Oscar (film) 170
Ossztanc (Let's dance together)
(musical) 161
Otto I (Holy Roman Emperor)
8
Ottoman Empire 21 *see also*
Turkey and Turks

Ózd (town) 114
Ozsda, Erika 169

P

Palffy, Fidel 42
Pannonia *see* Roman Empire
paprika (spice) 13, 124i, 135
Paris x, 35
Party of Hungarian Life 45
Party of National Will 42, 43
Pataki, George vii, 177
peasants 8, 12, 13, 14, 29–31,
32, 37, 38i, 55, 159, 163, 183,
194c
Pechengs 5
Pécs (city) vim, xii, 26
Peko Steel Industrial Works
115–117
PepsiCo (beverage company)
118
Pest (town) *see* Budapest
Peto, János 175
Petőfi Club 69
Petőfi, Sandor 69, 157
anti-Hapsburg poem 16i
Petrenko, János 115–117
Petri, György 159
Pizza Hut (fast–food chain)
118, 184
poetry *see* literature
Pokorni, Zoltan 106
Poland and Poles vii, 6, 12, 19,
44, 45, 69, 137, 142, 148, 152,
163, 169, 176, 189
current Hungary relations
141–142, 198c
Czech, Hungary economic
comparison 113–114, 114i,
120
foreign debt 132–133
military issues 147
Russia "friendship treaty"
140–141
"shock therapy" economic
reforms 114, 120
population viii, x, xii, 7, 14, 20,
36, 46i, 53, 75, 182
Portugal 38, 152
potatoes viii
Pozsgay, Imre 85
press vii, x, 21, 29, 49, 69,
97,152, 155, 160, 174–176,
177, 191
objectivity issue 174, 176
Princip, Gavrilo 21
prostitution 179–180
Proust, Marcel 161
Prussia. *See* Germany

Psalmus Hungaricus (Zoltán
Kodály) 164

R

"Red Terror," period of 30i,
31–33, 56, 195c
Racial Defense Socialist Party
42
radio 71, 74, 111, 172–174
Radio Free Europe 172
railroads 27, 129, 132
Rajk, László 56, 62,
Rákosi, Mátyás 54, 56, 58–62,
61i, 64, 66, 68–69, 196c
Reagan, Ronald 117
Reform (newspaper) 174
Renoir, Pierre-Auguste 168
Revolt of Job, The (film) 169
Revolutionary Ruling Council
30i. *See also* "Red Terror,"
period of
Ribbentrop, Joachim von 44
Ringier Rt (media company)
175
rivers vim, viii, xi, 12
Romania and Romanians vim,
viii, x, 11, 14, 15, 21, 27, 28,
32–33, 36, 45, 46, 54, 80, 88,
129, 137, 149, 183 195c
current Hungary relations
143, 146, 199c, 200c
military issues 146
Russia "friendship treaty" 140
Roman Catholic Church 7–10,
14, 31–32, 35, 55, 64, 73, 103,
181 193c
as percentage of populace x,
182
Roman Empire 5 *see also* Holy
Roman Empire
Romany *see* Gypsies
Royal Hungary 12–13, 194c
RTL Group (broadcasting conglomerate) 171, 173
Russia and Russians x, 3, 16,
17, 19, 21, 32, 81, 134, 149,
151, 169, 181
"shock therapy" economic
reforms 120
in World War I 21, 23–24,
56
Yeltsin in Hungary 141,
198c

S

St. Gellert. *See* Gerard
St. Stephen. *See* Stephen
(István) I

Sarajevo (city) 21
Saxony. *See* Germany
Schwartzenberg, Felix 17
science 178–179
Scientology, Church of 182
Scythe Cross Movement 42
Scythians 5
Security and Cooperation in
Europe, Organization for. *See*
Organization for Security and
Cooperation in Europe
(OSCE)
September 11, 2001, anniver-
sary. *See* Budapest; New York
City; United States
Serbia and Montenegro *vim*,
viii, x, 6, 8, 11, 14, 15, 16, 21,
24–25, 36 24*i*, 129, 189
current Hungary relations
145–146
Kosovo conflict 148, 150,
200*c*
Serbs. *See* Serbia and Montenegro
Showgirls (film) 170
Siklos Castle 186
Silent Revolution, The (Imre
Kovacs) 157
silver 7
Simonyi-Semadam, Sándor 35
skinheads (young neo-fascists)
104
slavery 4, 6, 8, 14
Slavs x, 4<\3208>6, 8, 12, 18,
20, 21, 24–27, 28, 36, 156,
195*c*
Slovakia and Slovaks *vim*, viii,
x, 6, 8, 12–13, 14, 27, 32, 36,
40, 44, 120
current Hungary relations
142, 143–144, 198*c*, 199*c*
nuclear smuggling issue
180
Slovenia and Slovenes *vim*,
viii, 6, 14, 16, 21, 36, 142
current Hungary relations
143, 144
smoking 150, 184
Social Democratic Party 26, 29,
31, 33, 37, 49, 55, 59
merger with Communists
60, 196*c*
socialism 28, 33, 64, 84–85,
197*c*
Socialist Party, Hungarian 106,
174. *See also* Socialist Workers' Party, Hungarian
in 1990 elections 88, 198*c*

in 1994 elections 95, 96,
145*i*, 199*c*
in 2002 elections 99, 100*i*,
200*c*
creation 85, 197*c*
economic reform policies 97,
110, 123–126, 131, 199*c*
Kádár ouster 80–81, 80*i*,
197*c*
Marxism-Leninism shift
84–85, 197*c*
political monopoly lost 86,
197*c*
privatization dispute 97,
111, 199*c*
profile of 102
renaming of 85, 197*c*
Socialist Workers' Party (ca.
1925) 39
Socialist Workers' Party (ca.
1994) 105
Socialist Workers' Party, Hungarian (1956–89) 72, 74, 76,
95, 118, 158
Sonata in B Minor (Franz Liszt)
164
Southern Illinois University
112
Soviet Union (USSR) and
Soviet bloc viii, 37, 54–55,
59, 60–62, 69, 81–83, 88, 106,
135, 137–141, 189
Hungarian uprising xii,
70–75, 70*i*, 197*c*
Hungary nuclear arms basing
147
nuclear materials smuggling
180
troops exit Hungary 139,
140*i*, 147, 198*c*
war strategy 146–147
in World War II 45, 46, 47,
49, 50–51, 53–54, 66, 168,
196*c*
Spain 152. 167
Spiro, György 160
Stalin, Joseph 54–55, 60,
61–62, 69, 70
steel 64, 65*i*, 67, 114, 114–117,
135
Stephen (István) I (St.
Stephen) (king of Hungary
and Roman Catholic saint)
9–10, 11*i*, 46*i*, 193*c*
stocks and bonds 40, 119, 198*c*
strikes 26, 39, 56
Suchman, Tamás 97
Suez Canal 74

sugar beets viii
Suleiman II ("The Magnifi-
cent") (Ottoman sultan) 12
sunflowers viii
Suranyi, György 125
Suslov, Mikhail 71
Suzuki (automaker) 118, 120
Sweden 49
Switzerland 27, 35, 38,
109–110, 175
Sylvester II (pope) 9
Szábo, Albert 104
Szábo, István 189
Szakasits, Árpád 59
Szálasi, Ferenc 42, 43, 46, 50,
51, 58, 104
Szechenyi, István 15
Szeged city *vim*, xii, 5, 7, 33, 54
Szeles, Gabor 117
Szell, George 163
Szikra Printing House Rt 175
Szilagyi, József 83–84, 197*c*
Szilard, Leo 179
Szótjay, Dome 49–50, 58
Szuros, Mátyás 86

T
Taszar (town) 150, 152
Teleki, Pál 33, 37, 40, 44–47
telephones and telecommunica-
tions 27, 111, 118, 120–121,
122
television vii, 77, 86, 111, 155,
170–174, 175, 191
Teller, Edward 179
Tepes, Vlad ("The Impaler")
183
Terminator 2 (film) 170
theater 20, 48*i*, 79, 155, 156,
157, 197*c*
Vigszinhaus reopening
161–163
Visegrad Palace Festival 183
Thunderstorms (Géza Feja) 157
Thurmer, Gyula 105
Tildy, Zoltán 41, 54, 56, 58–59
Tisza, István 21–22, 24–26
Tisza River *vim*, viii, 32, 53
cyanide spill 146, 200*c*
Tiszataj (journal) 159
Tocsik, Marta 98
Tokaj (town) 187
Torgyan, József 101
tourism and travel 76, 77, 79,
84, 129, 144, 167,179–181,
186, 187, 197*c*
Transcendental Studies (Franz
Liszt) 164

Transdanubia (region) 185
transportation 31, 73, 116, 118, 120, 130, 135, 151, 179–181, 198c
Transylvania (region) 8, 12–13, 16, 28, 32, 36, 46, 47, 53, 88, 146, 183, 198c
Trianon, Treaty of (1920) 35–37, 40, 42, 43, 47, 53, 59, 195c
Tripartite Pact (1940) 47, 196c
Trocadero (Budapest nightspot) 182
Tungsram (light-fixtures company) 120, 122
Turkey and Turks x, 4, 5, 11, 16, 20, 21,180, 187, 194c
  Hungary occupation 12–13, 13i, 194c
25, Firemen's Street (film) 169

U

Ugro-Finnish (language group) x, 3
Ukraine and Ukrainians vim, viii, x, 8,14, 27, 44, 53, 74, 117, 143, 189
  current Hungary relations 143
  Joseph Magyar interview 66
UN. See United Nations (UN)
Underberg Group 117
Under the Frog (Tibor Fischer) 160
Unification Church 182
United National Socialist Party 42
United Nations (UN) 39, 74, 134, 151
United States viii, xii, 23, 32, 42, 66–67, 84, 93–94, 98, 109–110, 133, 134, 138–139, 138i, 149–150, 151, 167, 168–170, 177, 179, 197c, 198c
  Bosnia peace deployment 150, 199c
  Hungarians in vii, xii, 177, 179
  investments in Hungary 109–110, 116, 117, 118, 120, 122, 125, 167
  Iraq war 151–153, 200c
  Mindszenty asylum 74, 181

September 11, 2001, anniversary vii
United Technologies 118
Unity Party 38, 40, 41, 42
Updike, John 161
Ural Mountains 3–4
uranium ix, 180
U.S. West (telecommunications company) 118

V

Valo Vilag (Real world) (TV show) 170–172
vampires 170, 183
Vamos, Miklós 160
Vatican see Roman Catholic Church
Videoton (electronics company) 117
Vienna 18i, 37
"Vienna Awards" (1838, 1940) 44, 46 195c
Vigszinhaus Theater (Budapest) 161–163
Visegrad 141, 183
Visegrad alliance (Czech Republic, Hungary, Poland, Slovakia) 135
  formation 141–142, 198c
Visitor, The (George Konrad) 159
Volkswagen (automaker) 120

W

Wałesa, Lech 141
Wallenberg, Raoul 49–50
Wall Street Journal 152
Warsaw Pact 75, 88, 137–139, 146–147, 196c
  dissolution of 147, 149, 198c
weapons, military. See armed forces; military reorganization
Wekerle, Sándor 26
Welch, John 122
Westel (U.S.-Hungarian joint venture) 121
West Germany 66, 77, 78, 84, 197c. See also Germany and Germanic Peoples
West Side Story (musical) 162
wheat viii, 61i
"White Terror," period of 31, 33, 37, 56, 195c

Wilhelm II (emperor of Germany) 21
Wilson, Woodrow 23
wines 187
Wisconsin 116
Wooden Prince, The (Béla Bartók) 164
Workers' Party, Hungarian 60, 68, 69, 70, 72 see also Socialist Workers' Party, Hungarian
World Bank 134
World National Popular Rule Party 104
World Trade Center (New York City). See New York City
World War I (1914–18) 19, 20, 23–27, 24i, 35, 104, 157, 195c
World War II (1939–45) 35, 37, 45–51, 46i, 48i, 53, 66, 159, 162, 163, 168, 196c

X

Xcel Energy, Inc. 110

Y

Yeltsin, Boris N. 82
  in Hungary 141, 198c
Young Democrats, Alliance of 98, 102, 174. See also Fidesz–Hungarian Civic Party
  in 1990 elections 102
  in 1994 elections 96, 102
Yugoslavia viii, 36, 47, 66, 143, 144–146. See also Serbia and Montenegro; former republics (e.g., Croatia, Slovenia)
  airspace military incursions 149, 198c
  Kosovo conflict 148, 150, 200c
youths and youth issues x, 50, 66, 73, 98, 99i, 101, 102, 104–105, 150, 159, 163, 171–172, 174, 178, 184, 185i, 186i

Z

Zhivkov, Todor 80
Zinner, Paul E. 60, 62, 75
Zwack Unicum Ltd. 117
Zwack, Peter 117